INFORMATION RIGHTS AND OBLIGATIONS

Markets and the Law

Series Editor:
Geraint Howells
Lancaster University, UK

Markets and the Law is concerned with the way the law interacts with the market through regulation, self-regulation and the impact of private law regimes. It looks at the impact of regional and international organizations (e.g. EC and WTO) and many of the works adopt a comparative approach and/or appeal to an international audience. Examples of subjects covered include trade laws, intellectual property, sales law, insurance, consumer law, banking, financial markets, labour law, environmental law and social regulation affecting the market as well as competition law. The series includes texts covering a broad area, monographs on focused issues, and collections of essays dealing with particular themes.

Other titles in the series

Cyber Consumer Law and Unfair Trading Practices
Cristina Coteanu
ISBN 0 7546 2417 X

Consumer Protection Law
Geraint Howells and Stephen Weatherill
ISBN 0 7546 2338 6 (Pbk)
ISBN 0 7546 2331 9 (Hbk)

Information Rights and Obligations

A Challenge for Party Autonomy and Transactional Fairness

Edited by

GERAINT HOWELLS
Lancaster University, UK

ANDRÉ JANSSEN
University of Münster, Germany

REINER SCHULZE
University of Münster, Germany

ASHGATE

Published by
Ashgate Publishing Limited
Gower House
Croft Road
Aldershot
Hants GU11 3HR
England

Ashgate Publishing Company
Suite 420
101 Cherry Street
Burlington, VT 05401-4405
USA

Ashgate website: http://www.ashgate.com

British Library Cataloguing in Publication Data
Howells, Geraint G.
Information rights and obligations : a challenge for party autonomy and transactional fairness. - (Markets and the law)
1. Disclosure of information - Law and legislation - Europe - Congresses 2. Liberty of contract - Europe - Congresses
3. Law - Europe - International unification - Congresses
4. Obligations (Law) - Europe - Congresses
I. Title II. Janssen, André III. Schulze, Reiner
346.4'022

Library of Congress Cataloging-in-Publication Data
Information rights and obligations : a challenge for party autonomy and transactional fairness / [edited] by Geraint Howells, André Janssen and Reiner Schulze.
p. cm. -- (Markets and the law)
Includes bibliographical references and index.
ISBN 0-7546-2432-3
1. Liberty of contract--European Union countries. 2. Contracts--European Union countries. 3. Disclosure of information--Law and legislation--European Union countries. I. Howells, Geraint G. II. Janssen, André, 1972- III. Reiner, Schulze, 1948- IV. Series.

KJE1640. I54 2004
342.240662--dc22

2004018318

ISBN 0 7546 2432 3

Printed and bound in Great Britain by TJ International Ltd, Padstow, Cornwall

Contents

List of Contributors

Dr. Edoardo Ferrante
Lecturer in Law, Dipartimento di Scienze Giuridiche, University of Turin, Italy

Dr. Paola Gozzo
Assegnista di Ricerca, Dipartimento di Scienze Giuridiche, University of Turin, Italy

Geraint Howells
Professor of Law, School of Law, Lancaster University, Barrister, Gough Square Chambers

Dr. André Janssen
Assistant Professor, Chair for German and European Private Law, University of Münster, Germany

Dr. Katarzyna Michałowska
Adiunkt, Chair for Comparative Civil Law, Law Faculty, Warsaw University, Poland

Annette Nordhausen, LL.M. (Eur)
Lecturer in Law, Centre for European, Comparative and International Law, University of Sheffield

Iain Ramsay
Professor of Law, Osgoode Hall Law School, York University, Toronto, Canada

Dr. Reiner Schulze
Professor of Law, Chair for German and European Private Law, University of Münster, Germany

Dr. Ruth Sefton-Green
Maître de conférences, University Paris I (Panthéon-Sorbonne), France

Dr. Christian Twigg-Flesner
Lecturer in Law, Law School, The University of Hull

Dr. Bettina Wendlandt, LL.M. (Chicago)
Assistant Professor, Chair for International Private Law and Civil Law, University of Münster, Germany

Dr. Chris Willett
Professor of Consumer Law, School of Law, De Montfort University

Foreword

This publication collects the contributions of a conference, which were presented in November 2003 hosted by the Centre for European Private Law (Münster) and the Centre for European Comparative and International Law (Sheffield). The conference concerned the topic 'Information Rights and Obligations – The Impact on Party Autonomy and Contractual Fairness' and was held in Münster.

The decision was taken not to reproduce the relevant Directives since they have been made available in various compendiums (cf. Oliver Radley-Gardner, Hugh Beale, Reinhard Zimmermann, Reiner Schulze, *Fundamental texts on European Private Law*, Hart Publishing, Oxford/Portland 2003; Ulrich Magnus, *Europäisches Schuldrecht, Verordnungen und Richtlinien*, Sellier, Munich/Berlin 2002).

The results of the conference should also contribute to the development of a common European legal terminology in the field of contract law.

We would like to thank the Marie Curie Training Site 'Harmonization of Business and Consumer Law in the EU' and the TMR Research Network 'Uniform Terminology for European Private Law' for financing the publication of this book. The Research Network consists of the partner universities of Turin (co-ordination), Barcelona, Lyon III, Münster, Nijmegen, Oxford und Warsaw and is supported by the European Commission.

In addition, we would like to thank those who assisted in the editing of this book, especially Martin Weitenberg.

Münster and Sheffield, June 2004

Geraint Howells André Janssen Reiner Schulze

Introduction

When the Centre for European Private Law at Münster and Sheffield's Centre for European Comparative and International Law came together with the idea of organizing a joint seminar on a contemporary European Private Law issue, the theme of information obligations easily came to mind. Information obligations have become an important technique at the European level. Certainly this is obvious in consumer law, but as this collection of chapters demonstrates it applies in other fields too. Information obligations are seen as useful tools for harmonization. They interfere less with national traditions than substantive regulation. The information approach also fits in with the jurisprudence of the ECJ in free movement cases. This shows a preference for information as a more proportionate response to legitimate national concerns than bans or controls on substance.

This topic has been subject to increased scrutiny following publication of the excellent collection edited by Grundmann, Kerber and Weatherill, *Party Autonomy and the Role of Information in the Internal Market*. That book sets out very well both the traditional justifications for information obligations to overcome information asymmetries and also the insights of behavioural economics into how the traditional economic assumptions may not match up to reality.

The present book has two functions to continue that debate. One task is to reflect more on the implications of information obligations for private law theory and particularly the concept of party autonomy. Viewed in classical terms, information obligations might be a threat to party autonomy, as the offeror is no longer free to make offers in whatever manner he pleases, but has to conduct his business in a certain way respecting duties to inform which are imposed directly (and indirectly) by the law. However, an alternative vision could be suggested, whereby if party autonomy is viewed in terms of both parties being able to make free and informed choices, then the information obligations actually promote party autonomy by enabling the recipient of the information to act in an informed manner to further his own interests. Another task of this collection is to look in detail at certain areas and to see how in practice the insights gained can be used to improve information regimes.

This collection includes eleven chapters from colleagues at Münster and Sheffield and other universities within Europe and North America. It starts with Chris Willett putting forward two versions of party autonomy – the traditional freedom-oriented perspective focusing on the intention of the parties and promoting self-reliant freedom and an alternative fairness-oriented perspective, which is more concerned with the distinctive interests and expectations of the parties. He then goes on to examine the particular issue of liability for public statements and considers that where two parties could both be potentially liable consideration should be given to channelling liability towards the party who can best maintain his autonomy. In the context of advertising he considers the producer is better able to do this than the trader as the producer can exercise quality control over the advertising.

Paola Gozzo describes the development of information obligations within the EC. She argues that party autonomy is a useful 'vague notion' around which everyone can agree and yet it lacks a specific meaning. The real work of harmonization is undertaken by concrete information obligations that operate under the banner of party autonomy. Katarzyna Michałowska tells how party autonomy has become accepted in Poland as a principle for the basis of legal regulation of the new market order. She uses the Package Travel Directive as an example of the new style of regulation.

A set of chapters look at problems of applying the information model to best effect, particularly given the insights of behavioural economics. Iain Ramsay notes the problems of disclosure in the context of consumer credit and cautions us to take a more considered and nuanced approach to the impact of information. In particular he points out that the value of information may lie not so much in affecting decision-making, but rather in the use it can be put to during the course of the agreement to help address problems that arise. He also notes the development of the responsible lending principle, but cautions that lenders may be just as susceptible to making irrational decisions as consumers. Bettina Wendlandt deals with the limited capacity of individuals to process information and looks for ways of improving the Timeshare Directive, by drawing some lessons from the Commercial Agents Directive. She concludes that only key information should be contained in a brochure, but detailed information should be retained in the contract. Annette Nordhausen adopts a similar approach in relation to electronic contracts. She seeks to draw upon the proposed Directive on Unfair Commercial Practices to identify what is key material information. She notes that under that proposed Directive such information is subject to a different sanctions regime, since not providing it is considered automatically unfair and subject to that Directive's sanction regime, but otherwise the lack of information needs to be tested against the proposed Directive's general unfairness test.

Edoardo Ferrante points to the importance of disclosure in the Unfair Contract Terms Directive. For him the difficulty is in finding the appropriate sanctions when terms have not been set out transparently. Christian Twigg-Flesner covers somewhat similar ground to Chris Willett, as he is also concerned with the Sale of Goods Directive. He is primarily interested in the extent to which the Sale of Goods Directive encourages the seller to disclose information about the product to prevent it being treated as defective. He is anxious lest the consumer is too readily denied recovery in circumstances where he does not understand the consequences of the information. This links nicely to the concerns of Geraint Howells about the ability to avoid product liability through the use of warnings. He argues that consumers should not be asked to play a game of Russian roulette when they cannot predict whether a risk is likely to affect them or the product they use. Information might fashion expectations, but care should be taken lest it slips too easily into a superficial indirect means of excluding liability. Product liability is nowadays tortious rather than contractual, but similar issues of party autonomy arise.

In a wide-ranging chapter Ruth Sefton-Green contrasts the approach of the French and English courts to the duties to inform. She shows us that these issues arise not only in consumer cases, but also in commercial contexts (such as franchising), as well as medical law. She points out that the person required to provide information may actually be the stronger party overall, just informationally weak. This is most obvious perhaps in the context of insurance contracts. She too draws a distinction between a view of contract based on individual adversarialism and co-operation, but suggests that the duty to inform might give rise to a new model of contractual fairness where people at least know what they are doing when making choices. The last chapter underlines the point that information duties do not only exist in consumer law. André Janssen looks at the different information requirements in commercial agency, distribution and franchise agreements. He includes in an Annex the 'Principles of European Private Law Long-Term Commercial Contracts'. He is cautiously optimistic that these principles could form the basis of a European Code. That is a major debate for another day, but what is interesting is the ability of lawyers contributing to this collection from a range of legal backgrounds within Europe to recognize the same trends and the need to address common concerns. In some modest way we hope this book adds to the increasingly impressive array of materials available for the students of European private law.

Geraint Howells André Janssen Reiner Schulze

Chapter 1

Autonomy and Fairness: The Case of Public Statements

Chris Willett

Introduction

In this chapter I consider what we mean when we refer to 'autonomy' in the context of regulating relationships between traders and consumers; and how this relates to freedom of contract thinking and more fairness-oriented thinking.[1] The basic argument made is that autonomy has a meaning that is in line with freedom of contract thinking; but that it has an alternative meaning, one that is more in line with fairness-oriented thinking. I try to explain what autonomy means when understood from a freedom of contract perspective; and how, from a freedom-oriented perspective, autonomy is thought to be best realized in various contexts. I also try to explain what autonomy means when understood from a fairness-oriented perspective; and how, from a fairness-oriented perspective, autonomy is thought to be best realized in these contexts. The discussion then focuses more specifically on autonomy, freedom and fairness in the context of public and advertising statements made by traders to induce consumers to enter contracts.

Basically, the argument is that freedom-oriented autonomy is about maximizing the self-reliant freedom of the parties in relation to who they contract with and on what terms. This involves strong adherence to the intention of the parties. Basing both obligation and liability on the intention of the parties is viewed as guaranteeing respect for party autonomy and respect for the expectations of the parties. In contrast, a fairness-oriented approach to autonomy is less concerned with the pursuit of a self-reliant version of freedom. It is also less concerned with the intention of the parties. More attention is given to the distinctive interests and expectations that a party such as a consumer is likely to have when entering relationships. Obligations and liabilities should be determined more by reference to these distinctive interests and expectations. Fairness-oriented autonomy may be

---

1 Issues relating to freedom, fairness and autonomy are being given considerable attention in academic literature at present. See, e.g., Trebilcock (1993); Beatson and Friedmann (1995); Brownsword, Hird and Howells (1999); Collins (1999); Grundman, Kerber and Weatherill (2001).

better secured by determining obligations and liabilities by reference to these distinctive interests and expectations than by reference to self-reliance and intention.

In the context of public and advertising statements the law has traditionally taken a more freedom-oriented approach to autonomy by focussing on the intention of the parties. However, recent rules on public and advertising statements seem to be more fairness-oriented and to pay more heed to the distinctive interests and expectations of consumers. As a consequence of this, fairness-oriented consumer autonomy is better achieved.

However, measures such as these (which seek to instate a fairness-oriented version of autonomy for the benefit of the consumer) inevitably restrict the autonomy of the traders with whom consumers deal. Refusing to base obligation and liability on the intention of traders means a restriction on the autonomy of traders. However, there may be choices available in relation to which traders should suffer the restrictions (or at least the greatest restrictions) on autonomy, for the benefit of consumers. If this is the case, and if there is an agenda to maintain trader autonomy where possible, then it is argued that the rules might seek to impose the restrictions on autonomy on those traders who are in the best position to find alternative means of exercising autonomy. In the case of trader liability for public and advertising statements there do appear to be choices in terms of which traders should bear the brunt of the autonomy restrictions. There is a choice as to the relative burdens to be borne by retailers and producers. It is argued that (at least where producer advertising statements are concerned) producers are in the best position to retain a degree of autonomy by alternative means, i.e. by exercising quality control over the advertising statements generated. There may, therefore, be some justification for developing the legal rules in such a way as to shift as much of the burden as possible away from retailers and towards producers.

Autonomy and Expectation

What do we mean, in general, when we refer to parties having autonomy or being autonomous in the context of a contractual relationship?[2] It seems that we are referring to control or influence. Contractors surely have autonomy, when they have control or influence over their actions in relation to the formation, contents and performance of a contract.

What about expectation?[3] Expectations seem to represent a perception as to whom one is entering a relationship with, and what one anticipates having to give to, and what one will get from, a relationship. So expectations are a conglomerate of the performance one imagines will be expected of oneself; who will expect such a performance; the burdens involved in providing this performance; the performance that can be expected of the other party; the benefits hoped to be

2 Generally on autonomy see Raz (1986); Grundman, Kerber and Weatherill (2001).

3 Generally on expectations see Steyn (1997).

derived from this performance; and what will happen if one party does not perform as expected.

There is, therefore, a close relationship between autonomy and expectation. A party exercises autonomy in deciding who to contract with; on what terms to contract; and how to behave in the course of performance. Making decisions on these matters will be influenced by the expectations that a party has as to who he is entering a relationship with and what he owes and is owed by virtue of being in this relationship.

The law cannot be neutral in a moral sense in matters relating to the balance of interests between parties to a contract.[4] The law must decide what expectations to enforce. To the extent that the law is concerned to promote autonomy, the law must also decide upon the degree of control or influence that is to be required before it is said that a party has exercised autonomy. The law must decide when a party should be able to claim that the degree of control or influence that he possessed is insufficient for him to have made an autonomous decision. In so deciding the law will have to choose what relevance information should have. When, if ever, should a lack of information mean that the party did not have sufficient control or influence over his decision so that it can be said that an autonomous decision was not made? Then there is the situation where positive information has been provided, has raised expectations, but is incorrect (whether these are expectations as to what one will get or who one will get it from). When, if ever, should it be said that this undermines the control or influence (and therefore the autonomy) of the recipient of the information? In making these various choices the law may discover that the parties have different expectations and that the type of autonomy that is valued by the parties is different. So, a trader may expect obligation and liability to be based upon intention, as this involves maximization of his (self reliant) control or influence (autonomy) in relation to who he is bound to and on what terms. By contrast, consumer expectations as to what they will get, and from whom, may be influenced by factors that go beyond what the traders in question intended. If expectations have been raised by information that is incorrect then the view may be that a truly autonomous decision has not been made.

Autonomy, Expectation, Freedom and Fairness

As I have suggested both autonomy and expectation are very open textured and indeterminate concepts. For example, I have argued that autonomy is about control or influence over decisions. So, a consumer might be said to be acting autonomously when entering a contract with imperfect information – the consumer still acts autonomously in the sense that a free choice is made to take the risk that the information may be imperfect. On the other hand it might be said that a

---

4 See Brownsword (1999), pp. 13, 38.

consumer only has a real chance of acting autonomously where he is in a position to make a more fully informed decision.[5]

Then we turn to expectations. It might be said that the expectations of the consumer should be determined by the formal terms of the contract. The formal terms are what the trader has agreed to; and they should determine what the consumer expects to get from the contract. In contrast, it could be argued that consumer expectations are (quite legitimately) formed by a much broader set of signals, including those coming in the form of advertising statements.[6] These signals must be taken into account in determining the reasonable expectations of the consumer; and the accuracy of these signals play a role in determining whether the consumer has had the chance to make a fully autonomous decision.

We can only engage in meaningful debate as to these concepts, and how they translate into concrete legal rules, once we have recognized that different types of autonomy and expectation are possible; that these different types of autonomy and expectation are based on different underlying philosophies of contract; and then gone on to work out which versions of autonomy and expectation seem to be in evidence in the context of the rules under consideration.

It seems that both autonomy and expectation take on particular types of meaning when viewed from a perspective that is more oriented to traditional freedom of contract values. Autonomy and expectation take on different meanings when viewed from a perspective that is more oriented to fairness values. From a classical freedom-oriented perspective *autonomy* is achieved by maximizing the (essentially *self-reliant*) freedom of the parties in relation to what is contracted for and with whom (if anyone) a contract is made. On this approach the autonomy of both parties is maximized by basing their obligations and liabilities on what they intended (or appeared to intend) to promise and who they intended (or appeared to intend) to make these promises to.

This connects with *expectation*. The expectations of a party as to what is being promised (and by whom) are viewed as being fixed by what the other party appears to have intended to promise, and who he appears to have made these promises to. So, for example, a consumer cannot expect that a trader will be liable except to the extent that the trader appears to have intended to promise to be bound. If a trader appears to intend to be bound to obligation 'X', but not to obligation 'Y' then the consumer cannot legitimately expect the trader to be bound to obligation 'Y'. In addition, if a trader appears not to intend to be bound to the consumer at all, then the consumer cannot legitimately expect the trader to be bound. The trader may send out inaccurate signals. However, if the trader does not appear to intend to be bound by these signals the inaccuracy will not be viewed as being a significant compromise of the autonomy of the consumer.

Then we turn to the role of vitiating factors. From a freedom-oriented perspective, once we have established what the parties appear to have intended to commit to, the intention to promise is only likely to be viewed as not genuinely autonomous where it has been induced by fairly extreme vitiating factors blatantly

---

5 Wein (2001), p. 80; Weatherill (2001), p. 180.

6 Brownsword, Howells and Wilhelmsson (1996), pp. 25, 41; Wightman (2003).

undermining the ability to make an autonomous decision. This preserves a high degree of (self reliant) autonomy for the parties. A party is free to make commitments except where his free agency has been seriously undermined by force or misinformation. A party is also free to use as broad a range of tactics as possible in order to secure the commitment of the other party; his freedom to do so only being restricted where he has been guilty of using blatantly exploitative tactics.

However, from a fairness-oriented perspective both autonomy and reasonable expectation must be read in light of the need to take account of distinctive consumer needs, perspectives and interests. This means recognizing a number of points. The first point is that consumers are likely to have less information than traders about products and services and the terms on which they are sold.[7] Secondly, consumers are likely to be placing a strong degree of reliance on advertising and marketing signals. These are much more transparent to the consumer than are the formal terms.[8] In addition, consumers are fairly infrequent purchasers of major items (at least by comparison with traders). As such, their expectations are less likely than many business contractors to have been shaped by experiences of 'problem' transactions and the way in which these are resolved.[9] In most cases their purchases will have been relatively trouble free. As such, their experience is of products and services that are value for money and live up to the promises made about them in advertising and marketing. It might, then, be said to be hardly surprising that a strong degree of reliance should be placed on these signals by comparison with the formal terms. A third point, relating specifically to substantive consumer interests, is that consumers buy products and services for use in the private sphere of life. If they do not live up to expectations there is a potentially serious impact upon the private sphere of life; rather than simply on the profitability of a firm. When cars, washing machines or televisions do not work according to what is normal or what was promised, there is a real impact on the private sphere of life, family etc.[10] There may also be less scope than that possessed by a trader to absorb the losses that result from such problems.[11]

This sort of analysis then leads a fairness-oriented perspective to view autonomy and expectation in particular ways; ways that are different from the way in which autonomy and expectation are viewed from a freedom-oriented perspective. This may involve the adoption of positive (or more indirect) transparency requirements. The consumer is then viewed as being in a more realistic position to exercise autonomy, through better informed consent.[12] It may involve refusing to enforce agreements based on the existence of factors that are considered to have vitiated the (fairness-oriented) autonomy of the consumer (consumer autonomy may have been restricted by a lack of transparency that

7 See Wein (2001), pp. 83-85; Weatherill (2001), p. 180.
8 See Brownsword, Howells and Wilhelmsson (1996); Wightman (2003).
9 See Wightman (2003), pp. 176-177.
10 See Wightman (1996), p. 97.
11 See Wightman (1996), pp. 97-98.
12 See Weatherill (2001).

compromises the ability to give informed consent; by the fact that no alternative terms were available; or by the fact that the consumer was in a much weaker bargaining position and so could not bargain for an improvement in what was on offer).[13]

A fairness-oriented approach may, where appropriate, involve supplementing the responsibilities of traders vis-à-vis consumers (by the imposition of substantive contractual obligations on traders). These obligations may be imposed on the grounds that they reflect the reasonable expectations of the consumer; these being expectations that may have been generated by signals that go beyond what is said in the formal terms.[14] These expectations may relate to matters that will have a serious impact on the private sphere of life. Giving legal recognition to these expectations can also be viewed as a way of enhancing the autonomy of the consumer. A consumer may have based his decision to enter a contract on an expectation that has been raised by incorrect information that has been provided to him. If this is the case, it might be suggested that the decision to enter the contract was not a fully autonomous decision, given that it was based on incorrect information. In addition, it is particularly important for the consumer to have the opportunity to make autonomous decisions, given the impact that the decision will have on the private sphere of life.

Such measures clearly restrict what, from a freedom-oriented perspective, would be understood to be the autonomy and expectations of traders. Traders are restricted in their ability to choose how to bring about contractual relationships. If obligations are imposed on a trader (to reflect the reasonable expectations and enhance the autonomy of the consumer) which the trader did not voluntarily undertake, then the autonomy of the trader has been restricted.[15] Equally, if obligations are imposed in relation to parties to whom the trader did not intend to oblige himself to it is clear that there is a restriction on the autonomy of the trader. Finally, the expectations of the trader are compromised. The trader is bound to terms that there was no intention to be bound to, and perhaps to parties that there was no intention to be bound to. The trader only expects, from a freedom-oriented perspective, to be bound to terms that have been agreed to and to parties to whom a commitment has been made.

In some cases there may be a choice as to which traders should suffer the restrictions (or at least the greatest restrictions) on autonomy. When such a choice exists then (to the extent that there is an agenda to maintain trader autonomy where possible) the rules should arguably seek to channel liability towards the party who is in the best position to find alternative means of exercising autonomy.

---

13 This approach can be argued to be taken in the regulation of consumer contract terms. On this see Willett (1999), pp. 82-83.

14 Willett (1996), p. 126.

15 See Willett (1996), p. 126.

Liability for Public and Advertising Statements

Art. 2 (2)(d) of the Consumer Sales Directive[16] provides that goods are presumed to be in conformity with the contract if they

> show the quality and performance which are normal in goods of the same type and which the consumer can reasonably expect, given the nature of the goods and taking into account any public statements on the specific characteristics of the goods made about them by the seller, the producer, or his representative, particularly in advertising or in labelling.

It should be noted that the provision refers to statements as to the 'specific characteristics' of the goods. This seems to exclude what lawyers in the UK would describe as 'sales puffs', i.e. statements that are not objectively verifiable.[17] However, it seems to cover objectively verifiable (or factual) statements (both those that describe the essential identity of the goods and those that describe other characteristics e.g. statements as to particular inspections that have been carried out, durability, fitness for different purposes and general performance capabilities).[18] In terms of the source of the relevant statements, what seems to be covered are (i) statements made solely by the seller in brochures, notices, labelling and general advertising; (ii) statements originally made by the producer or his representative (in brochures, notices, labelling and general advertising) but then passed on, displayed or otherwise conveyed to the consumer by the seller; (iii) statements by the manufacturer or his representative in brochures, notices, labelling and general advertising which have not been passed on to the consumer by the seller, but rather conveyed directly to the consumer via the media, billboard advertising, direct mailing, text messaging etc.[19]

The liability for these statements rest with the seller of the goods, and not with the producer.[20] Of course, even before this provision sellers in most Member States owed a general quality obligation of some type to the consumer. In the UK, for example, there is an implied term to the effect that goods will be of satisfactory quality.[21] This is an updated (and more 'consumerized') version of the old 'merchantable quality' obligation owed since the Sale of Goods Act 1893 and before in the common law. This quality obligation is itself based on a fairness-oriented approach to expectation. The obligation is imposed by law. The consumer has not acted autonomously (in a self-reliant sense) to extract a promise that the goods be of satisfactory quality. The seller does not intend to make a contractual

16 Directive 1999/44/EC, on certain aspects of the sale of consumer goods and associated guarantees, OJ 1999 L 171/12. Generally on the Directive and the concept of autonomy see Riesenhuber (2001).

17 See the English cases of *Dimmock* v. *Hallett* [1927] A.C. 177, PC, and *Hummingbird Motors* v. *Hobbs* [1986] R.T.R 278, CA.

18 See Willett, Morgan-Taylor and Naidoo (2004), pp. 94, 97.

19 See Oughton and Willett (2002), pp. 299, 311.

20 Directive 1999/44/EC, Art. 2 (1).

21 Sale of Goods Act, Section 14 (2).

promise to the effect that the goods are of satisfactory quality. It makes more sense to say that the consumer has a reasonable expectation that the goods will be of satisfactory quality.[22] Particularly in the case of modern, complex products consumers are unlikely to have sufficient information about potential defects to enable them to know what promises to seek to extract in relation to quality. Even if they did have this information they would usually lack the bargaining strength to persuade the seller to make such a promise. However, if goods are sold at their normal price they will normally be of satisfactory quality. This is the signal received by most consumers, and this is what is likely to be expected.

The satisfactory quality obligation has now been amended so as to indicate that one of the circumstances to be taken in to account in determining whether goods are of satisfactory quality is 'public statements on the specific characteristics of the goods made about them by the seller, the producer, or his representative, particularly in advertising or in labelling'.[23] As suggested, this would seem to cover the three categories of statement set out above. The pre-existing satisfactory quality obligation already covered statements falling into categories (i) and (ii) above, i.e. statements emanating solely from the seller and statements emanating from the producer, but passed on by the seller. Such statements might create independent liability for the seller. However, they would also be relevant to the general satisfactory quality obligation. 'Description' was always one of the factors to be taken into account when deciding whether the goods are of satisfactory quality.[24] This includes descriptions identifying the basic nature of the goods. However it also includes descriptive statements more generally and if such statements are made by the seller (whether they originate from the seller or the manufacturer) they could be taken into account under the heading of 'description'.[25] Again, this cannot be said to be based upon a freedom-oriented notion of autonomy. The seller is not responsible for such statements on the basis that he intends to promise to be liable for them. He is liable because the statements have influenced the expectations of consumers as to what can be expected in terms of quality. This brings us to the consumer side of the equation. As just indicated, taking account of the statements in categories (i) and (ii) in determining the scope of the quality obligation involves recognition that these statements may raise expectations that should be given some force of law. This is obviously a fairness-oriented version of expectation. It is grounded in statements that the seller has not necessarily intended to promise to be bound to; but which might nevertheless reasonably have influenced someone in the position of a consumer. There is also a fairness-oriented, rather than a freedom-oriented approach, to autonomy. The consumer has not exercised his autonomy in such a way as to elicit a promise from the seller to the effect that the statements are accurate. Rather, there are statements

---

22 See Willett (1996).

23 Sale and Supply of Goods to Consumers Regulations 2002, Regulation 3, which amends Section 14 of the Sale of Goods Act 1979 by the insertion of a new subsection (2D).

24 Sale of Goods Act, Section 14 (2A).

25 See *Rogers* v. *Parish* [1987] Q.B. 933.

that have raised expectations and, in this sense, influenced his decision to enter the contract. To the extent that these statements are incorrect, the ability of the consumer to make an informed decision is compromised. In this sense the autonomy of the consumer is compromised.

The real significance of the new provision (certainly in the UK) is that the statements in category (iii) above are now part of the quality obligation owed to the consumer. It is at least uncertain as to whether such statements would previously have been relevant to the quality standard in many Member States and certainly in the UK. When Section 14 refers to 'description', it seems unlikely that this covers statements made by the manufacturer or his representative that the seller has in no way conveyed or passed on to the consumer. It seems likely that the courts would have adhered to a more freedom-oriented approach and denied that a seller should have his autonomy and expectations restricted by holding him liable for statements made by another party. So it seems unlikely that statements made by the manufacturer or his representative would previously have been relevant to the Section 14 obligation owed by the seller. Making these statements relevant seems to fortify the fairness-oriented approach to consumer expectations and autonomy. The reality of modern marketing suggests a strong degree of reliance by consumers on statements by manufacturers.[26] Statements from manufacturers seem likely to play a significant role in determining consumer expectations. The expectations raised by such statements seem likely to be at least as powerful, and often more powerful, than expectations that are raised by statements made by sellers. Therefore, if the statements made by manufacturers are inaccurate this could be argued to have a particularly debilitating effect on the autonomy of the consumer in the sense of his ability to make an informed decision.

Not only is it unlikely that this would have been recognized previously by the satisfactory quality obligation, but the consumer would have found it difficult to obtain recognition of these interests by any other legal means. Again in line with a freedom-oriented approach to seller autonomy and expectation the courts would not find the seller liable in misrepresentation or breach of contract for statements which he has played no part in passing on to the consumer; and therefore clearly did not intend to be bound to. Direct manufacturer liability has also been difficult to obtain. The courts in the UK have been extremely reluctant in the past to impose direct contractual or tortious liability upon the manufacturer for his advertising statements. Where contractual liability has been in question the benchmark has, once again, been intention. A manufacturer will certainly be contractually bound where he makes a clear promise to do something (e.g. pay a sum of money or provide a service) in exchange for the consumer entering into a contract with a retailer to buy the product.[27] However, the courts are much more cautious where general advertising statements are concerned, even where these are factual statements that seem likely to have been relied upon and reasonably influenced the expectations of the consumer. The manufacturer will probably be liable where he

---

26 Riesenhuber (2001), p. 356, refers to the 'reliance [by the consumer] on the accuracy of information [contained in advertising] about the quality of the goods'.

27 See *Carlill* v. *Carbolic Smoke Ball Co.* [1893] Q.B. 256.

confirms the statement in response to an enquiry by a consumer contemplating entering a specific transaction.[28] However, in the absence of such confirmation, the courts have tended to deny that there is the requisite intention to undertake a contractual obligation.[29] Where liability in tort is in question, a fundamental requirement is that there should have been a special relationship of proximity between the parties giving rise to a duty to take care in relation to the making of the statement.[30] The courts have not tended to find that such a special relationship exists and have not chosen to ground liability on the compromise of the autonomy or expectations of the consumer.[31]

So, the new rule is a significant step towards a fairness-oriented notion of reasonable expectation and consumer autonomy in consumer contracting. The rule might also be said to make a significant contribution to a broader framework of EC rules that are concerned with ensuring respect for fairness-oriented notions of autonomy. Fairness-oriented autonomy might be said to be the concern of the various EC consumer law provisions that impose positive transparency and disclosure requirements.[32] Fairness-oriented autonomy also seems to be the goal of provisions granting cancellation rights to consumers.[33] Here the idea seems to be that we should guard against the danger that consumers may not have fully thought through the implications of certain important commitments. As such, the consumer should be given time for further reflection, in the hope that a more genuinely autonomous decision can be made. Fairness-oriented autonomy and expectation are also in evidence where rules on unfair contract terms are concerned. Under the Unfair Contract Terms Directive written terms must be expressed in plain and intelligible language.[34] In addition, whether a term is fair must be assessed by reference, *inter alia*, to whether the term was transparent.[35] The agenda seems to be to give the consumer an opportunity to make a more informed, and so autonomous, decision.

Seller Autonomy

For all this, the new rule clearly compromises the autonomy of the seller. He is liable for statements that have been made by another party and that he has not

---

28 See, e.g., *Shanklin Pier Ltd.* v. *Detel Products Ltd.* [1951] 2 K.B. 854; Beale (1996), pp. 137, 151.

29 See, e.g., *Lambert* v. *Lewis* [1982] A.C. 225.

30 *Caparo Industries plc.* v. *Dickman* [1990] 2 A.C. 605.

31 *Lambert* v. *Lewis* [1982] A.C. 225.

32 e.g., pre-contractual disclosure of certain specified information is required by Directives 90/314/EC (Package Travel), 94/47/EC (Time-Sharing) and 97/7/EC (Distance Selling).

33 e.g., 'cooling off' periods are provided for by Directives 85/577/EC (Doorstep Selling) and 94/47/EC (Package Travel).

34 Art. 5 (1).

35 See Willett (1999).

necessarily passed on to the consumer. The seller clearly does not intend to make a binding promise in relation to a statement that has come from a third party and that he has not even passed on to the consumer. He will only be able to escape this liability if he shows that:

> (a) at the time the contract was made, he was not, and could not reasonably have been, aware of the statement,
>
> (b) before the contract was made, the statement had been withdrawn in public or, to the extent that it contained anything which was incorrect or misleading, it had been corrected in public, or
>
> (c) the decision to buy the goods could not have been influenced by the statement.[36]

An example of defence (a) might be where the statement formed part of an advertising campaign which was aimed at another part of the EU and which the seller in question would not have known about at the time when he sold the goods to the consumer. Defence (a) seems to recognize that the seller should not be liable where he had no opportunity whatsoever to exercise autonomy in relation to the statement, because he was not aware of it.

Defence (b) refers to the statement being 'withdrawn' or 'corrected'. Presumably this can be done either by the seller or the producer. Presumably also the withdrawal or correction will need to refer clearly to the original statement and be clear about the fact that it is being withdrawn and/or the manner in which it is being corrected. Finally, it will be insufficient if the withdrawal or correction is in an obscure trade magazine; the publicity must be effective to alert consumers. Defence (b) allows the seller the opportunity to exercise a degree of autonomy in that he can be on the lookout for statements that may be incorrect and look to correct them. However, he may not know that they are incorrect; and this is no defence.

Defence (c) will surely be very difficult for the seller to establish in the face of the reliance that consumers arguably place upon manufacturers' statements; which statements are of course intended to induce exactly such reliance. Presumably this provision will protect the seller where he can show that the consumer could not have known of the statement.

We can see, then, that the rule on seller liability for producer statements is especially compromising of the autonomy of the seller. It is, of course, the producer who is in the best position to exercise his autonomy to prevent the problem in the first place; at least where the statement emanates from him. The producer can take autonomous action by exercising quality control over the advertising statements generated. Above I argued that if there is a choice between limiting the autonomy of one trader in the interests of protecting the consumer and limiting the autonomy of another trader for the same reasons then the law should seek to channel liability towards the party who is in the best position to exercise autonomy by alternative means. In our present context this means considering

---

36 Art. 2 (4).

ways in which liability can be channelled towards the producer. This will involve consideration of the best ways in which the rules of contract and tort can be used by the retailer against the producer in cases where the retailer has been held liable to the consumer for statements made by the producer. Of particular relevance in this context is Art. 4 of the Consumer Sales Directive, which says that:

> Where the final seller is liable to the consumer because of a lack of conformity resulting from an act or omission by the producer, the final seller shall be entitled to pursue remedies against the person or persons liable in the contractual chain. The person or persons liable against whom the final seller may pursue remedies, together with the relevant actions and conditions of exercise, shall be determined by national law.

There is considerable uncertainty as to what precisely this requires. How much freedom does it actually give to national law? Are producers entitled to contract out of any liabilities that may be imposed on them? These points cannot be developed in this chapter.[37] However, I would simply suggest that if retailer autonomy is thought to be an important principle in EC law then this provision should be interpreted (in so far as is possible in keeping with the text) in such a way as to oblige Member States to provide retailers with a remedy where they are held liable for the statements of producers. There is a quite separate means of channelling liability towards producers to which we shall now turn.

Guarantees and Associated Advertising

Where goods are sold or supplied to a consumer with such a guarantee, the guarantee is deemed to take effect at the time of delivery 'as a contractual obligation owed by the guarantor under the conditions set out in the guarantee statement and the associated advertising'.[38] The idea that the guarantee should be binding seems to fit both with a freedom-oriented and a fairness-oriented approach to autonomy. The party providing the guarantee clearly intends to be bound by it, so that, from a freedom-oriented perspective, holding him liable means simply holding him to his autonomously given promise. The consumer clearly expects the guarantee to be binding, so that, to the extent that he has been influenced to buy the product by the guarantee, the enforceability of the guarantee involves respect for the expectations and autonomy of the consumer.

However, what is of particular interest is that what is binding are the 'conditions laid down in the guarantee statement and the associated advertising'. Presumably what is meant here is that statements in leaflets, brochures and general advertising which add to or elaborate upon the formal contents of the guarantee should be binding along with these formal contents. This could expand the range of statements for which sellers and producers will be liable, especially within systems

37 For a full discussion of Art. 4 see Bridge (2002).

38 Art. 6 (1).

(such as those within the UK) which have been very reluctant to impose liability for producer's statements. Of course, this provision goes further than the provision discussed above which makes producers' advertising statements relevant to the overall assessment of satisfactory quality. An advertising statement will only be one factor to be taken into account in deciding on whether the goods are of satisfactory quality. However, the provision in relation to guarantees now under discussion seems to create 'stand alone' liability for advertising statements which are associated with guarantees. It seems therefore that the rule on associated advertising is reflective of a fairness-oriented notion of reasonable expectation and autonomy. The trader probably does not intend to be bound to these statements. However, the consumer may reasonably expect that the trader will be responsible for them; and if the statement is untrue or misleading the consumer has not, from a fairness-oriented perspective, made a fully autonomous decision to enter the contract. Of course, it will often be the producer who has given the guarantee and who will therefore be liable for both the guarantee and the associated advertising. There is therefore an opportunity for the consumer to hold the producer directly liable for at least some of his advertising statements. This may divert some of the liability for producers advertising away from the retailer and towards the producer. This means that the liability is focussed on the party (the producer) who is best placed to exercise autonomy to take autonomous action to prevent the problem arising in the first place.

However, the provision may actually go further than is obvious at first glance. Perhaps there is liability even where the advertising statement does not actually build on a particular provision in the formal guarantee. Rather there may be liability where the statement makes a 'guarantee' type promise itself, or even just a statement of fact? Does there even need to be a guarantee? Can the statement be one that is 'associated' simply with the goods? If we are interested in diverting as much liability as possible to the party best placed to exercise autonomy in relation to advertising statements then it is suggested that the rule should be interpreted to place as much liability for advertising statements as possible on the producer who has made the statements. This would reduce the need for the consumer to take action against the seller under Art. 2 (2)(d) above; so relieving the seller of the burden of liability that he is not best placed to take autonomous action to avoid. There might, indeed, be attractions to the consumer in taking action against the producer in cases where the complaint is not one relating to quality in a general sense; but rather simply that the goods do not live up to a particular statement in the producer's advertising. It must be remembered that the action against the seller is based on a general quality problem. A statement made by the producer may be incorrect, but this will not, in itself, guarantee that there will be a nonconformity for which the seller will be liable (or to put this in UK terminology, that the goods will be of unsatisfactory quality). The expectations raised by a statement are only one factor to be taken into account in deciding whether the goods are in conformity (or are of satisfactory quality). There may be an incorrect statement, but it may be concluded, on an overall assessment of the goods, that they are in conformity / are of satisfactory quality.

A Brief Comment on Autonomy in Commercial Contracts

Of course, questions of autonomy arise in relationships in cases other than where there is a consumer protection agenda. Where commercial contracts are concerned, there tends to be more controversy over rules that are restrictive of traditional freedom-oriented notions of autonomy. This is partly because there is less acceptance of the idea that either party to a commercial contract is inherently weaker and therefore in need of the assistance of the law. It is also often argued that certainty and traditional freedom-oriented autonomy and self-interested dealing should be prioritized in commercial contracts.[39] Intervention is probably least controversial where it can be said to be enhancing the autonomy of the 'protected' party (albeit that this is a fairness-oriented notion of autonomy); rather than refusing to enforce certain types of term or activity on purely substantive grounds. One way in which this can be said to occur is when the law bases the enforceability of standard terms on transparency. An example of this is the common law rule to the effect that particularly onerous or unusual terms should be drawn fairly to the attention of the other party if they are to be deemed to have been incorporated into the contract.[40] The idea, then, is that the term will not be impugned on substantive grounds as long as the other party had a fair chance of knowing of it; and therefore making a more fully informed decision as to whether to accept it. This is thought to be of importance in the case of unusual terms in particular as these depart from the general expectations of those in the contracting community in question. As such there is a suspicion that truly informed (autonomous) consent was not given.

Interpretation of contracts is another topical issue in English contract law at present. There appears to be a trend in interpreting contracts less in accordance with the literal meaning and more in accordance with the expectations of parties with the knowledge and experience of dealing as part of a particular contracting community.[41] So it might be rationalized that the provisions are not interpreted in a particular way simply so as to produce a substantively fair outcome. The agenda, rather, might be said to be to secure the autonomy of the parties by enforcing what parties in that contracting community would reasonably understand themselves to have agreed to.

References

Beale, H. (1996), 'Customers, Chains and Networks', in Willett, C. (ed.), *Aspects of Fairness in Contract* (London: Blackstone), pp. 137-155.

Beatson, J. and Friedmann, D. (eds.) (1995), *Good Faith and Fault in Contract Law* (Oxford: Clarendon Press).

---

39 See Brownsword (1999), pp. 16-19.

40 *Interfoto Picture Library Ltd.* v. *Stiletto Visual Programmes* [1989] Q.B. 433.

41 See Brownsword (2003), p. 104.

Bridge, M. (2002), 'Article 4 Right of Redress', in Bianca, M. and Grundman, S. (eds.), *EU Sales Directive Commentary* (Antwerp, Oxford, New York: Intersentia), pp. 179-204.

Brownsword, R. (1999), 'Positive, Negative and Neutral', in Brownsword, R., Hird, N.J. and Howells, G. (eds.), *Good Faith in Contract: Concept and Context* (Aldershot: Ashgate), pp. 13-40.

Brownsword, R. (2003), 'After *Investors*: Interpretation, Expectation and the Implicit Dimension of the "New Contextualism"', in Campbell, D., Collins, H. and Wightman, J. (eds.), *Implicit Dimensions of Contract* (Oxford and Portland, Oregon: Hart), pp. 103-141.

Brownsword, R., Hird, N.J. and Howells, G. (eds.) (1999), *Good Faith in Contract: Concept and Context* (Aldershot: Ashgate).

Brownsword, R., Howells, G. and Wilhelmsson, T. (1996), 'Between Market and Welfare: Some Reflections on Article 3 of the EC Directive on Unfair Terms in Consumer Contracts', in Willett, C. (ed.), *Aspects of Fairness in Contract* (London: Blackstone), pp. 25-59.

Collins, H. (1999), *Regulating Contracts* (Oxford: Oxford University Press).

Grundman, S., Kerber, W. and Weatherill, S. (eds.) (2001), *Party Autonomy and the Role of Information in the Internal Market* (Berlin: de Gruyter).

Oughton, D. and Willett, C. (2002), 'Quality Regulation in European Private Law', 25, *Journal of Consumer Policy*, pp. 299-328.

Raz, J. (1986), *The Morality of Freedom* (Oxford: Oxford University Press).

Riesenhuber, K. (2001), 'Party Autonomy and Information in the Sales Directive' in Grundman, S., Kerber, W. and Weatherill, S. (eds.), *Party Autonomy and the Role of Information in the Internal Market* (Berlin: de Gruyter), pp. 348-370.

Steyn, J. (1997), 'Contract Law: Fulfilling the Reasonable Expectations of Honest Men', 113, *Law Quarterly Review*, pp. 433-442.

Trebilcock, M.J. (1993), *The Limits of Freedom of Contract* (Cambridge, Massachusetts: Harvard University Press).

Weatherill, S. (2001), 'Justifying Limits to Party Autonomy in the Internal Market – EC Legislation in the Field of Consumer Protection', in Grundman, S., Kerber, W. and Weatherill, S. (eds.), *Party Autonomy and the Role of Information in the Internal Market* (Berlin: de Gruyter), pp. 180-196.

Wein, T. (2001), 'Consumer Information Problems – Causes and Consequences', in Grundman, S., Kerber, W. and Weatherill, S. (eds.), *Party Autonomy and the Role of Information in the Internal Market* (Berlin: de Gruyter), pp. 80-97.

Wightman, J. (1996), *Contract: A Critical Commentary* (London: Pluto).

Wightman, J. (2003), 'Beyond Custom: Contract, Contexts and the Recognition of Implicit Understandings', in Campbell, D., Collins, H. and Wightman, J. (eds.), *Implicit Dimensions of Contract* (Oxford and Portland, Oregon: Hart), pp. 143-186.

Willett, C. (1996), 'Fairness in Sale of Goods Act Quality Obligations and Remedies', in Willett, C. (ed.), *Aspects of Fairness in Contract* (London: Blackstone), pp. 123-136.

Willett, C. (1999), 'Good Faith and Consumer Contract Terms', in Brownsword, R., Hird, N.J. and Howells, G. (eds.), *Good Faith in Contract: Concept and Context* (Aldershot: Ashgate), pp. 67-89.

Willett, C., Morgan-Taylor, M. and Naidoo, A. (2004), 'The Sale and Supply of Goods to Consumers Regulations', *Journal of Business Law*, pp. 94-120.

Chapter 2

The Strategy and the Harmonization Process within the European Legal System: Party Autonomy and Information Requirements*

Paola Gozzo**

Introduction

Normally discussions about European law follow two different approaches. On one hand they look at national systems and compare them in order to find a common set of rules or values.[1] On the other hand, they look at the relationship between national laws and Europeans laws in order to find out if and to what degree national legal systems meet the requirements of the European directives.[2] In both cases, however, the perspective focuses on the national level.

* This publication has been written within the Research Network 'Uniform Terminology for European Private Law'. The member universities are Turin (Coordinator), Barcelona, Lyon, Münster, Nijmegen, Oxford and Warsaw. The research network is part of the Improving Human Potential (IHP) Programme financed by the European Commission (Contract no. HPRN-CT-2002-00229).

** I wish to thank Professor Roy Pateman for helping me to write the English version of this chapter.

1 A leading project on this regard is the University of Trento's initiative on The Common Core of European Private Law. This is a scholarly initiative launched in 1994 by Mauro Bussani and Ugo Mattei. The project seeks to unearth the common core of the body of European Private Law within the general categories of contract, tort and property. The search is for what is different and what is already common in the different legal forms of European Member States. See generally Bussani and Mattei (1995); Caruso (1995); Curran (2002). For a description of different scholarly initiatives on European Private Law see Pasa (2002).

2 The Bibliography on Community Law adoption within Member States is large. For general discussions see van Caenegem (2002); Zimmermann (2002); Werro (1998); Sacco (1993); Schulze (1995); Benacchio (2001); Schulze and Schulte-Nölke (2000); Hartkamp and Hesselink (1998). A forthcoming book on European Law gives a much more complete coverage and bibliography of EU directives and their adoption in Member States. See Benacchio and Pasa (2004).

In this chapter, I reverse this standpoint and put at the core of my argument the European legal system. Moreover, the chapter is based on an understanding of how the European legal system is shaped at two different levels: the Community law and the *ius commune*.[3] My concern is devoted to showing the strategy employed by European institutions, such as the Commission or the Council, to pursue European law harmonization. Because of this concern, I draw attention especially to EU documents. In order to underline the harmonization strategy adopted by the EU I took as a case study a diachronic perspective on the relationship between party autonomy and information requirements.

My argument is as follows. First, I look at the strategy adopted by the EU to harmonize the laws of Member States, especially those related to commercial exchanges. In this regard, I wish to make two initial observations. The EU has used the legislative tool widely in connection with specific areas of contract such as consumer law. This has been called the *'sector-specific approach'*. Starting in 2001, the European Commission begun to be more concerned about contract law in general and, therefore, in stressing a common shared concept such as party autonomy. This development is connected with the debates concerning the introduction of a European Civil Code, and with the European Commission's current agenda, which expressly calls for an official discussion on the topic. I am referring, in particular, to the Communication of July 2001 'On European Contract Law'[4] and to the Communication of February 2003 entitled 'A More Coherent European Contract Law – An Action Plan'.[5]

Taking into account the different normative policies of European institutions, I provide an understanding of party autonomy and information requirement relationships at Community law and at *ius commune* levels over the last two decades. I argue that during the nineties, party autonomy and information requirement were used by the European Commission as *strategic tools* to pursue its harmonization policies, and to penetrate the space occupied by the laws of the Member States. In this context I stress the fact that at Community law level party autonomy has taken on the language of traditional contract theory but not the context. In particular, I suggest that at the Community level, party autonomy is now an unformalized expression or a *vague notion*.[6] Moreover, I stress the fact that party autonomy is employed by the EU as a vague notion in order to avoid cultural resistance and problems within Member States' legal systems and therefore, to foster its new policy of general European contract law.

This article is divided into three parts. The first part provides the basic framework about the European harmonization process and its context. The second part discusses the questions regarding the role occupied by party autonomy and information requirements within the EU legal system. The third part deals with the

---

3 For existing relations between Community Law and *ius commune* see Somma (2003).

4 COM (2001) 398 final.

5 COM (2003) 68 final.

6 For vague notion related to legal transplants and transition processes see Ajani (2003), p. 3. For vague notion in language and logic see Williamson (1994).

concept of the *vague notion* and the EU harmonization process, providing an analysis of the strategy underpinning it.

The EU Legal System and the Harmonization Process on Contract Law

The emerging European legal system is a complex phenomenon shaped by different forces. On one hand is the modern *ius commune*, and on the other hand, the *Community law*.[7]

Ius commune lacks a modern definition, but is widely represented by soft law recognized by market actors,[8] by domestic courts' judgments and by texts stressing a common European legal tradition.[9] This drives a bottom-up harmonization process.

Community law consists of an enormous volume of legislative measures, such as directives, communications and resolutions, produced by EU institutions driving a top to bottom harmonization process.[10]

Recently, some authors have pointed out that with regard to private law the *ius commune* and Community law adopt different approaches: in particular, Somma has claimed that the *ius commune* is pursuing a solidaristic dimension of the law of contract while Community law is stressing an individualistic one.[11] His analyses

---

7 For existing relations between *ius commune* and Community law see Somma (2003).

8 Soft law is a term generally employed to refer to a great variety of instruments such as declarations of principles, codes of practice, guidelines, standard forms, that lack legal status and are not legally binding, but there is a strong expectation that their provisions will be respected and followed. In *ius commune* it can be represented by Unidroit principles or by Principles of European Contract Law.

9 For common understanding of modern *ius commune* I refer to Professor van Gerven's collection *Ius commune casebooks for the Common Law of Europe* where all publications are based on text, cases and materials on national, supranational and international laws. See generally Devroe and Droshout (2004); Larouche (2000); van Gerven (1996); for further information see http://www.rechten.unimaas.nl/casebook or http://www.law.kuleuven.ac.be/casebook/.

10 The entire body of European law is known as *acquis communautaire*. It includes all treaties, regulations, directives passed by European institutions as well as ECJ judgements. The Glossary of EU defines it as follow: 'The Community *acquis* is the body of common rights and obligations which bind all Member States together within the European Union'. See http://europa.eu.int/scadplus/leg/en/cig/g4000.htm.

11 See Alpa (2000); Somma (2003), p. 16: 'Il diritto comune europeo mostra di preferire il dialogo con le scienze sociali e difatti valorizza i concetti di classe e di ruolo – i quali alludono a schemi comportamentali fortemente eterodiretti – mutuati specialmente dall'analisi sociologica. Laddove il diritto comunitario mostra di voler dialogare prevalentemente con quelle scienze economiche che utilizzano come punto di riferimento per le loro costruzioni un modello umano capace di affrancarsi dai condizionamenti del reale. [...]. In tal modo il diritto comune europeo si presenta come un ordinamento capace di consolidare il percorso storico compiuto dalla civilistica, che ha abbandonato il riferimento a modelli di impronta individualistica per valorizzare

are based upon a comparison between domestic courts and legislation, and European directives in various fields.[12]

In my opinion analyses such as Somma's, focusing on individuals as market actors, underline the general trust of Community law in sustaining a free capital market shaped by the needs of major enterprises.

The complex European scenario depicted above leads me to investigate in detail the actual relationship between party autonomy and information requirements in Community law separately from the *ius commune*. Moreover, I will investigate it from a dynamic perspective within the harmonization process.

Today, in the EU there are two major problems on the agenda. The first concerns harmonization; the second concerns the principles that animate or could animate it. Regarding the latter there are two basic approaches: one search is for the common core of different domestic laws (Common Core Project),[13] the other seeks to identify the existence of the principles already present in Community law (Acquis Group).[14]

Recent debates on harmonization stress two different but interconnected points: the first concerns harmonization itself, and the second the law of contract.[15]

Regarding the latter it has been pointed out that the law of contracts assumes, at the Community level, an extraneous connotation compared to domestic context or a *policy oriented* nature. As it has been written:

> It is true that European contracts law, unlike national laws, opts for a stronger *policy* attitude (consumer protection, internal market construction....).[16]

Indeed, the justification for contract law harmonization is expressly stated in the need to assure competition in the European internal market.

With regard to harmonization, it has also been noted that a distinction must be made between harmonization as a product and harmonization as a process. Particularly, discussions invite to valorise the role of law-making institutions.[17]

---

costruzioni di marca solidaristica. Diversamente il diritto comunitario [...] si presenta come un ritorno all'individualismo'.

12 Somma (2003). The author analyses: standard forms, medical and environmental liability.

13 See *supra*, n. 1.

14 The *Acquis Group* was founded in 2002 and currently consists of more than 30 legal scholars from (nearly) all EC Member States. Professor Ajani (University of Turin, Italy) represents the group as speaker and Professor Schulte-Nölke (University of Bielefeld, Germany) co-ordinates the activities. The *Acquis Group* targets a systematic arrangement of existing Community law which will help to elucidate the common structures of the emerging Community private law. It concentrates its work upon existing EC private law which can be discovered within the *acquis communutaire*. See Pasa (2002). For more information on Acquis Group see www.Acquis-Group.org; Schulte-Nölke (2003).

15 Cafaggi (2003).

16 Cafaggi (2003), p. 203.

17 Cafaggi (2003); Joerges (2003).

Examining the EU as a law making institution, we can distinguish two different phases: the first covering the period from the end of the eighties and the beginning of the nineties, and the second beginning with the Tampere (Finland) meeting of 15-16 October 1999.[18]

In the first period, the EU proceeded with the formation of the *acquis communautaire*. Until the Tampere meeting the EU had employed a *sector specific approach* to strengthen the construction of a set of common rules assuring competition within the internal market. From 1999, as a result of Tampere Council conclusions, a claim for a *greater convergence in civil law* among Member States was put on the agenda.[19] The Commission's Communications of 2001 and of 2003, which were focused on European contract law, furthered the European Council's new policy.

The Communication of 2001 in particular was intended to broaden the debate on European Contract Law and was concerned to gather information on the need for far-reaching EU action in the area of contract law. The Communication posed three questions. Whether the proper functioning of the Internal Market was affected by problems regarding the conclusion, interpretation and application of cross-border contracts. Whether different national contract laws discourage or increase the costs of cross-border transactions. Finally, whether a sectorial harmonization approach to contract law could lead to possible inconsistencies in European laws or to problems of non-uniform application and transposition into national legal systems.[20]

The Communication of 2003 maintains the consultative character stated in the previous communication. It confirms that there is no need to abandon the sector specific approach but

> seeks to obtain feedback [...] whether non-sector specific measures such as an optional instrument may be required to solve problems in the area of European contract law.[21]

Particularly, the Commission wished to elaborate a *common frame of reference* for European contract law that must provide for best solutions in terms of common terminology and rules, such as the definition of fundamental concepts and abstract terms or of the rules governing aspects of contract law, such as non-performance. Moreover, a common frame of reference must become the base for further reflection on an optional general instrument in the area of European contract law. Regarding the latter, the Commission intends to launch a debate

---

18 Tampere Council conclusions 'Towards a Union of Freedom, Security and Justice' (Bulletin EU 10-1999).

19 Chapter VII of Tampere Council conclusions entitled 'Greater convergence in civil law' states: 'As regards substantive law, an overall study is requested on the need to approximate Member States' legislation in civil matters in order to eliminate obstacles to the good functioning of civil proceedings. The Council should report back by 2001'.

20 COM (2001) 398 final, p. 3.

21 COM (2003) 68 final, p. 4.

on the opportunism, the possible legal form, the contents and the legal basis for possible solutions.[22]

Party Autonomy, Information Requirements and Community Law

In the Treaty of the European Community there is no explicit reference to party autonomy. Nevertheless, it is expressly stated that the Union is found upon the market economy. In Art. 4 (1) of the Treaty it is written:

> For the purposes set out in Article 2, the activities of the Member States and the Community shall include, as provided in this Treaty and in accordance with the timetable set out therein, the adoption of an economic policy which is based on the close coordination of Member States' economic policies, on the internal market and on the definition of common objectives, and conducted in accordance with the *principle of an open market economy* with free competition.[23]

Moreover, Art. 3 EC Treaty speaks about an internal market based upon free movements of goods, persons, capitals and services.

Art. 153 (ex-Art. 129a) EC Treaty, on consumer's protection, deals with information and states:

> In order to promote the interests of consumers and to ensure a high level of consumer protection, the Community shall contribute to protecting the health, safety and economic interests of consumers, as well as to promoting their right to information, education and to organise themselves in order to safeguard their interests.

In the Draft Treaty Establishing a Constitution for Europe, Art. 3 affirms that the Union shall offer an area of freedom, security and justice and a single market where competition is free and undistorted; Art. 4 reaffirms fundamental freedoms. In the preamble to Part II can be read:

> Conscious of its spiritual and moral heritage, the Union is founded on the indivisible, universal values of human dignity, freedom, equality and solidarity; it is based on the principles of democracy and the rule of law. It places the individual at the heart of its activities, by establishing the citizenship of the Union and by creating an area of freedom, security and justice [...].

Title IV on solidarity provides for a right to information *in good time* to workers.[24] Right to information is also provided in the section devoted to consumer protection.[25]

---

22 COM (2003) 68 final, point 2.

23 Emphasis added.

24 Art. II-27 Draft Treaty Establishing a Consitution for Europe.

25 Art. III-130 Draft Treaty Establishing a Consitution for Europe.

Regarding the secondary legislation level, I consulted the directives listed below:

- Directive 1999/44/EC on certain aspects of the sale of consumer goods and associated guarantees;[26]
- Directive 93/13/EEC on unfair terms in consumer contracts;[27]
- Directive 90/314/EEC on package travel, package holidays and package tours;[28]
- Directive 85/577/EEC to protect the consumer in respect of contracts negotiated away from business premises;[29]
- Directive 87/102/EEC for the approximation of the laws, regulations and administrative provisions of the Member States concerning consumer credit (as modified by Directive 90/88/EEC and 98/7/EEC);[30]
- Directive 97/7/EC on the protection of consumers in respect of distance contracts;[31]
- Directive 94/47/EC on the protection of purchasers in respect of certain aspects of contracts relating to the purchase of the right to use immovable properties on a timeshare basis.[32]

They all represent directives on consumer protection mentioned in the first European communication on contract law already adopted by Member States.[33] I am referring to the Communication from the Commission to the Council and the European Parliament *On European Contract Law* of 11 July 2001 and, in particular, to Annex I on *Important community acquis in the area of private law.*[34]

All Directives, at least in their recitals stress the need to foster market transactions among and between Member States and freedom of personal, goods and services movements. However, no one makes an explicit reference to party autonomy or to it contents.

By contrast, in consumer contract law, many directives contain information requirements as an obligation of the parties providing services or goods.[35] For instance, many directives stipulate that the information has to be given in writing,[36]

26 OJ L 171 of 7 July 1999, pp. 12-16.

27 OJ L 095 of 21 April 1993, pp. 29-34.

28 OJ L 158 of 23 June 1990, pp. 59-64.

29 OJ L 372 of 31 December 1985, pp. 31-33.

30 OJ L 042 of 12 February 1987, pp. 48-53.

31 OJ L 144 of 4 June 1997, pp. 19-27.

32 OJ L 280 of 29 October 1994, pp. 83-87.

33 I omitted the Proposal for a Directive concerning the distance marketing of consumer financial services.

34 COM (2001) 398 final.

35 On the importance of information requirements within European Private Law and consumer policy see Schulze, Ebers and Grigoleit (2003); Reich and Woodroffe (1994); Micklitz and Weatherill (1993).

36 Art. 4 Directive 85/577/EEC on Contracts Negotiated away from Business Premises; Arts. 4 and 6 (1) Directive 87/102/EEC on Consumer Credit; Art. 4 Directive

or that the information must be given in a clear and comprehensible manner.[37] The Directives on Timesharing[38] and on Package Travel[39] stipulate that the information given becomes an integral part of the contract and binds the supplier of the service. In the same directive there are provisions concerning modifications of the information and the communication of these to the consumer.[40] Moreover, many directives concerning consumer protection provide for information requirements to be given prior to the conclusion of the contract.[41] Basically, such information, concerns the major characteristics of the goods or services, price and additional costs, arrangements for payment, rights and obligations of the consumer, as well as the procedures required to finalize the contract and to take redress. Information requirements can be also provided at the time of the conclusion of the contract, as in the case of the Directive on Legal Assistance[42] or after its conclusion, such as Art. 4 of Cross Border Credit Transfer Directive.

However, a significant point to mention is that nowhere in Community directives is there a clear definition or a general clause concerning information requirements.

The only places where the European community officially makes express reference to party autonomy are in some recent documents, dealing with the European contract law in general. I am referring, particularly, to the Communication on the European contract law of 2001 (already mentioned) and to the more recent Communication of February 2003 entitled 'A More Coherent European Contract Law – An Action Plan'.[43]

For instance the 2001 document refers to party autonomy in these terms:

> Generally, national contract law regimes lay down the principle of contractual freedom. Accordingly, contracting parties are free to agree their own contract terms. However, each contract is governed by the laws and court decisions of a particular state. Some of these national rules are not mandatory and contracting parties may decide either to apply these rules or to agree different terms. Other national rules, however, are

---

90/314/EEC on Package Travel; Arts. 3 (1) and 2 (4) Directive 94/47/EC on Timesharing; Art. 5 Directive 97/7/EC on Distance Contracts.

37 Art. 10 (1) Directive 2000/31/EC on Electronic Commerce; Art. 5 Directive 97/7/EC on Distance Contracts; Art. 4 Directive 85/577/EEC on Contracts Negotiated away from Business Premises; Art. 4 (1) Directive 90/314/EEC on Package Travel; Art. 3 (2) Directive 94/47/EC on Timesharing.

38 Art. 3 (2) Directive 94/47/EC on Timesharing.

39 Art. 3 (2) Directive 90/314/EEC on Package Travel.

40 Art. 3 (2) Directive 94/47/EC on Timesharing; Art. 3 (2) Directive 90/314/EEC on Package Travel; Art. 6 (2) Directive 87/102/EEC on Consumer Credit.

41 For instance: Arts. 4 and 5 Directive 97/7/EC on Distance Contracts state that information must be given in good time during the performance of the contract or at least at the time of delivery; Art. 6 Directive 87/102/EEC on Consumer Credit states that information might also be given at the agreement's time.

42 Directive 87/344/EEC on Legal Assistance.

43 COM (2003) 68 final.

mandatory, in particular where there is an important disparity between the positions of the contracting parties, such as contracts with tenants or consumers.[44]

In the same documents, the EU also deals with information requirements. Annex III, *on the structure of the Acquis and relevant binding instruments,* provides a list of the directives containing information requirements. It inserts them in the paragraph on pre-contractual and contractual obligations and, in particular under the label: *obligations of the party providing the services or the goods.* It organizes them with regard to the point at which they must be delivered: prior to the conclusion of the contract, at the time of the conclusion of the contract and after the conclusion of the contract.

In its 2003 communication the European Commission confirms its understanding of party autonomy as a principle of Member States' legal systems. Moreover, in the part where it discusses the opportunity to promulgate non specific-sector measures on European contract law it is written:

> It is the opinion of the Commission that contractual freedom should be one of the guiding principles of such a contract law. Restrictions on this freedom should only be envisaged where this could be justified for good reasons. Therefore it should be possible for the specific rules of such a new instrument, once it has been chosen by the contracting parties as the applicable law to their contract, to be adapted by the parties according to their needs.[45]

Information requirements are not mentioned anywhere else.

Party Autonomy, Information Requirements and *Ius Commune*

In the words of the European Commission, party autonomy constitutes something inherent in the economic and cultural background (or substrata) of the domestic legal orders and, therefore, of the European legal system. Being more precise, the Commission refers to freedom of contract and affirms that it must be put at the core of the future European law of contract. However, by contrast with its high declaratory value, party autonomy is quite absent in the Community law.

The Commission ruling can be compared with what happens in the domestic laws where party autonomy represents the rule laid down as forming the basis of the law of contract, under the technical and the interpretative profiles, both in legislation and case law.

An example from the Italian experience, Art. 1322 of the Italian Civil Code formulates the principle.[46] This Article is the pivot of the entire general part of

44 COM (2001) 268 final, point 27.

45 COM (2003) 68 final, point 93.

46 Art. 1322 Italian *Codice civile*: Autonomia contrattuale. 'Le parti possono liberamente determinare il contenuto del contratto nei limiti imposti dalla legge. Le parti possono anche concludere contratti che non appartengono ai tipi aventi una disciplina

contract law; it refers to the agreement, the cause, and the content of the contract as well as the contract's interpretation or resolution.[47] Italian monographs on private law face the matter both in order to show its importance and to indicate its limits.[48]

The only textbook devoted to European Contract Law dedicates a chapter to freedom of contract and to its limits.[49] As with the Italian Civil Code, the Principles of European Contract Law[50] provide a definition of Freedom of Contract:

> (1) Parties are free to enter into a contract and to determine its contents, subject to the requirements of good faith and fair dealing, and the mandatory rules established by these Principles.
> (2) The parties may exclude the application of any of the Principles or derogate from or vary their effects, except as otherwise provided by these Principles.[51]

As it has been seen in section two, information requirements are a key concept in Community law. They constitute a list of obligations imposed on those parties providing goods or services and constitute part of the vocabulary of Community law.

However, as far as legal scholarship is concerned, the category of information requirements is meaningless. Private lawyers, whether in the civil or common tradition, refer to duties and rights and, therefore, about a duty to inform, or to disclose, and a right to information. But, Italian law does not provide for a special article in the Civil Code concerning information requirements. Rather these requirements are discussed in connection with other issues such as pre-contractual liability, good faith, and, more recently, consumer contracts.[52] There is though a claim by some scholars for a *contratto informato*.[53]

The tendency to deal with information requirements in connection with other institutions of the law of contract is also shown in the textbook on European

---

particolare, purché siano diretti a realizzare interessi meritevoli di tutela secondo l'ordinamento giuridico'.

47 Agreement (Arts. 1326-1342 Italian Civil Code); cause (Arts. 1343-1345 Italian Civil Code); object (Arts. 1346-139 Italian Civil Code); interpretation (Arts. 1362-1371 Italian Civil Code); resolution (Arts. 1453-1469 Italian Civil Code).

48 See for instance Trimarchi (2003); Galgano (2001); Gazzoni (2000).

49 Flessner and Kötz (1997), Chapter 8 'The limits of contractual freedom', p. 124. The chapter is devided as follows: I. Introduction; II. Regulated contracts: 1. Tenants, 2. Employees, 3. Consumers, 4. Costs and Benefits; III. Unfair Contracts; IV. The Control of General Conditions of Business.

50 Lando and Beale (2000); Lando and Clive (2003). On General Principles of European Contract Law see Castronovo (2001); Gentili (2001).

51 Art. 1:102 Principles of European Contract Law.

52 Pre-contractual liability (Art. 1337 Italian Civil Code); good faith (Art. 1375 Italian Civil Code); consumer's contract (Arts. 1469bis-1469sexies Italian Civil Code).

53 A general claim for a *contratto informato* by Italian scholars can be found in De Nova and Sacco (2002); Musy (1999).

contract law.[54] Also the Principles of European Contract Law do not spell out information requirements in detail.[55] Even if Art. 4:106 deals with the particular case in which the information given by a party to the other was incorrect[56] the law adopts a traditional approach to questions arising from the violation of information requirements and reframes them in terms of pre-contractual liability,[57] general good faith, fair dealing,[58] or co-operative duties.[59] This does not mean that information requirements do not exist at an academic level and debates. This simply means that they are not part of a traditional approach to contract law.

At this stage in my argument, the relationship between party autonomy and information requirements can be illustrated through this image: in *ius commune* party autonomy is included in codification or general contract doctrines, while information requirements are not. On the contrary, in the Community law party autonomy has no place in written law, whereas information requirements occupy considerable space within the incoherent corpus of the community documents, and are explicitly recognized as a category by the European Commission.

Depending on the perspective taken, the relationship between party autonomy and information requirements can be radically different. In Community law information requirements play a central role in consumer contract law. In contrast, at the *ius commune* level they are duties and rights built around general rules on party autonomy. Moreover, if party autonomy is analysed within *ius commune*, it is a rule with certain contents and constraints, whereas it is impossible to give it a precise meaning within Community law.

Party Autonomy, Information Requirements and the EU's Harmonization Strategy

I will pose a number of questions. What was the impact of the adoption of EU directives on Member States legal systems? What was the normative policy

54 Flessner and Kötz (1997). Duties of information are treated in the chapter devoted to deceit and duress under different labels such as right of information or duty to disclose. See section II: 'Non-disclosure as Deceit', p. 198.

55 Reasons are two. The first one regards the fact that the Principles of European Contract Law only deal with the general part of contract law and not with specific contracts while information requirements have been developed in connection with specific contracts and not with general contract law theory. The second reason is connected with the remedies oriented nature of the Principles of European Contract Law. See Storme (2003), p. 231.

56 Art. 4:106 Principles of European Contract Law states: 'A party who has concluded a contract relying on incorrect information given it by the other party may recover damages in accordance with Art. 4:117 and even if the information does not give rise to a right to avoid the contract on the ground of mistake under Art. 4:103, unless the party who gave the information had reason to believe that the information was correct'.

57 Art. 4:117 Principles of European Contract Law.

58 Art. 1:201 Principles of European Contract Law.

59 Art. 1:202 Principles of European Contract Law.

pursued by the EU during the past year's promulgating directives? Why are there so many information requirements listed in consumer law directives? Why do recent Communications on European contract law stress the concept of freedom of contract as a general principle of all Member States? What kind of relationship affects party autonomy and information requirements within the European harmonization process?

From the EU perspective the first result of the adoption of EU directives is their enactment into domestic law. Information requirements are seen as strictly connected with consumer law, and consumer law is generally seen as a product of EU directives.[60] Moreover, the style adopted by European legislators in designing rules on consumer law focuses on listing precise information obligations on those providing goods and services.

From a law making perspective, consumer law represents one of the most interesting results of the *sector-specific approach* of Community law as well as one of the most important chapters of the *acquis communitaire*. Besides persisting differences between domestic legal systems, it penetrates into the tissue of the legislation of all Member States, especially founding members, at least with regards to information requirements.

Party autonomy is a principle inherent in Community law, but without any specific definition. It is inherent both because the EU was founded upon the ideology of market economy and because all Member States base their contract theory on it. Its contents and its limits are not established at Community law level, but within domestic legal systems.

To avoid 'legal irritants',[61] Community law sticks to broad principles without addressing any normative content. In the domestic context, freedom of contract takes a precise normative dimension through the rules governing contracts and their interpretation. At Community level it loses its content and remains

> the centrepiece of contract law in all Member States and enables contracting parties to conclude the contract which most suits their particular needs. This freedom is restricted by certain compulsory contract law provisions or requirements resulting from other laws. However, compulsory provisions are limited and parties to contract enjoy a significant degree of freedom in negotiating the contract terms and conditions they want.[62]

With the 2001 document, party autonomy is placed firmly at the top of Community law, and paradoxically it is at the top at a time which is characterized

---

60 It is true that consumer protection was a doctrine already known in some Member States before the promulgation of the first directive of this kind. However, it is also true that consumer protection was greatly helped through the adoption of European directives in all Member States. Moreover, it is true that consumer protection was a quite new field also for those countries, as France and Germany and England that begin to regulate this sector before European intervention. Reich and Woodroffe (1994); Micklitz and Weatherhill (1993).

61 Teubner (1998), p. 23.

62 COM (2003) 68 final.

by a decline in the importance of information requirements among other issues in domestic law.

But in which way is it placed at the top? Not as a rule, as it is at *ius commune* level, but as an unidentified and unformalized concept or, using Gianmaria Ajani's words: a *vague notion*.[63] Professor Ajani has used this term in debates on the circulation of legal models and legal transplants. In particular, he stresses that vague notions are useful in pursuing legislative policies starting from a distinctive base. His argument is founded upon a difference between the symbolic and the empirical meaning of concepts[64] and goes on to affirm that once these concepts are received in borrowing countries they lose their original empirical meaning and take on a symbolic relevance. In this way, *a priori* legitimated models, based on concepts widely recognized as development market factors, became tools with which to pursue legal reforms. Moreover, macro-transnational notions, or hyper-notions, due to their vagueness and consequent flexibility, can influence local laws without interfering with particular cultural and social contexts.

Following a strategy already taken by other law-making institutions around the world, the EU is also stressing standards generally agreed upon to reach a consensus on items in its legislative agenda.

Conclusions

In his book devoted to law of contract, Sacco affirms that the jurist desires and has always desired that the contract regulated by the law corresponds to criteria of justice and fairness.[65] The author explains the idea through a description of the contract that must fit three requirements. In Sacco's view the contract, must be *libero, ponderato e informato*.

Other authors echo the need for a 'just contract': for example, in France, Ghestin wrote about *l'utile et le juste* as fundamentals of the general theory of contract.[66] Common law doctrine is concerned with *fairness in the exchange*, to underline the need that the contract must correspond to this criterion.[67]

Without digressing too far, it is evident that within the academic world the discussions concerning the relationship between party autonomy and information requirements follow the debates on contract's justice. With respect to the role occupied by party autonomy and by information requirements inside the

---

63 Ajani (2003), p. 3. For a definition of vague notion see Rossi (2003): a vague notion is a notion where the boundaries of its application are not clearly delineated.

64 Such as *rule of law, corporate governance* and *good faith*. Ajani (2003), p. 3, concentrates his analysis on the strategic use of vague notions on countries in transition from planned to market economies such as the Russian Federation and countries of Central Europe. Moreover, he stresses the action of some institutions such as World Bank, International Monetary Fund and the EU.

65 De Nova and Sacco (2003).

66 Ghestin (1981).

67 Atiyah (1979).

Community law, I believe that the first one constitutes a *vague notion* and that the second one represents rules with a high degree of formalization useful to penetrate different national contexts.

Examining the data related to directives on consumer contracts in parallel with normative policies pursed by EU the different strategies adopted in the two phases of European harmonization is evident. The first phase is marked by sector-specific harmonization and by the diffusion of information requirements into domestic boundaries. The second phase is one of pursuing harmonization in a field intimately involved with the cultural and historical background of single legal systems. Shifting party autonomy from its rule's role to that of a vague notion gives the EU the opportunity to open discussions on a wider level on the codification of a civil law on principles shared by all Member States.

The absence, in the whole corpus of Community law of a definition of party autonomy together with the contextual absence of a general theory of contract, allows the Community to avoid cultural resistance from Member States following different legal traditions. At the same time, the new policy for a general European Civil Code is being pursued on two tracks. On one hand, through the manifold directives already adopted by Member States and, on the other, by concentrating on concepts already existing within national legal systems, but cleansed of their local specificity.

References

Ajani, G. (2003), 'Navigatori e giuristi. A proposito del trapianto di nozioni vaghe', in Bertorello, V. (ed.), *Io comparo, tu compari, egli compara: che cosa, come, perchè?* (Milan: Giuffrè).

Alpa, G. (2000), *La cultura delle regole. Storia del diritto civile italiano* (Rome and Bari: Laterza).

Atiyah, P.S. (1979), *The Rise and Fall of Freedom of Contract* (Oxford: Clarendon Press).

Benacchio, G.A. (2001), *Diritto privato della Comunità europea. Fonti, modelli, regole*, 2nd edn. (Padua: Cedam).

Benacchio, G.A. and Pasa, B. (forthcoming 2004), *The Enlarged Union: A Guide to European Private Law* (Budapest: CEU Press).

Bussani, M. and Mattei, U. (1995), *The Common Core Approach to European Private Law*, at http://www.jus.unitn.it/dsg/common-core/Approach.html.

Caenegem, van, R.C. (2002), *European Law in the Past and in the Future* (Cambridge: Cambridge University Press).

Cafaggi, F. (2003), 'Una *Governance* per il diritto europeo dei contratti?', paper presented at *Europeanization of contract law?* Conference held at the European University Institute, Florence, 24-25 October 2003, reproduced at http://www.iue.it/LAW/ResearchTeaching/EuropeanprivateLaw/Conferences.shtml.

Caruso, D. (1995), *The Common Core of European Private Law*, Common Core Meeting, Trento, 6-8 July 1995, reproduced at http://www.jus.unitn.it/dsg/common-core/papers/europe.html.

Castronovo, C. (2001), 'Il contratto nei "Principi di diritto europeo"', 4, *Europa e diritto privato*, pp. 787-823.

Curran, V. (2002), 'On the Shoulders of Schlesinger: The Trento Common Core of European Private Law Project', 2, *Global Jurist Frontiers*, no. 2, reproduced at http://www.bepress.com/gj/frontiers/vol2/iss2/art2.
De Nova, G. and Sacco, R. (2002), 'Obbligazioni e contratti', in Rescigno, P., *Trattato di diritto privato* (Turin: Utet).
Devroe, W. and Droshout, D. (2004), *The Ius Commune Casebook Project*, reproduced at http://www.law.kuleuven.ac.be/casebook/.
Flessner, A. and Kötz, H. (1997), *European Contract Law* (Oxford: Clarendon Press).
Galgano, F. (2001), *Diritto privato* (Padua: Cedam).
Gazzoni, F. (2000), *Manuale di diritto privato* (Naples: Edizioni Scientifiche Italiane).
Gentili, A. (2001), 'I principi di diritto contrattuale europeo: verso una nuova nozione di contratto?', *Rivista di diritto privato*, pp. 42 *et seq.*
Gerven, van, W. (1996), 'Casebooks for the Common Law of Europe: Presentation of the Project', 4, *European Review of Private Law*, pp. 67 *et seq.*
Ghestin, J. (1981), 'L'utile et le juste dans les contracts', 26, *Archives de philosophie du droit*, pp. 35-57.
Hartkamp, A.S. and Hesselink, M.W. (eds.) (1998), *Towards a European Civil Code* (The Hague: Kluwer Law International).
Joerges, C. (2003), 'Europeanization as Process: Tensions between the Logic of Integration and the Logic between Codification', paper presented at *Europeanization of contract law?* Conference held at the European University Institute, Florence, 24-25 October 2003, reproduced at http://www.iue.it/LAW/ResearchTeaching/EuropeanprivateLaw/Conferences.shtml.
Lando, O. and Beale, H. (eds.) (2000), *Principles of European Contract Law*, Part I and Part II combined and revised (The Hague: Kluwer Law International).
Lando, O. and Clive, E. (eds.) (2003), *Principles of European Contract Law*, Part III (The Hague: Kluwer Law International).
Larouche, P. (2000), 'Ius Commune Casebooks for the Common Law of Europe: Presentation, Progress, Rationale', 8, *European Review of Private Law*, pp. 101 *et seq.*
Micklitz, A.W. and Weatherill, S. (1993), 'Consumer Policy in the European Community: Before and After Maastricht', *Journal of Consumer Policy*, pp. 285 *et seq.*
Musy, A.M. (1999), *Il dovere di informazione* (Trent: Università degli Studi di Trento).
Pasa, B. (2002), 'I progetti di ricerca sul diritto privato comune: il nuovo "Acquis Group"', 1, *Contratto e Impresa Europa*, pp. 654-662.
Reich, N. and Woodroffe, G. (eds.) (1994), *European Consumer Policy after Maastricht* (The Hague: Kluwer Academic Publishers).
Rossi, P. (2003), *Ontologie applicate e comparazione giuridica: alcune premesse*, reproduced at http://www.dsg-unito.it/ut/papers.htm.
Sacco, R. (1993), 'The System of European Private Law: Premise for a European Code', *Italian Studies in Law*, I, pp. 71-80.
Schulte-Nölke, H. (2003), 'The Commission's Action Plan on European Contract Law and the Research of the Acquis Group', paper presented at *Europeanization of contract law?* Conference held at the European University Institute, Florence, 24-25 October 2003, reproduced at http://www.iue.it/LAW/ResearchTeaching/EuropeanprivateLaw/Conferences.shtml.
Schulze, R. (1995), 'Le droit privé commun européen', 47, *Revue internationale de droit comparé*, pp. 7 *et seq.*
Schulze, R., Ebers, M. and Grigoleit, C. (eds.) (2003), *Informationsplichten und Vertragsschluss im Acquis communautaire* (Tübingen: Mohr Siebeck).
Schulze, R. and Schulte-Nölke, H. (eds.) (2000), *Casebook zum Europäischen Privatrecht* (Baden-Baden: Nomos).

Somma, A. (2003), *Diritto comunitario vs. diritto comune europeo* (Turin: Giappichelli).
Storme, M. (2003), 'Information Requirements and Remedies in the Principles of European Contract Law', in Schulze, R., Ebers, M. and Grigoleit C. (eds.), *Informationspflichten und Vertragsschluss im Acquis communautaire* (Tübingen: Mohr Siebeck), pp. 231-244.
Teubner, G. (1998), 'Legal irritants. Good Faith in British Law or How Unifying Law Ends up in New Divergencies', 61, *Modern Law Review*, pp. 23 *et seq.*
Trimarchi, P. (2003), *Istituzioni di diritto privato* (Milan: Giuffrè).
Werro, F. (1998), *L'Européanisation du droit privé – vers un code civil européen?* (Fribürg: university publisher).
Williamson, T. (1994), *Vagueness* (London and New York: Routledge).
Zimmermann, R. (2002), *Comparative Foundations of a European Law of Set-Off and Prescription* (Cambridge: Cambridge University Press).

Chapter 3

Evolution of Party Autonomy in a Legal System under Transformation – Recent Developments in Poland under Special Consideration of the Package Travel Directive

Katarzyna Michałowska

Introduction

Transformation of the Polish economic system after 1989 was facilitated by the reform of the civil law. Free market, entrepreneurship, and competition would not have been possible without recognition of the basic premise of party autonomy and freedom of contract. This chapter examines the evolution of the concept of party autonomy in contract law of a country which not only created, during the last years, a legal environment for a free market, but also embarked on 'Europeanization' of its legal system in the eve of its membership of the EU. The implementation of the Package Travel Directive is used to illustrate the latter aspect of law reform and its practical results.

Party Autonomy and Freedom of Contract under Polish Law

The Code of Obligations 1933

After the First World War, civil law relations in the territory of the newly independent Polish state were governed by several legal systems, which was a legacy of more than a hundred years of partitions. In the various regions of Poland there applied laws of German, Austrian, Hungarian, French and Russian origin. The Polish Parliament promptly appointed a Codification Commission and entrusted it with the task of drafting uniform laws for the whole of the country, and subsequently with elaborating a new codification. The Codification Commission, composed of pre-eminent Polish jurists, both academics and practising lawyers, began its work in 1919. Starting from a law which resolved internal conflicts of law questions, the Commission drafted new laws relating to copyright, patents, unfair competition, bills and cheques, rules of civil procedure. In their work, the commissioners relied on a comparative analysis of the European legal systems, and strove to produce modern legislation. The year 1933 saw the adoption, by Presidential decree, of the new Code of Obligations, and 1934 of the Commercial Code. Work on the codification of matrimonial and property law continued, but did not result in codification of these areas of the law during the inter-war period; however, the drafts prepared at that time were used in the 1940s and 1950s in further unification and codification efforts.

The Code of Obligations expressed the concept of freedom of contract in its Art. 55 as follows:

> The parties which enter into a contract may arrange the legal relation between them as they deem appropriate, provided that its contents and purpose are not contrary to public order, the law or bona mores.[1]

This provision was well suited to serve the needs of a free market economy and clearly expressed the liberal values of the time. It later served as a source of inspiration to the drafters of the present formulation of the concept in Polish law.

The Post-War Period

Further law unification and codification efforts undertaken after the Second World War resulted in the adoption of several decrees, including the Decree on general principles of civil law of 1946, later substituted by a Law of the same title of 1950. One of the general principles stipulated in the Law of 1950 was the principle that a juridical act which breaches statute or the rules of community life is invalid. Therefore, a wider concept, that of a 'juridical act', comprising both contracts and unilateral declarations was used. Also, the criterion to be applied to judge the validity of a juridical act was described as 'rules of community life', a new phrase to enter the Polish legal language. This latter development was a result of some influence of Soviet law concepts, and was also present in the legal systems of other countries of the region.

The Civil Code of 1964 – A Rule with Some Exceptions

Codification of the Polish civil law was completed in 1964 with the adoption of a Civil Code. Comprised of four books (general principles, property, obligations, and inheritance), it left family law to be regulated in a separate code, also of 1964. The

---

1 Rozporządzenie Prezydenta Rzeczypospolitej z dnia 27 października 1933 r., Kodeks zobowiązań (Dz.U. R.P. Nr 82, poz. 598), Art. 55: 'Strony, zawierające umowę, mogą stosunek swój ułożyć według swego uznania, byleby treść i cel umowy nie sprzeciwiały się porządkowi publicznemu, ustawie ani dobrym obyczajom' (translation by Katarzyna Michałowska).

Civil Code abrogated the former Code of Obligations of 1933, the provisions of the Commercial Code which governed business transactions, and the general principles of civil law adopted in 1950. The express recognition of the idea that parties are free to shape their contracts as they wish, subject to certain statutory limitations, did not find its way to the new Code. Instead, the Code addressed the general concept of 'juridical acts' and provides in its Art. 58 that a juridical act which breaches statutory law or is intended to circumvent statutory law is null and void, unless the law provides for other consequences. A breach of the 'rules of community life' was put on an equal footing with a breach of statutory law, and it also results in nullity of a juridical act.

As mentioned above, the term 'rules of community life' supplanted the terms used in the former statutory enactments, such as 'bona mores', 'good faith', 'loyalty and integrity of an entrepreneur'. All of them refer to some general values which are rooted in moral beliefs shared by the community and ensure that these values are respected in the process of application of statutory law. However, the meaning of the general clause of 'rules of community life' was at that time determined by Art. 5 of the Civil Code. It used to provide that such rules should be interpreted as those prevailing in the Polish People's Republic, thus giving them an ideological dimension. The debate over the present meaning of the 'rules of community life' continues to date, with the participation of the legal writers and the courts. Some see it as remnants of the past. The law-makers have decided not to change the numerous provisions of the Code which refer to the rules of community life and have not generally replaced them with the traditional concepts. Instead, piecemeal law reform is made, and whenever there is a need nowadays for a general clause in order to 'open' the statute to extra-systemic values, bona mores and good faith are as a rule used in the newly formulated provisions, while the general clause referring to the 'rules of community life' appears in the provisions formulated earlier.

During the entire period from the adoption of the Civil Code in 1964 until the major amendment of July 1990, party autonomy and freedom of contract have always been recognized as basic premises of Polish civil law. Although no express recognition of the parties' autonomy to arrange their contract as they wished was to be found in the Code, this remained to be considered a rule, albeit with exceptions. It was derived from the provisions of the Code which states that a juridical act has not only the effects it expressly provides for, but also those which follow from statute, the rules of community life and from an established custom, as well as the rule that a juridical act is null and void only if it breaches statutory law, or is intended to circumvent it, or where it breaches the rules of community life. Hence, where there is no such breach, the will of the parties prevails. The various laws of the time, designed to ensure that state-owned companies enter into contracts with one another in an organized manner, consistent with the needs of a centrally planned economy, were regarded as an exception to the rule. Also, even if they were subject to some form of administrative control and regulation, state-owned companies were supposed to actually enter into contracts, i.e. the contract remained the basic mechanism to ensure the exchange of goods and services.[2]

Much of the law relating to business transactions among state-owned companies, representing the largest group of 'professional' economic players of the time, was to be found in secondary legislation. The Council of Ministers was authorized to issue special regulations to govern such transactions in a manner different than that stipulated under the Code. This power could be delegated to other administrative agencies. Hence, a special legal regime could, and, to some extent, was indeed developed. On the other hand, the Civil Code remained intact. The classical civil-law mechanism applied in relations between all other subject, i.e. individuals and entities of the small private sector, as well as between the 'units of socialized economy' and such other subjects. This explains why the Code could continue with only some modifications in the 1990s, consisting mainly in the removal of several ideologically-driven provisions, while the basic institutions of civil law remain in the Code as they used to be regulated before, in many cases their roots going back to the former codification. In fact, according to one of the authors it could be said without much exaggeration that the Polish Civil Code, except for these 'deformations', which were rather easy to remove, could apply in any European country.[3] Also, at present, when the number of new laws passed in Poland every year is considerable and ever growing, the Civil Code is rightly seen as the ideal of clarity and brevity.

The Law Reform of 1990 – Freedom of Contract stated in the Code in Express Terms

The belief that there should exist a special category of subjects and a unique legal regime to organize economic relations among them was abandoned once Poland began its economic, political and legal reforms in 1989-1990. However, it should be noted that liberalization of business began earlier, with the adoption in 1988 of a new law on economic activity, based on the premise that everyone is free to engage in business and that the same rules should apply to all businesses operators. The reform of the Civil Code, in particular that known as the 'July Amendment' of 1990,[4] was an important step in the creation of a legal environment for a free market. It was part of the first phase, intended to cover only such changes which could be implemented fairly quickly and were necessary in order to ensure that market mechanisms can work. Further refinement was scheduled to be made later; this started in 1996 and continues to date, the latest amendments being effective as of September 2003.

During the first phase of law reform, the Polish Civil Code only needed some adaptation; the basic institutions of civil law regulated in the Code did not need to

---

2 For a presentation of selected aspects of Polish contract law see Wagner (1968).

3 Kordasiewicz (2002), p. 56. The author presents a review of Polish civil and commercial law in the context of systemic transformation and European integration.

4 Ustawa o zmianie ustawy - Kodeks cywilny z dnia 28 lipca 1990 r. (Dz. U. Nr 55, poz. 321).

be changed, which also proves its high legislative quality. Focus will be made here on the fact that the idea of freedom of contract found its clear expression in the Code. However, also the remaining amendments made at that time served that objective.[5] These included abolishment of the idea that the property of the state deserves stronger protection than the property of other subjects, of the requirement that interpretation and application of the Code should be made in accordance with the basic principles of the social and political system of the country. The *rebus sic stantibus* clause was introduced, as well as a mechanism for a contractual and judicial adjustment of contractual performance consisting in the payment of a sum of money; changed were the rules concerning limitation of claims. The procedure for the resolution of disputes between business parties was reformed. The concept of 'units of socialized economy' was abandoned, and the privatization processes which followed, coupled with the growth of the number of new private firms, totally changed the economic structure of the country.

A new article on freedom of contract was added in Book 3 of the Civil Code, i.e. that part of the Code which regulates contractual relations. This suggests that the parties are restricted by mandatory provisions in arranging their property relations or those in the area of the law on inheritance. As provided for in Art. 353^1:

> The parties which enter into a contract may arrange the legal relation between them as they deem appropriate, provided that its contents and purpose are not contrary to the nature of the relationship, statutory law or the rules of community life.

The rule has been tested by the courts in a number of cases. Some of the themes in the case law include:[6] the question of the freedom to create abstract obligations (considered in the context of unconditional bank guarantee payable on demand), the termination of contracts made for specified time and modification of the terms of long-term contracts by one of the parties, the legal effects of a contract to transfer ownership of a thing as collateral security, the nature of some innominate contracts (e.g., franchise and – before it became a nominate contract regulated in the Civil Code – that of leasing). The cases also demonstrate a tendency to uphold the agreement reached by the parties as far as possible and reluctance of the courts to intervene, save for situations where the contract clearly does not satisfy the criteria set out in Art. 353^1.

Standard Terms Contracts and Consumer Contracts

Standard terms contracts were first regulated in Polish law in the Code of Obligations of 1933. The Civil Code of 1964 originally authorized the Council of Ministers and other administrative agencies to set out general terms and standard terms contracts to apply between state-owned companies and in contracts between

5 Safjan (1993).

6 Trzaskowski R. (2002) reviews the case law of the Supreme Court and Courts of Appeal accumulated during 10 years from the adoption of Art. 353^1 of the Civil Code.

such companies and 'other persons'. This resulted in the creation of a body of normative rules, a *lex specialis* which bound a certain category of subjects. With respect to contracts made with general public, these regulations concerned mainly the provision of services. The law reform of 1990 recognized that the authorization for the Council of Ministers to issue secondary legislation to set out the detailed rules for the creation and performance of contracts 'with the participation of consumers' was to be limited to the situations which call for the protection of the interests of the consumers. This authorization was used in 1995 when a regulation concerning contracts of sale of movables to consumers was passed.[7] The Code did not provide a definition of the consumer. It was to be found in the said regulation which defined a consumer as

> anyone who acquires goods for purposes not connected with business activity.

There applied three types of general terms: (i) those passed as normative acts, (ii) those passed by competent parties, authorized to do so under special authorization envisaged in the law, binding on the other party if they were handed to her upon the formation of the contract or – where it was customary to use them in a relationship of a given type – if the other party could easily take notice of their provisions, (iii) other general terms, issued with no special authorization, binding if the other party agreed to include them in the terms of the contract.

Later developments, in particular those connected with the implementation of European consumer protection directives, which was part of the second phase of law reform, resulted in further changes to the standard terms contract regime. The Code now provides that standard terms, set out by one of the parties to a contract, are binding upon the other if they were given to her upon the formation of the contract or – if it is customary to use general terms in a given type of contract – also where the other party could easily take note of them. However, in consumer contracts the latter rule applies only to contracts commonly made to deal with minor matters of ordinary life.

This 2000 amendment to the Code[8] also included a definition of the consumer, added to the Code as a subsection in the article dealing with standard term contracts. According to that formulation, a consumer was

> a person who entered into a contract with a professional business entity for a purpose which is not directly connected with business operations.

---

[7] Rozporządzenie Rady Ministrów z 30 maja 1995 r. w sprawie szczegółowych warunków zawierania i wykonywania umów sprzedaży rzeczy ruchomych z udziałem konsumentów (Dz. U. Nr 64, poz. 328).

[8] Ustawa z dnia 2 marca 2000 r. o ochronie niektórych praw konsumentów oraz o odpowiedzialności za szkodę wyrządzoną przez produkt niebezpieczny (Dz. U. Nr 22, poz. 271). It implemented into Polish law the regime for control of abusive contractual terms and product liability.

This gave rise to the interpretation that a legal person also was a consumer, in the meaning of this provision, in each case where the legal person was not involved in business operations and where it was indeed involved in such operations, it used to enjoy the status of a consumer if the contract in question was made outside of its professional activity. Therefore, the notion of the consumer was wider than that under European law and covered also legal persons; as a result, a certain category of subjects enjoyed greater protection than that guaranteed under Community legislation. On the other hand, the definition did not cover professional activity. This led to further legislative changes.

The latest amendments to the Civil Code[9] resolved the difficulty and finally harmonized Polish civil law in this respect with European law. According to the new Art. 22^1 in Book 1 of the Code, i.e. that setting out the basic concepts for the entire area of civil law, a consumer is

> a natural person who performs a juridical act which is not directly connected with that person's business operations or his or her profession.

There is no doubt now that the notion of a 'consumer' relates to natural persons only. The new definition is of a general nature and applies to all juridical acts performed by consumers, not only those under the Civil Code, but those of a civil law character in general.

Overview of the Process of Implementation of Community Law in Poland

From Association to Membership

The Europe Agreement establishing association between the Republic of Poland on the one part and the European Communities and their Member States on the other part,[10] made in Brussels on 16 December 1991, in force since February 1994, was a major stimulus for law reform. The Europe Agreement was from the very beginning considered – at least by Poland – to be the initial step towards full integration. The parties recognized that approximation of present and future Polish legislation to EC legislation was a precondition for economic integration, and Poland was to use its best endeavors to ensure this. To this end, Poland was to approximate its laws, in particular those in the areas listed in Art. 69. These included, by way of example, banking law, financial services, competition, consumer protection. Approximation was to result in meeting the 'European standard' at a satisfactory level, while closer harmonization was to follow at a later stage.

---

9 Ustawa z dnia 14 lutego 2003 r. o zmianie ustawy- Kodeks cywilny oraz niektórych innych ustaw (Dz. U. Nr 49, poz. 408).

10 Dz. U. 1994, Nr 11, poz. 38, [1993] OJ L348. For an overview of the Europe Agreements see Macleod, Hendry and Hyett (1996), pp. 375 *et seq.*

Progress made in the efforts to prepare the country for full membership of the EU allowed accession negotiations to open in March 1998. They closed during the summit of the European Council in Copenhagen in December 2002. The Accession Treaty of 16 April 2003, ratified by Poland after a referendum held in June 2003, following its ratification by the Member States, will come into force on 1 May 2004. Poland will be one of the ten acceding countries. This presupposes absorption of the *acquis communautaire* accumulated to date.

Procedures and Results

A project of such a massive scope could not be achieved without employment of special procedural measures. There still existed in the mid 1990s the need to continue 'regular' law reform to modernize Polish law. The international obligations under the Europe Agreement and, later on, the obligations assumed in the course of the accession negotiations with respect to legal harmonization were the second major reason for further change. Third, the system of sources of law had to be adapted to the provisions of the new Constitution of 1997, which also resulted in revisions to some already existing normative acts.

In 1996, a new Commission for the Codification of Civil Law was created. The Commission is a body composed of outstanding Polish jurists who elaborate drafts of new laws to be later presented to the Parliament as government bills. The responsibilities of the Commission were defined in its original founding instrument as follows:

> To elaborate the general principles for changes in the civil, family and business law, to determine general principles and to draft laws of basic importance in the system of civil, family, and business law, in particular those amending the Civil Code, the Code of Civil Procedure, the Family and Guardianship Code and the Commercial Code, due regard being given to the need to harmonize Polish law with European law.[11]

The Commission prepared amendments to the Civil Code and the major codification of company law, the Commercial Companies Code of 2001, as well as a number of legislative enactments regulating specialized areas of private law.

Other institutional mechanisms for the adoption of harmonized laws include a special bills review procedure by the government agency entrusted with coordination of pre-accession actions. Since 1994 each government bill has been opined by the Committee for European Integration before it was sent to Parliament in order to ensure that it dealt with the relevant questions arising under EC law in an appropriate manner. Since 1999 also bills presented by the parliamentarians

---

[11] Uchwała Nr 109/96 Rady Ministrów z dnia 17 września 1996 r. w sprawie powołania i organizacji Komisji Kodyfikacyjnej Prawa Cywilnego, reproduced in *Kwartalnik Prawa Prywatnego* 1997, vol. 1, pp. 175-177. The regulation that now governs the work of the Commission for the Codification of Civil Law defines its tasks in a similar way, Rozporządzenie Rady Ministrów z dnia 22 kwietnia 2002 r. w sprawie utworzenia, organizacji i trybu działania Komisji Kodyfikacyjnej Prawa Cywilnego (Dz. U. Nr 55, poz. 476).

have been subject to such review. Each bill was screened for compliance with European law and with government integration policy; the bills were also accompanied with excerpts from EC legislation on the matter. Special commissions were created in the two Houses of Parliament in 2000 to ensure that bills dealing with harmonization issues are processed fast. This resulted in a considerable acceleration of work.

In practice, community legislation in the area of private law has been implemented either in the Civil Code, or by way of separate statutes. Incorporation of consumer law in the Code is preferred as far as it is possible to introduce the changes without compromising the integrity and coherence of the Code. Therefore, unfair contract terms and product liability have become part of the Code, while contracts negotiated away from business premises, distance contracts, consumer sale, consumer credit, timesharing are set out in separate laws. The electronic signature and electronic services directives were implemented in the same manner, i.e. as separate statutes.

Question of Interpretation

Adoption of black-letter law does not exhaust the problem of harmonization and implementation of EC law in an acceding country. It is equally important to ensure that the law enforcement authorities, administrative agencies, professional and consumer organizations, and the citizens themselves, are aware of their respective responsibilities and their rights and know how to exercise them.

Pro-European interpretation was expressly advocated by the Supreme Administrative Court in its two cases in 1999 and 2000.[12] The Court stated that the Europe Agreement created an obligation to harmonize Polish law with EC law, therefore, if there were several potential interpretations of a law, the one closest to European law should be preferred.

In this respect, as far as general awareness in particular of consumer law and the ramifications of the transposition to Polish law of the numerous EC directives in the field, much criticism has been voiced.[13] There is a need to better disseminate information about the case law of the ECJ and of the courts of other European countries in order to facilitate development of the practical standard of protection. The constitutional norm which binds the public authorities to protect consumers against threats to their health, privacy, security and unfair market practices should be interpreted in light of the *acquis communautaire*, thus also other interests of the consumer, e.g., the right to information, should be upheld.[14] A criticism of the courts which are said to be too cautious and uncreative in their reliance on general

---

12 V S.A. 434/99, V S.A. 1658/99, cited in Czapliński W. (2002), 'Harmonizacja prawa we Wspólnocie Europejskiej i zbliżanie ustawodawstwa polskiego do prawa wspólnotowego', in Matey-Tyrowicz M. (ed) *System prawa RP w procesie europeizacji*, Europejska Wyższa Szkoła Prawa i Administracji, Warszawa 2002, pp. 35-52.

13 Łętowska (2002), especially pp. 76 *et seq.*

14 Łętowska (2002).

clauses, is balanced with some hope that the casuistic approach used in the EC directives in regulating consumer protection, if followed in the domestic law, would produce good results in that it would help the courts.[15]

The Case of the Package Travel Directive – The Case of a 'Mixed' Statute

The Package Travel Directive

Council Directive 90/314/EEC on Package Travel, Package Holiday and Package Tours of 13 June 1990 set out the minimum standards concerning the information provided to the consumer, formal requirements for package travel contracts, regulated certain contractual obligations and security in case of insolvency.

The general rule that the information provided must not be misleading (Art. 3 (1)) is supplemented by the specific requirements as to the minimum contents of brochures, should they be provided (Art. 3 (2)) and the minimum information to be provided to the consumer (Art. 4 (1)).

As stated in the preamble to the Directive, services under package tours are often provided in a state other than that in which the consumer is resident. Thus, the consumer is often exposed to a foreign environment which he or she does not know, and advance information as to the type and the level of services offered by the organizer of the tour and the local conditions on the spot is important. The required provision of information about the basic features of the 'holiday infrastructure', e.g., the means of transport, the location, tourist category or degree of comfort and the main features of the accommodation, as well as the visits, excursions or other services which are included in the total price, helps to eliminate the risk that only the attractive features of the package offered to the consumer are presented, while those which are less pleasant are concealed. Therefore, the consumer has a real choice, and the information gap between the service organizer or the retailer and the consumer is reduced.

The information to be exchanged between the parties can be grouped as follows: (i) that which may be provided in any descriptive matter, i.e. in a brochure, and, if so provided, is binding on the organizer or the retailer unless special circumstances prevail (Art. 3), (ii) the information to be provided before the contract is concluded (Art. 4 (1)(a)), (iii) that to be included in the contract where appropriate depending on the type of the package (Art. 4 (2)), i.e. that listed in the Annex to the Directive, (iv) as well as the information to be provided in good time before the start of the journey (Art. 4 (1)(b)).

However, the Directive also envisages further exchange of information as part of the obligations of the parties to cooperate prior to or during the performance of the contract. The Directive guarantees that the consumer has a right to transfer his booking to another eligible person, if he is prevented from proceeding with the package, but is required to give the organizer or the retailer reasonable notice of his

---

15 Sukiennik (2000).

intention to do so (Art. 4 (3)). The obligation on the part of the organizer to notify the consumer – as quickly as possible – of the circumstances which compel him to change any of the essential terms in the circumstances set out in Art. 4 (5), enabling the consumer to withdraw without penalty or to accept the revised terms, is coupled with the obligation on the part of the consumer to notify his decision in this respect to the organizer or the retailer as soon as possible. As part of the rules concerning liability of the organizer for the proper performance of the contract, the Directive provides that in the case of any failure in the performance of a contract which the consumer perceives on the spot, the consumer should communicate them to the supplier of the service concerned and to the organizer and/or the retailer in writing or any other appropriate form at the earliest opportunity, and such obligations must be stated clearly in the contract (Art. 5 (4)). Finally, the question of the security for the refund of money paid over and for the repatriation of the consumer in the event of insolvency set out in Art. 7 of the Directive, also has an information aspect, as the organizer and/or the retailer must provide sufficient evidence of such security.

The Commission's Report on the implementation of the Package Travel Directive,[16] while pointing out some imprecise provisions and the concern for the transposition of the Directive in the domestic legislation of the Member States, did not record major difficulties with the transposition and operation of the basic information requirements set out in Arts. 3 and 4 and in the Annex. However, some of the problems encountered arose due to the use in the Directive of open-ended terms such as 'reasonable' ('reasonable notice' to the organizer in Art. 4 (3) to be observed by the consumer where they transfer their booking to another person). The Report suggests that a three-week notice originally envisaged in its domestic legislation by Luxembourg, seemed to be too restrictive. The Report also shows that some Member States implemented Art. 3 (2)(a) and 4 (1)(a) too narrowly in that it was only their own citizens who could take benefit of the obligation of the organizer and/or the retailer to provide information on passport and visa requirements.

The Act of 29 August 1997 on Tourist Services – A Mixed Statute

The Polish Act on Tourist Services of 29 August 1997[17] combines administrative regulation of the tourist industry (the licensing procedures, the professional qualifications and experience required of persons involved in the tourist industry, classification of hotel facilities), and private law matters, grouped in a separate chapter entitled 'Protection of the Client'. This is a first general Act under Polish law to regulate tourist services, and it implements the provisions of the Directive.[18]

---

16 Report on the Implementation of Directive 90/314/EEC on Package Travel and Holiday Tours in the Domestic Legislation of EC Member States, SEC (1999) 1800 final.

17 Ustawa z dnia 29 sierpnia 1997 r. o usługach turystycznych (Dz. U. z 2001 r. Nr 55, poz. 578).

18 Nesterowicz and Bagińska (1999); Wendlandt-Gwoździcka (2000); Nesterowicz (2001).

The proposals to regulate the contract of 'travel' in the Civil Code has not been implemented. The term 'client' used in the Act has essentially the same meaning as 'consumer' in the Directive. The Act implements the provisions of the Directive with respect to the information to rights and obligations, applicable at the pre-contractual stage and in the course of entering into and the performance of the contract for the provision of package travel, package holidays and package tours.

To the extent that the Act does not provide otherwise, contracts between organizers and the clients are governed by the provisions of the Civil Code and of other laws concerned with consumer protection. Contractual provisions less favorable to the consumer than those provided for in the Act are null, and replaced with statutory terms. There is also an administrative sanction for an organizer which breaches its obligations provided for in the Act, in particular those concerned with the information requirements, namely his license to operate in the tourist industry may be withdrawn. Upon payment by the client of the price or of an advance for more than ten per cent of the price, the organizer shall hand in to the client a written confirmation of a bank or insurance guarantee or of an insurance policy taken for the benefit of the clients to cover repatriation or refund of money in the case where the organizer does not perform the contract, together with the information as to the applicable claims procedures.

Some of the rules under the Directive, such as the rule providing for the liability of the organizer for the performance of all of the obligations under the contract had been firmly in place in the Polish Civil Code. Therefore, the Directive does not represent a higher standard of protection in this field.

On the other hand, the development brought about by implementation of the provisions concerned with pre-contractual information ensures transparency of the contract and enables the consumers to make informed decision. This is a welcome development, since Polish law lacked such regulations.

Polish legislation on tourist services, shaped also by implementation of the Package Travel Directive, illustrates both continuity and change in Polish law, market liberalization which translates into greater freedom of contract and, at the same time, the necessary protection of the consumer.

References

Kordasiewicz, B. (2002), 'Polskie prawo cywilne i handlowe w dobie przemian ustrojowych i integracji europejskiej', in Matey-Tyrowicz, M. (ed.), *System prawa RP w procesie europeizacji* (Warsaw: Europejska Wyższa Szkoła Prawa i Administracji), pp. 53-89.

Łętowska, E. (2002), *Prawo umów konsumenckich* (Warsaw: Beck).

Safjan, M. (1993), 'Zasada swobody umów (Uwagi wstępne na tle wykładni Art. 353^1 k.c.)', *Państwo i Prawo*, vol. 4, pp. 12-19.

Macleod, I., Hendry, I.D. and Hyett, S. (1996), *The External Relations of the European Communities* (Oxford: Clarendon Press).

Nesterowicz, M. (2001), 'Umowa o podróż', in Rajski, J. (ed.), *System prawa prywatnego. Prawo zobowiązań – część szczegółowa.*, vol. 7 (Warsaw: Beck), pp. 621-652.

Nesterowicz, M. and Bagińska, E. (1999), 'The approximation of Polish law to Directive 90/314/EEC of 13 June 1990 on package travel, package holidays and package tours', *Comparative Law Review*, vol. 9-10 (Torún: Nicholas Copernicus University), pp. 309-318.

Sukiennik, P. (2000), 'Prawo wspólnotowe a umowy', in Mik, C. (ed.), *Europeizacja prawa krajowego. Wpływ integracji europejskiej na klasyczne dziedziny prawa krajowego* (Toruń: Dom Organizatora), pp.169-184.

Trzaskowski, R. (2002), 'Swoboda umów w orzecznictwie sądowym', *Przegląd Sądowy*, vol. 3, pp. 63-86, vol. 5, pp. 116-152, vol. 6, pp. 95-122.

Wagner, W.J. (1968), 'Introduction to Polish Reports and Annotations with Particular Reference to the Law of Contracts', in Schlesinger, R.B. (ed.), *Formation of Contracts. A Study of the Common Core of Legal Sytems* (New York: Oceana Publications, London: Stevens & Sons), pp. 309-317.

Wendlandt-Gwoździcka, M. (2000), 'Polskie prawo turystyczne na tle dyrektywy europejskiej o podróżach i wycieczkach turystycznych sprzedawanych w formie pakietu usług' in Mik, C. (ed.), *Europeizacja prawa krajowego. Wpływ integracji europejskiej na klasyczne dziedziny prawa krajowego* (Toruń: Dom Organizatora), pp. 197-222.

Chapter 4

From Truth in Lending to Responsible Lending*

Iain Ramsay

Introduction

Consumer credit law is a paradigm for contemporary consumer law. Its provisions include information transparency, the right of the consumer to withdraw from a credit contract, the opportunity for adjustment in the light of changed circumstances, the control of unfair terms, and screening of lenders.[1] A combination of private and public regulation, consumer credit law mixes economic and social concerns: the former represented by the interest in a transparent, competitive market, the latter by a concern for the potentially adverse social consequences of over-indebtedness. The recent proposal for a new EU Directive on Consumer Credit is representative of this paradigm with its combination of proposals to increase competition in the credit market while at the same time addressing problems of over-indebtedness that might lead to 'economic exclusion and costly action on the part of Member States' social services'.[2] I discuss in this chapter the role of information obligations in consumer credit law as a technique for achieving a transparent and competitive credit market and also in addressing over-indebtedness – a phenomenon of current concern in a number of EU

---

* This chapter benefited from the comments of participants at the Symposium 'Information Rights and Obligations: the Impact on Party Autonomy and Contractual Fairness', University of Münster, 21-22 November 2003. In addition, Toni Williams provided helpful comments.

1 Many of these provisions are found in the proposal for a new EU Directive on Consumer Credit (see *infra*, n. 2) and they exist in a variety of manifestations in national legislation in both Europe and North America. For further analysis of the economic and social dimensions of consumer credit law see Ramsay (1995).

2 See Proposal for a Directive of the European Parliament and of the Council on the Harmonization of the Laws, Regulations and Administrative Provisions of the Member States concerning Credit for Consumers (Brussels, COM (2002) 443 final 2002/0222 (COD) at para. 2.4.) My comments are based on the original draft proposal of the EU Commission. This has been substantially criticized by the European Parliament. See European Parliament, Committee on Legal Affairs and the Internal Market, Notice to Members 2/2004.

countries.[3] I proceed by describing and evaluating the experience of disclosure regulation in credit transactions, then probe its assumptions in the light of psychological findings on consumer decision making associated with behavioural economics. Given the limits on consumer decision making suggested by this approach I analyze the recent EU proposal of a responsible lending standard as a possible response to information deficits in the consumer credit market and outline the potential for economic irrationality on the part of lenders.

The Development and Experience of Credit Disclosure

Required disclosures of information by credit suppliers were adopted by many countries in the late 1960s and 70s,[4] with the primary objective of achieving a more transparent, competitive market through the discipline of informed and confident consumers. Disclosures may be required at several stages in a consumer credit transaction: in advertising, before a contract is executed, in the contract document, and during performance or on default. A central aspect – truth in lending – is the pre-contractual disclosure of the cost of borrowing stated as a cash figure and as a standardized percentage rate – the APR (Annual Percentage Rate). Disclosure of the APR is intended to provide a low cost, reliable signal for individuals wishing to compare different credit products. If sufficient individuals search by using this signal then this will induce competition in the market and reduce price dispersions. In addition, it should facilitate new entrants to the credit market. In the absence of regulation lenders would be unlikely to voluntarily develop such a standard.[5] Standardized disclosures may prevent market discrimination by credit providers between marginal (active searchers) and infra-marginal consumers.[6] It is sometimes claimed that disclosure of the standardized APR and other terms will prevent consumers becoming over-indebted.[7] This is reflected in the warning function of truth in lending, alerting a consumer to particularly high costs of credit or the severe consequences, such as loss of a home,

3 See generally Leitão Marques and Frade (2003), Chapter 6 and Introduction 2-4. For the UK see DTI (2003a); DTI (2003b), Chapter 5. For France see Assemblée Nationale (2003), p. 5: 'surendettement ... ce problème social grandissant'. For a recent study of over-indebtedness in the EU see OCR Macro (2001).

4 For US history see Rubin (1991); see also Duggan (1986).

5 See Beales, Craswell and Salop (1981), p. 523.

6 The issue of market discrimination is raised as an important issue by Schwartz and Wilde (1979), p. 666.

7 See National Commission on Consumer Finance (1972), p. 174; Crowther Committee (1971), para. 3.8.13. '[F]aced with the temptation to spend people need to be made fully aware of the limits of their own capacity to make repayments, the cost and availability of borrowing and the rules and regulations surrounding credit trading, so that they do not over-extend their financial resources by ill-informed and rash use of credit facilities.'

for a consumer who defaults on the agreement.[8] It also provides a standardized synopsis of credit terms for future reference by the consumer in the event of a dispute, and facilitates enforcement of regulatory legislation (such as interest rate ceilings).[9]

Several points stand out in assessing the experience of truth in lending. First, it is characterized by adaptation and experimentation. There has been adaptation over time to the growth of variable rate loans and open-ended credit such as credit cards. There has been experimentation with different forms of disclosure such as the 'wealth warning' on loans secured against a home,[10] the 'Schumer box' that provides a concise statement of credit card costs and fees on solicitations for credit,[11] disclosures by credit card companies of the length of time required to pay an unpaid balance if a consumer only pays the minimum balance on the credit card,[12] and the requirements of heightened disclosures to potentially vulnerable groups.[13] Lenders have also attempted to avoid regulation through techniques such as the development of leasing in the US, shifting advertising to unregulated forms,[14] or burying disclosures in fine print. Regulators respond by further regulation, for example, requiring that the APR be more prominent than any other interest rate disclosure and that in some solicitations it appear in 18-point type.[15] This detailed nature of disclosure regulation underlines its characteristic as a form of bureaucratic regulation, dependent on technical expertise and empirical knowledge where regulators write detailed rules[16] that are incorporated into the contracts of the private bureaucracies that dominate the market for consumer credit in many countries. The development of disclosure rules in credit markets epitomizes Bourgoignie and Trubek's description of consumer law as a 'continuous, flexible, and often particularistic form of activity more than a fixed body of rules'.[17] It is one example of the materialization and differentiation of modern contract law.

---

8 See, e.g., the UK Consumer Credit (Content of Quotations) and Consumer Credit (Advertisements) (Amendment) Regulations 1999, Statutory Instrument 2725 s.3.

9 See Landers and Rohner (1979), pp. 740-741.

10 See *supra*, n.8.

11 This box is named after Senator Charles Schumer who promoted this reform in the US Congress. See Regulation Z § 226.5a (2).

12 In the US, California introduced legislation to this effect. See Cal Statutes 2001, adding California Civil Code s1478.13, at ch711. Although this legislation was subsequently held to be invalid under the Federal pre-emption doctrine the idea behind the legislation has become influential. For recent English proposals to introduce a similar requirement in the UK see DTI (2003b), para. 2.32.

13 DTI (2003b), para. 2.15.

14 See *Jenkins* v. *Lombard North Central PLC* [1994] 1 WLR 1468 (CA).

15 This is required in solicitations for credit cards in the US so that individuals are not misled by a temporary initial rate. See Regulation Z § 226.5 (b)(1). A recent UK Select Committee proposes the introduction of a similar rule in the UK. See House of Commons Treasury Committee (2003), para. 36.

16 Regulation Z and its appendices runs to approximately 200 pages.

17 See Trubek (1987), p. 9.

Assessments of truth in lending have often pointed to its limitations.[18] Commentators have argued that it has provided benefits primarily to middle class consumers and not low-income consumers,[19] that consumers only have a vague idea of how to use the APR effectively, and may focus on monthly payments rather than the APR. Consequently it may have had only a modest effect on consumer shopping behaviour. Criticisms of the impact of truth in lending are sometimes based on fairly dated research from the 1970s, but recent research does suggest a continuing lack of awareness among significant numbers of consumers concerning the concept of an APR.[20] Although it is not necessary for individuals to understand the concept if it is a reliable signal of comparative credit costs, the APR may mislead unsophisticated consumers as to the actual money cost of credit.[21]

In truth, it is not easy to measure the impact over time of truth in lending and to distinguish it from other influences on consumer behaviour. Studies often focus on individual knowledge rather than actual behaviour. The impact of disclosure must be viewed in the context of a market where it is not necessary for all consumers to be informed for a market to behave competitively, although there may be potential problems where lenders can discriminate between active searchers and other consumers. Recent research indicates that consumers feel more confident because truth in lending signals that creditors' behaviour is being monitored.[22] Most research has investigated the impact of pre-contractual disclosures on shopping behaviour rather than assess the value of disclosures at a later stage of the transaction, such as in relation to default or disputes. It is probable that consumers may find detailed information on their rights and responsibilities valuable at this stage.

Credit grantors and enforcement agencies in the UK have criticized the complexity of certain aspects of truth in lending[23] and some jurisdictions have questioned the value of the APR as a useful disclosure in relation to open ended credit such as lines of credit,[24] but there is little broad support for the dismantling of disclosure regimes. Current reforms in the UK, EU, Canada and New Zealand represent consolidation, modernization and rationalization of existing disclosure

---

18 See, e.g., Rubin (1991); and see discussion in Ramsay (1989), pp. 329-333.

19 See, e.g., Wilhelmsson (1997), p. 223; Howells and Wilhelmsson (2003), pp. 380-382.

20 See MORI (2003) finding that 38 per cent of those interviewed did not know what the term APR stands for.

21 An APR may give consumers a misleading sense of the actual money cost of credit leading them to assume that a short term loan with a higher APR is much more costly than the same loan amortized over a longer period of time.

22 See Durkin (2002).

23 See Office of Fair Trading (1994), p. 15. The recent White Paper on consumer credit reform in the UK proposes simplification of the advertising regulations. See DTI (2003b), p. 7. There was pressure to simplify the Truth in Lending Act in the US that resulted in the Truth in Lending Simplification and Reform Act 1980. This was in response to the growth of class actions by consumers based on violations of Truth in Lending Act provisions. See Rohner (1981).

24 New Zealand has jettisoned the concept of the APR as a standardized measure of all credit costs. See Macpherson and McBride (2003).

law. A political economy of consumer credit regulation might suggest that the absence of pressure for radical reform is because disclosures have only a modest effect on business practices, may advantage larger financial institutions in terms of compliance costs, and are more widely acceptable than regulation of contract terms. Whatever the explanation, information disclosures are viewed currently as central to the development of a competitive credit market of informed consumers who are no longer confused by the increasing range and complexity of credit products available on the market. This approach is captured in the recent UK proposals on credit disclosure whose objectives are 'to enable consumers to compare products with confidence, make informed decisions and therefore drive competition between lenders'.[25]

Assumptions of Disclosure Regimes and the Contribution of Behavioural Economics

Credit disclosure regimes have not generally been premised on systematic theorizing about the role of information in markets beyond the idea of the importance of transparency to the workings of consumer markets. Neo-classical economics assumes a rational consumer who searches for information until the costs of search exceeds the benefits and the literature on information failure has identified situations where the high costs of search may lead to significant consumer detriment. It has also drawn attention to the fact that it is not necessary for all consumers to be informed for a market to function competitively. If a significant number of so-called marginal (searching) consumers search then the market will respond and other consumers may benefit, assuming that suppliers are not able to discriminate between marginal and infra-marginal consumers. The neo-classical approach also underlines the potential costs and unintended consequences of regulation and exhibits a preference for information remedies (disclosures, cooling-off periods) over more intrusive regulation (as represented by bans on terms). This approach is similar to that adopted by the ECJ in *Cassis de Dijon*[26] where the court exhibited a preference for information remedies and placed the burden of proof on those who proposed more extensive regulation.

Neo-classical economics recognizes that consumers may not pay attention to information in contracts at the time of contracting through 'rational ignorance', a form of cost/benefit calculation that concludes that the information relates to a later event that may be unlikely to occur. However, behavioural economics has drawn attention to systematic deviations from the model of the rational utility maximizing individual in neo-classical accounts of economic behaviour.[27] Its findings have been applied to a variety of markets but they have particular salience to consumer

---

25 See DTI (2003b), para. 2.1.

26 ECJ C-120/78 *REWE-Zentral-AG* v. *Bundesmonopolverwaltung für Branntwein* [1979] ECR 649.

27 For a comprehensive survey see Hanson and Kysar (1999a); Sunstein (2000); Conlisk (1996).

credit markets where individuals generally do not rely on professional advice. The conclusion that many of these systematic irrationalities in consumer behaviour do not seem to be corrected through repeat purchasing behaviour underlines their significance to regulation of credit markets. There are a large number of propositions associated with behavioural economics and it is a burgeoning field of research. What follows is a brief list of some propositions relevant to consumer credit.

First, individuals make systematic errors in assessments of risk, over estimating risks that can be recalled easily, for example vivid incidents (plane crash) that are newsworthy, and underestimating those which are less vivid (the possibility of a stroke). Unemployment is a primary cause of debt default. If we assume that the potential loss of a job and its impact on credit commitments is not highly salient among the public then individuals may underestimate the probability of debt default. While it is true that there are many media stories about the perils of debt over-commitment, the high visibility of credit advertising that connects credit to the good things of life may tend to crowd out information on the potential for default. These intuitions are borne out by a recent survey of credit consumers by the National Consumer Council that concluded:

> Most of our respondents suppressed the risks involved, and felt confident (possibly over-confident) that in their ability to stay out of trouble [...] consumers were aware that unexpected events could seriously affect their ability to pay but felt that this was something that happens to others. Most felt losing their jobs, suffering a serious accident or illness were remote possibilities.[28]

This quotation reflects a second finding in behavioural economics, that individuals are overoptimistic and therefore more likely to filter out information on the potential risks of credit at the time of entering the credit transaction.

Individuals may not act rationally and make consistent decisions over time.[29] We have time-inconsistent preferences that affect our willingness to delay gratification. Experiments indicate that an individual faced with the choice of receiving \$100 in six years or \$200 in eight years will choose the latter alternative, whereas an individual faced with the choice between receiving \$100 now or \$200 in two years, will invariably take the \$100. Yet they are the same choice framed differently. This finding recognizes that we may be 'multiple selves' with a tension existing between the impulsive and the planner self. Individuals might wish to protect the planner self from the impulsive self by 'hands tying' strategies such as automatic transfers to savings accounts, joining diet clinics that prevent exit, making public statements that one is quitting smoking and so on.

There is also the concept of 'information overload'.[30] This refers to the idea that as the amount of information provided to a consumer increases, she will use decision-making strategies that are more prone to error. It may be desirable

---

28 National Consumer Council (2002), p. 4.

29 See O'Donoghue and Rabin (1999); Loewenstein and Elster (1992).

30 For a survey of the literature on information overload see Paredes (2003).

therefore to present less information. Finally, there is one of the most robust findings in the literature-the framing effect-illustrated above in relation to the decision whether to accept money now or later. Individuals make different decisions depending on how a choice is framed. For example, individuals are more averse to a choice framed as a loss than the same choice framed as forgoing a gain.

Economists have applied the concepts of behavioural economics to the market for credit cards where credit card companies make the bulk of their profits from individuals who carry an outstanding balance on their cards.[31] Lawrence Ausubel concludes that individuals' bounded rationality – as reflected in their underestimation of the extent of their future credit card borrowing – explains the supra-normal profits of credit card operations in the 1980s, notwithstanding the existence of a large number of credit card providers in the US market.[32] His central argument is that there are substantial numbers of overoptimistic consumers who do not intend at the outset to borrow on their cards but who subsequently do so. These consumers are unlikely to be interest rate sensitive since they do not intend to use the card as a borrowing mechanism.[33] In later research Ausubel argues that consumers do not act rationally in response to low interest introductory offers of credit, overrating the importance of the introductory rate as compared to its duration or the ensuing post introductory rate.[34] David Gross and Nicholas Souleles note potential irrationality in consumers' response to an increase in credit card limits. Contrary to conventional economic analysis the extra credit was not used solely by consumers who were close to their credit limit. Other consumers also increased significantly their use of credit card debt. Individuals borrowed on credit cards even though they had access to alternative, cheaper sources of credit such as low cost home equity debt and checking and savings accounts.[35] Further research by David Laibson, Andrea Repetto and Jeremy Tobacman[36] suggests that US consumers seem to exhibit contrasting selves: acting irrationally in borrowing at high interest rates on credit cards while at the same time patiently accumulating significant amounts of long terms assets such as pensions.

Credit card companies, as profit maximizers, seek to identify these systematic irrationalities in consumer behaviour, and regularly conduct 'experiments' on consumers to identify the most profitable selling techniques,[37] for example,

---

31 The following comments on credit cards draws on Ramsay (2003).

32 Ausubel (1991).

33 Ausubel's argument on this issue has been challenged by other writers. See Cargill and Wendell (1996); Brito and Hartley (1995); Zywicki (2000).

34 See Ausubel (1999).

35 See Gross and Souleles (2002), p. 180: 'Most puzzling of all, over 90 per cent of people with credit card debt have some very liquid assets in checking and savings accounts, which usually yield at most 1-2 per cent'.

36 Laibson, Repetto and Tobacman (2001).

37 For example the US credit card company Capital One continually experiments with fees or collection methods to understand how they affect different types of consumers. In 2000 it conducted 46,000 product, price, marketing and distribution channel and service tests. See 'Capital One: Fanaticism that Works' US Banker, August 2001, Vol. III, Issue 8, p. 24.

automatically raising credit card ceilings, offering payment 'holidays', or reducing the minimum payment rate (now two per cent of the outstanding balance in some cases). This is of course not different from the behaviour of many businesses selling goods to consumers. Businesses accumulate a large 'private sociology' of consumer behaviour as part of their attempt to influence consumer preferences.[38] Hanson and Kysar describe the many psychological techniques used by businesses to manipulate consumer preferences, coining the idea that there exists a distinctive market failure that they call 'market manipulation'.[39] The particular danger for consumers in the case of credit is that the practices of credit card companies may increase the risk of over-indebtedness.

Researchers on insolvency in North America have shown that individuals faced with an adverse change of circumstance often use credit card borrowing as a substitute for the limits of public support systems and as a mechanism for maintaining a lifestyle.[40] Individuals expect that their problems will be temporary and some continue to borrow past a time when any rational individual would do so. Borrowing on a credit card is however very costly and in the event that the problem is not temporary an individual may become over-indebted. This behaviour seems to fit phenomena identified by behavioural economics, namely that individuals have a status quo bias, are averse to losses, and are overoptimistic. The willingness to incur the high costs of credit card debt may also reflect the fact that individuals seem to have difficulties in understanding the effects of interest compounding leading them to underestimate the costs of paying off the debt.

There are several points which may be drawn from the literature on behavioural economics. First, the findings raise questions about the objectives and efficacy of disclosure regulation. A policy of simply providing more information may be a policy of accidental wisdom. Policy makers have been intuitively aware of the limitations of consumer decision-making. The use of the APR as a signal reduces the potential for information overload. The introduction of the 'Schumer box' in credit card solicitations economizes on consumers' attention at a time when a consumer will not be committed to a particular transaction and these disclosures may stimulate competition in the credit card market. This could serve as a model for credit advertising generally. 'Wealth warnings' in relation to home mortgages exploit loss aversion, although any effects may be counteracted by consumers' tendency to minimize the risk of default. Targeted disclosures to groups with a statistically high chance of default seem a promising development. Behavioural economics suggests that policymakers, like advertisers and credit card companies, should design information remedies in the light of its insights about the importance of the framing effect, loss aversion and so on.

Second, it may be dangerous to over-generalize about the potential impact of information disclosures. Rather than making broad distinctions between middle income and low-income consumers we should recognize that all consumers suffer from bounded rationality. Historical studies of working class credit suggest a

38 I discuss this at greater length in Ramsay (1996), Chapter 3.

39 See Hanson and Kysar (1999b).

40 See, e.g., Sullivan, Warren and Westbrook (2000), p. 137.

relatively high degree of planning by working class consumers in relation to credit.[41] Over-indebtedness among lower income consumers may simply reflect a greater likelihood that they suffer from more insecure forms of employment and other cost barriers (e.g. travel costs) to searching for credit. The challenge is to extend the choices available to lower income consumers and education and information may be one part of a programme of 'positive welfare' that combines regulation, education and institutional alternatives.

Third, one might be sceptical of the effect of disclosures at the time of contracting on reducing subsequent problems of over-indebtedness. Many studies indicate that it is a change of circumstance after credit is granted that triggers over-indebtedness.[42] Even the existence of a general cooling-off period of 14 days, as outlined in the proposed EU Directive on Consumer Credit, may have a limited effect given the phenomenon of cognitive dissonance – namely that individuals justify to themselves *ex post* the choice that they have made rather than admit that the alternative choice not taken might have been a superior alternative. Casual empiricism might support this argument since the very extensive French disclosure and cooling-off provisions appear not to have prevented a growing problem of over-indebtedness in France.[43] The difficulties of countering over-optimism and mis-estimations of risk at the time of entering the contract point to the importance of disclosures at a later stage of the relationship. Information concerning over-indebtedness and an individual's rights and responsibilities might be more effective at this stage of the transaction. Thus warnings about the dangers of paying the minimum balance on a credit card might be triggered by minimum payments for a period of two months. Post-contractual disclosures that are made at a later stage of a credit transaction might be quite extensive. The concept of 'information overload' may be inapplicable here since a consumer will be very interested in information on her rights and responsibilities and less distracted by point of sale marketing.[44]

Fourth, behavioural economics raises issues in relation to autonomy and paternalism in regulation and the construction of consumer law as a form of interventionist regulation. In some recent writing on consumer protection in Europe a sharp contrast has been drawn between information rules that enhance autonomy and mandatory rules establishing the basic terms of consumer contracts that restrict consumer choice and represent paternalism. Stefan Grundmann, Wolfgang Kerber and Stephen Weatherill argue that information rules 'diverge fundamentally from traditional mandatory rules that fix the content of the contract [...] [T]hey are designed to enable party autonomy, they do not restrict the variety of products and contractual conditions available'.[45] However, the recognition of time-inconsistent preferences, risk mis-estimations, over-optimism, framing

41 See, e.g., Johnson (1985).

42 See, e.g., Sullivan, Warren and Westbrook (2000); Kempson (2002); European Credit Research Institute (2003), p. 4.

43 See Assemblée Nationale (2003).

44 See further on post-contractual disclosures Whitford (1973), pp. 466-467.

45 Grundmann, Kerber and Weatherill (2001), p. 3.

effects, and the potential limits on information disclosures in preventing subsequent default and over-indebtedness, suggest that mandatory rules on credit terms related to default might be justified in terms of preserving individual autonomy. The fear that credit default might substantially compromise an individual's autonomy has influenced both common law approaches to credit contracts[46] and US consumer bankruptcy law.[47] These laws may be justified as protecting the future freedom[48] or autonomy of the consumer.

We might draw from the discussion thus far that consumer preferences are fluid and malleable and that they may be formed by the framing of the decision making process. Consumers' preferences may be constructed in the process of decision making. Herbert Hart criticized John Stuart Mill's protests against paternalism as based on the characteristics of 'what a normal human being is like which does not correspond to the facts'. Mill endowed his 'normal human being' with 'too much of the psychology of a middle-aged man whose desires are relatively fixed, not liable to be artificially stimulated by external influences; who knows what he wants and what gives him satisfaction or happiness; and who pursues these things when he can'.[49] The resurgence of neo-liberalism in European policy making suggests that there is a danger in attributing to the consumer too much of the psychology of the middle aged (male) law professor or judge!

Finally, this discussion raises questions concerning the legal distinction between the average consumer and the vulnerable consumer that has been adopted in the case law of the ECJ. The 'average consumer who is reasonably well-informed and reasonably observant and circumspect'[50] evokes an image of consumer decision making quite different from that suggested by behavioural economics. The law has identified groups of consumers who may be particularly vulnerable and in need of protection[51] generally identified with poor consumers, immigrants and ethnic minorities, disabled and the unemployed, individuals with low educational attainment, and the elderly.[52] However, it is not only low-income consumers who may be manipulated in the credit marketplace, although the costs of irrationality are comparatively higher for these consumers. The 'reasonably circumspect' consumer is, of course, an ideal type rather than an empirical reality. However, one senses that there is a belief that the 'reasonable' consumer of the law has some connection with a scientific model of the rational consumer. However,

---

46 See, e.g., in the common law *Horwood* v. *Millar's Timber and Trading Company* [1917] 1 K.B. 305.

47 See *Local Loan Co.* v. *Hunt* [1934] 292 US 234.

48 See Smith (1996).

49 Hart (1963), pp. 32-33.

50 ECJ C-210/96 *Gut Springenheide* v. *Oberkreisdirektor des Kreises Steinfurt* [1998] ECR I-4567, para. 31.

51 See ECJ C-382/87 *Buet and Educational Business Services (EBS) SARL* v. *Ministère Public* [1989] ECR 1235, para. 13.

52 The UK Office of Fair Trading identified seven categories of vulnerable consumers: those on low income, the unemployed, those suffering long term illness or disability, those with low levels of educational attainment, members of ethnic minorities, older people and the young. Burden (1998).

the dissonance between the law's model and consumer decision making in everyday life, draws attention not only to the rival rationalities of the expert and the lay person but also to the ideological content of the 'reasonably circumspect consumer'. Undoubtedly this construction of the consumer is useful to a market integrationist strategy in the EU, another example of how conceptions of the consumer are hitched to the star of other groups' agendas,[53] but behavioural economics underlines the contested nature of images of the consumer in contemporary society.[54]

At this point let me add some caveats. I am not suggesting that consumer law and policy should adopt the prescriptions of behavioural economics *tout court*. Nor should the law relentlessly pursue a series of interventions to attempt to correct the biases identified by behavioural economics. There remains disagreement concerning the significance and implications of its findings. Nor am I attempting to deny the possibility of consumers making impulsive market purchases so that only 'rational' purchases would be permitted – a policy with clearly authoritarian overtones. Rather the ideas in behavioural economics may assist in the continuing process of understanding the scope and limits of disclosure regimes in addressing problems in markets such as consumer credit where there has been historically a perception that consumers may make costly mistakes that threaten their autonomy and may reduce overall social welfare.

Responsible Lending as an Information Strategy

The proposed EU Directive on Consumer Credit would introduce a 'responsible lending' obligation for lenders. This would require a credit supplier to gather information on the likelihood of a consumer being able to repay a credit obligation both at the time of entering an agreement and on any amendment of the agreement. This requires checking information held by credit bureaux. To facilitate this process cross border access to databases must be provided on the same terms as the access provided to local creditors.[55] The creditor must also choose the most appropriate form of credit for a consumer given the financial situation of the consumer, weighing the advantages and disadvantages associated with the product proposed and the purpose of the credit.[56]

Given the limits of consumer decision-making, the concept of responsible lending may be justified as a response to the limits of information disclosure to consumers as a technique for avoiding over-indebtedness. Under the proposed EU Directive the objective of the responsible lending obligation is to lessen the risk of consumers 'falling victim to disproportionate commitments that they are unable to meet, resulting in their economic exclusion and costly action on the part of

53 For an excellent historical discussion of this phenomenon see Hilton (2003).

54 For different models of consumer behaviour see Wilhelmsson (1996), pp. 53-65; Kysar (2003).

55 *Supra*, n. 2: EU Directive proposal, Arts. 8 and 9.

56 *Ibid.*, Art.6.

Member States' social services'. The premise of the proposals is that there are too many individuals defaulting on their debts and that lenders do not have sufficient incentives to reduce this level to a socially acceptable level because the costs of increased screening outweigh the benefits.[57] One commentator suggests that a similar Swiss provision is aimed at protecting vulnerable consumers[58] and those unable to resist the aggressive advertising of credit card companies. The concept of responsible lending has antecedents in existing national legislation and case law in the EU and previous Commission reports.[59] In the US the concept of 'improvident credit extension' was proposed by Vern Countryman as a response to the perception that consumer finance companies were contributing to the 'bankruptcy boom' of the 1960s in the US. A credit extension was improvident 'where it cannot reasonably be expected that the debtor can repay the debt according to the terms of the agreement under which the credit was extended in view of the circumstances of the debtor as known to the creditor and of such circumstances as would have been revealed to him upon reasonable inquiry prior to the credit extension'.[60]

There are already excellent analyses of the significance of responsible lending as a 'needs oriented' form of law[61] or as representing a more cooperative model of contract. I wish rather to analyze it in the context of information failures on the supply side of the consumer credit market. Credit suppliers may face information deficits in assessing credit risk. Economists identify the problem of adverse selection in relation to credit markets.[62] Adverse selection refers to the fact that suppliers have difficulty assessing important characteristics of borrowers such as their general willingness to repay, willingness to take risks which reduce probability of repayment, and willingness to repay debts in the event of difficulties. Absent reliable assessments of such traits suppliers may not be able to discriminate between high and low risk individuals. A lender who sets a fixed rate of interest will attract some higher risk individuals for whom the price is a bargain and low risk individuals for whom it is not. Increasing the interest rate to compensate for higher risk individuals may at a certain level attract larger numbers of high risks rather than good risks so that profits are reduced below the level that would be made at a lower interest rate. A lender will find it more profitable therefore to refuse to lend above a certain rate, resulting in credit being *rationed* rather than being offered at a higher rate. The market for credit does not clear, that is to say, there are presumably individuals willing to pay the high rate who do not get access to the market.

The economic literature on adverse selection and credit rationing was developed in relation to commercial lending markets. In consumer markets a major antidote to problems of adverse selection has been the development of credit

57 See Stauder (2003).
58 See Stauder (2003).
59 See COM (1995) 117, pp. 52-53, cited in Howells and Wilhelmsson (1997), p. 203.
60 See Countryman (1975), p. 23.
61 See, e.g., Wilhelmsson (1990). See also Howells (1997), pp. 271-274.
62 See Stiglitz and Weiss (1981).

scoring[63] – the application of standardized statistical prediction techniques to credit granting – and credit bureaux that provide information on consumers and credit scores. Although credit scoring was originally used to minimize defaults it is also used now to maximize profits so that pricing of a credit card will take into account differential levels of default as one factor in calculating profit from a particular portfolio of credit card users. Credit scoring has also facilitated risk based pricing in the credit card market where credit card companies differentiate more finely between customers in relation to the level of interest payable on outstanding balances.

The existence of information sharing through credit bureaux represents a potentially significant reputational sanction for borrowers.[64] However, the impact of this sanction may differ depending on the nature of the information held by a credit bureau. Within Europe there is a divide between those countries such as France where credit bureaux only include negative information and others such as the UK that include positive information on an individual's credit repayments. Jorge Padilla and Marco Pagano argue that a system of negative reporting that reports only payment delinquencies is likely to result in greater incentives on borrowers to repay than a system that includes additional positive information on an individual's credit balances and repayment history. In the latter system a borrower who knows that a financial institution will also release positive information may have a higher incentive to default since she knows that one default may be discounted by lenders who have access to other positive information on the credit file.[65] It is also possible that extensive information sharing may facilitate a deeper consumer credit market but not necessarily result in lower levels of indebtedness or even default. A research institute financed by the credit industry claims that 'countries with positive registries such as the UK, the US and Sweden [...] have high levels of indebtedness'.[66] The development of 'sub-prime' or 'non-status' credit markets in North America, where there are higher risks of default, were facilitated partly by sophisticated positive credit scoring systems. A negative information system might dampen the development of this form of market as well as preventing individuals with a history of negative information from 'graduating' into the mainstream consumer market. Finally, a negative information system may have an effect on competition in the credit market by reinforcing the informational dominance of banks. These comments suggest some ambiguity about the overall effects of more creditor information: greater competition that could create incentives to 'oversell', more democratization in access to credit but not necessarily a reduction in the level of default.

There is a tension between the thrust of the responsible lending standard and the development of credit scoring, particularly as practiced by credit card companies. The responsible lending standard envisages a more individualized lending process, perhaps based on a meeting with the borrower. Credit scoring

63 For an introduction to credit scoring see Thomas, Edelman and Crook (2002).

64 See discussion in Padilla and Pagano (1999).

65 *Ibid.*

66 European Credit Research Institute (2003), p. 5.

however permits a lender to grant credit without ever meeting the borrower. There are some advantages in the latter process since it reduces the potential for individual prejudice to affect a decision. However, critics of credit scoring argue that some credit scoring systems focus on a limited number of variables, in particular past payment history, and believe that additional information, such as income, should be taken into account.

It is also possible that lenders, like borrowers, may make irrational decisions. A potential failure on the supply side of the credit market is that of 'irrational exuberance'.[67] Lenders have on a number of occasions during the past thirty years exhibited irrational exuberance in lending (e.g. lending to third world countries). Credit scores do not (I believe) include data on the likelihood of the economy going into recession or an economic bubble bursting.[68] In a recent English report on over-indebtedness the credit risk department head of a major lender is quoted as stating in relation to the practice of automatically raising credit card limits that: 'You can't afford not to do it because all your competitors are doing it'.[69] Financial institutions may be under powerful short run pressures to generate profits, creating incentives to cut corners. When the bubble bursts it is the borrower who may suffer as firms cut back sharply on lending and take collection action in relation to increased delinquencies. Responsible lending could play a role here either in enforcing a collective 'hands tying' contract by lenders to restrain practices that might contribute to over-indebtedness or in stimulating credit scoring systems that are more sensitive to economic conditions that may affect repayment levels.[70]

If credit scoring has the potential to democratize access to credit then one benefit of the responsible lending standard is to focus attention on credit scoring systems and ensure greater transparency in their operation. Given the important role of credit in society there should be opportunity for democratic debate and accountability in relation to these technocratic systems that include and exclude consumers within the credit market and discipline individuals through 'credit ratings'.

Lenders may also lack good information about a borrower's circumstances at the time of a default by the borrower. An obligation of responsible lending could encourage greater attempts by lenders to understand the position of the debtor and reach an amicable settlement. Creditors currently make extensive use of collection agencies that are often uninterested in the reasons for default by the consumer and are only interested in the commission payable on collecting the debt. This creates incentives for aggressive and illegal behaviour by collectors. Contracting out collection permits lenders to divert any reputation sanction for draconian collection activities away from themselves and on to the agency. Reducing the ability to externalize this cost could generate more incentives to reach a settlement.

A further issue in relation to the responsible lending obligation is its impact on lower income credit markets such as rent-to-own stores (e.g., 'Crazy George' in the

67 See Shiller (2001).
68 See Avery, Calem and Canner (2004).
69 Kempson (2002), p. 40.
70 See Avery, Calem and Canner (2003).

UK), doorstep credit and other forms of 'sub-prime' or 'non-status lending'. Lenders in these markets do not necessarily check credit bureaux and, in any event, in England and the US are willing to lend to those with negative credit records. In these markets it is comparative information on relevant choices that may be of greatest use to a consumer. The real challenge for policy in this area is to increase the availability of normatively acceptable options for consumers.

A fundamental question in relation to responsible lending is the standard to be achieved. Presumably the goal is to reduce the level of over-indebtedness or debt default to a socially acceptable level. The most effective method of achieving this goal may be to establish a clear performance standard, in this case the socially acceptable level of default, and to sanction or tax those lenders that do not achieve this standard. This would leave credit companies free to adopt whatever method was most acceptable to achieve this objective. This would require greater transparency by lenders in the presentation of their delinquency and charge off rates. However, establishing an appropriate level of debt default in society assumes a social consensus on this issue, something that does not exist currently. It is possible that a responsible lending standard could stimulate discussion between stakeholders on methods to develop concrete guidelines for different consumer credit markets.

Conclusion

Truth in lending and disclosure legislation are instrumental forms of law intended to change market behaviour. We are perhaps more modest now than in the 1970s about the capabilities of instrumental law. One message of this chapter might seem to be a re-iteration of the limits of the information paradigm as the primary focus of consumer regulation.[71] However, I have suggested a nuanced approach to disclosure legislation that focuses on when and how consumers make decisions and when they will find information useful. Significant substantive disclosures on consumer rights in contract documents may be justified where those rights are likely to be exercised at a later stage of the transaction when individuals will have a strong interest in knowing their legal position. Such disclosure might reduce the overall social costs of adjustment to changed circumstances. We should also not assume that lower-income consumers would not benefit from disclosures, although issues of literacy and education ought also to be addressed. Since disclosures are unlikely to have a significant impact on over-indebtedness, more systematic regulation of default and development of over-indebtedness policy are necessary as part of consumer credit law. Consumer bankruptcy law is an integral part of consumer credit law and the right to declare bankruptcy is a mandatory default rule of all credit contracts in many countries.

Information disclosure is intended to promote consumer autonomy and increase social welfare through competitive markets. The concept of autonomy is

71 See Howells and Wilhelmsson (2003), pp. 380-382.

however a slippery concept. In one of the most thoughtful analyses of this concept Jon Elster concludes that 'I can offer no satisfactory definition of autonomy' and that autonomy is best understood 'as a residual, as what is left after we have eliminated the desires that have been shaped by one of the mechanisms on the short list for irrational preference formation'.[72] Other writers also point to the difficulties of specifying the conditions for an autonomous choice.[73] In this chapter I have outlined some of the difficulties posed by the literature of behavioural economics for developing conditions of autonomous choice by consumers in the credit market. It is certainly arguable that regulation of contractual terms and mandatory terms may increase consumer autonomy, defined as future freedom. It is potentially misleading to view these rules of consumer protection law as necessarily a limit on party autonomy. The 'planner' consumer may wish to protect herself from the 'impulsive' self in market decisions and the political process provides the opportunity for citizens to register this preference through regulation.

These points are not restricted to consumer credit law. There is much current interest in the concept of autonomy in contract law. Consumer protection is sometimes viewed as an interference with autonomy (or freedom of contract). However, both the concepts of autonomy and freedom of contract may be compatible with significant state intervention.[74] Cooling-off periods and prohibitions on unfair terms may be justified in terms of freedom from contract, protecting individuals' freedom to contract and make autonomous choices.

Finally, the decline of the welfare state and social safety net in many countries means that consumer credit is increasingly used as a substitute for state support or to finance activities, such as education, that once was wholly financed by the state. Theorists describe an increasing individualization of risk in society where individuals are required to 'write their own biographies' under conditions of uncertainty.[75] This public role of credit and debt regulation is most advanced in the US where consumer bankruptcy provides a safety net for many individuals who have used credit as a substitute for state financing of health care and unemployment. This public dimension of credit suggests that values from the public sphere such as democratic accountability and security against unnecessary risks for consumers should be relevant to the development of consumer credit law.

References

Assemblée Nationale (2003), *Avis présenté concernant la procedure de rétablissement personnel, 8 juillet 2003* (Paris: Assemblée Nationale).

Ausubel, L. (1991), 'The Failure of Competition in the Credit Card Market', 81, *American Economic Review*, pp. 50 *et seq.*

---

[72] See Elster (1983), p. 21.

[73] See Trebilcock (1993), p. 148.

[74] See Rakoff (2004).

[75] See, e.g., Beck (1992).

Ausubel, L. (1999), *Adverse Selection in the Credit Card Market* (Working Paper, University of Maryland).

Avery, R. Calem, P., and Canner, G. (2004), *Consumer Credit Scoring: Do Situational Circumstances Matter?*, Working Paper No. 146 (Basel: Bank for International Settlements).

Beales, H., Craswell, R. and Salop, S. (1981), 'The Efficient Regulation of Consumer Information', 24, *Journal of Law and Economics*, pp. 491 *et seq.*

Beck, U. (1992), *Risk Society: Towards a New Modernity* (translated by Mark Ritter) (Beverly Hills: Sage).

Brito, D. and Hartley, P. (1995), 'Consumer Rationality and Credit Cards', 103, *Journal of Political Economy*, pp. 400 *et seq.*

Burden, R. (1998), *Vulnerable Consumer Groups: Quantification and Analysis*, Research Paper No. 15 (London: Office of Fair Trading).

Cargill, T. and Wendell, J. (1996), 'Bank Credit Cards: Consumer Irrationality versus Market Forces', 30, *Journal of Consumer Affairs*, pp. 373 *et seq.*

Conlisk, J. (1996), 'Why Bounded Rationality?', 10, *Journal of Economic Literature*, pp. 669 *et seq.*

Countryman, V. (1975), 'Improvident Credit Extension: A New Legal Concept Aborning', 27, *Maine Law Review*, pp. 1 *et seq.*

Crowther Committee (1971), *Report of the Committee on Consumer Credit* (London: DTI).

Department of Trade and Industry (DTI) (2003a), *Task Force on Tackling Overindebtedness: Second Report* (London: DTI).

Department of Trade and Industry (DTI) (2003b), *Fair, Clear and Competitive: The Consumer Credit Market in the 21st Century* (London: DTI).

Duggan, A. (1986), 'Consumer Credit Rate Disclosure in the United Kingdom and Australia: A Functional and Comparative Appraisal', 35, *International and Comparative Law Quarterly*, pp. 87 *et seq.*

Durkin, T. (2002), 'Consumers and Credit Disclosures: Credit Cards and Credit Insurance', *Federal Reserve Bulletin*, pp. 201 *et seq.*

Elster, J. (1983), *Sour Grapes: Studies in the Subversion of Rationality* (Cambridge: Cambridge University Press).

European Credit Research Institute (2003), *Briefing on consumer credit, indebtedness and overindebtedness*, prepared for the EP Hearing on the Consumer Credit Directive, 29 April 2003 (Brussels: ECRI).

Gross, D. and Souleles, N. (2002), 'Do Liquidity Constraints and Interest Rates Matter for Consumer Behaviour? Evidence From Credit Card Data', *Quarterly Journal of Economics*, pp. 149 *et seq.*

Grundmann, S., Kerber, W. and Weatherill, S. (eds.) (2001), *Party Autonomy and the Role of Information in the Internal Market* (Berlin: de Gruyter).

Hanson, J. and Kysar, D. (1999a), 'Taking Behavioralism Seriously: The Problem of Market Manipulation', 74, *New York University Law Review*, pp. 630 *et seq.*

Hanson, J. and Kysar, D. (1999b), 'Taking Behavioralism Seriously: Some Evidence of Market Manipulation', 112, *Harvard Law Review*, pp. 1420 *et seq.*

Hart, H.L.A. (1963), *Law, Liberty and Morality* (Stanford: Stanford University Press).

House of Commons Treasury Committee (2003), *Transparency of Credit Card Charges, HC 125-1* (London: HMSO).

Hilton, M. (2003), *Consumerism in Twentieth-Century Britain: The Search for a Historical Moment* (Cambridge: Cambridge University Press).

Howells, G. (1997), 'Seeking Social Justice for Poor Consumers' in Ramsay, I. (ed.), *Consumer Law in the Global Economy* (Ashgate: Dartmouth).

Howells, G. and Wilhelmsson, T. (1997), *EC Consumer Law* (Ashgate: Dartmouth).

Howells, G. and Wilhelmsson, T. (2003), 'EC Consumer Law: Has it Come of Age?', *European Law Review*, pp. 370 *et seq.*

Johnson, P. (1985), *Saving and Spending: The Working Class Economy in Britain 1870-1939* (Oxford: Oxford University Press).

Kempson, E. (2002), *Over-indebtedness in Britain: A Report to the Department of Trade and Industry* (Bristol: Personal Finance Research Centre).

Kysar, D. (2003), 'The Expectations of Consumers', 103, *Columbia Law Review*, pp. 1700 *et seq.*

Laibson, D., Repetto, A. and Tobacman, J. (2001), 'A Debt Puzzle', at http://post.economics.harvard.edu/faculty/laibson/papers.html.

Landers, J. and Rohner, R. (1979), 'Functional Analysis of Truth in Lending', 26, *University of California at Los Angeles Law Review*, pp. 711 *et seq.*

Leitão Marques, M. and Frade, C. (2003), 'Searching for an Over-indebtedness Regulatory System for Portugal and the European Union' in Niemi-Kiesiläinen, J., Ramsay, I. and Whitford, W.C. (eds.), *Consumer Bankruptcy in Global Perspective* (Oxford: Hart).

Loewenstein, G. and Elster, J. (eds.) (1992), *Choice over Time* (New York: Russell Sage Foundation).

Macpherson, E. and McBride, N., (2003) *Recent Trends in Regulated Credit: Lessons from the New Zealand Experience*, at http://www.ciroap.org/apcl/credit/.

Market and Opinion Research International (MORI) (2003), *Consumer Awareness of Credit Issues – Research Study conducted for the Department of Trade and Industry, September 2003* (London: DTI).

National Commission on Consumer Finance (1972), *Report on Consumer Credit in the United States* (Washington: Government Printing Office).

National Consumer Council (2002), *Credit-Choice or Chance* (London: NCC).

OCR Macro (2001), *Study of the Problem of Consumer Indebtedness: Statistical Aspects Final Report* (London: OCR).

O'Donoghue, T. and Rabin, M. (1999), 'Doing it Now or Later', *American Economic Review*, pp. 103 *et seq.*

Office of Fair Trading (1994), *Consumer Credit Deregulation* (London: Office of Fair Trading).

Padilla, A.J. and Pagano, M. (1999), *Sharing Default Information as a Borrower Discipline Device* (University of Salerno: CSEF Working Paper).

Paredes, T. (2003), 'Blinded by the Light: Information Overload and its Consequences for Securities Regulation', 81, *Washington University Law Quarterly*, pp. 417 *et seq.*

Rakoff, T.D. (2004), 'Is "Freedom from Contract" Necessarily a Libertarian Freedom?', *Wisconsin Law Journal* (forthcoming).

Ramsay, I. (1989), *Consumer Protection: Text and Materials* (London: Law in Context).

Ramsay, I. (1995) 'Consumer Credit Law, Distributive Justice and the Welfare State', 15, *Oxford Journal of Legal Studies*, pp. 177 *et seq.*

Ramsay, I. (1996), *Advertising Culture and the Law* (London: Sweet and Maxwell).

Ramsay, I. (2003), 'Consumer Credit Society and Consumer Bankruptcy: Reflections on Credit Cards and Bankruptcy in the Informational Economy', in Niemi-Kiesiläinen, J., Ramsay, I. and Whitford, W.C. (eds.), *Consumer Bankruptcy in Global Perspective* (Oxford: Hart).

Rohner, R., (1981), 'Truth in Lending "Simplified": Simplified?', 56, *New York University Law* Review, pp. 999 *et seq.*

Rubin, E.L. (1991), 'Legislative Methodology: Some Lessons from the Truth-in-Lending Acts', 80, *Georgetown Law Journal*, pp. 233 *et seq.*

Schwartz, A. and Wilde, L. (1979), 'Intervening in Markets on the Basis of Imperfect Information', 127, *University of Pennsylvania Law Review*, pp. 630 *et seq.*

Shiller, R. (2001), *Irrational Exuberance* (Princeton: Princeton University Press).
Smith, S. (1996), 'Future Freedom and the Freedom of Contract', 59, *Modern Law Review*, pp. 167 *et seq.*
Stauder, B. (2003), *Le Prêt Responsable: L'Exemple de la Nouvelle Loi Suisse sur le Crédit de la Consommation* (Paper presented at 9th Conference, International Association of Consumer Law, Athens, on file with author).
Stiglitz, J. and Weiss, A. (1981) 'Credit Rationing in Markets with Imperfect Information', 71, *American Economic Review*, pp. 393 *et seq.*
Sullivan, T., Warren, E. and Westbrook, J. (2000), *The Fragile Middle Class: Americans in Debt* (New Haven: Yale).
Sunstein, C. (ed.) (2000), *Behavioral Law and Economics* (Cambridge: Cambridge University Press).
Thomas, L., Edelman, D. and Crook, J. (2002), *Credit Scoring and its Applications* (Philadelphia: Society of Industrial and Applied Mathematics).
Trebilcock, M.J. (1993), *The Limits of Freedom of Contract* (Cambridge, Massachusetts: Harvard University Press).
Trubek, D. (1987), 'Consumer Law, Common Markets and Federalism: Introduction and General Concepts', in Bourgoignie, T. and Trubek, D. (eds.), *Consumer Law, Common Markets and Federalism in Europe and the United States, Vol. 3: Integration through Law* (Berlin: de Gruyter).
Whitford, W. (1973), 'The Function of Disclosure Regulation in Consumer Transactions', *Wisconsin Law Review*, pp. 400 *et seq.*
Wilhelmsson, T. (1990), '"Social Force Majeure" – A New Concept in Nordic Consumer Law', 13, *Journal of Consumer Policy*, pp. 1 *et seq.*
Wilhelmsson, T. (1996), 'Consumer Images in East and West', in Micklitz, H.-W. (ed.), *Rechtseinheit oder Rechtsvielfalt in Europa? Rolle und Funktion des Verbraucherrechts in der EG und den MOE-Staaten* (Baden-Baden: Nomos).
Wilhelmsson, T. (1997), 'Consumer Law and Social Justice', in Ramsay, I. (ed.), *Consumer Law in the Global Economy: National and International Dimensions* (Ashgate: Dartmouth).
Zywicki, T. (2000), 'The Economics of Credit Cards', 3, *Chapman Law Review*, pp. 79 *et seq.*

Chapter 5

EC Directives for Self-Employed Commercial Agents and on Time-Sharing – Apples, Oranges and the Core of the Information Overload Problem

Bettina Wendlandt

Introduction

Information requirements contained in European secondary law have been implemented in national legislations in various areas of law. However, information requirements supposed to protect consumers have been facing more and more criticism. Especially, the respective provisions contained in the Time-Sharing Directive[1] (TSD) are under attack. In the following, these information requirements will be compared to the duties contained in the Commercial Agents' Directive[2] (CAD).

This comparison will show the very different structure of the information requirements concerned. They could be described as being as diverse as apples and oranges. Still, this comparison will also make a contribution to the discussion concerning the TSD in two respects:

First, the degree to which information requirements directly limit party autonomy does not necessarily correspond to the degree of how undesirable the regulation might be. Indirect effects on party autonomy can weigh much heavier.

Second, suggestions to improve the TSD made by several authors are backed up by the comparison with the CAD's information requirements.

This chapter will conclude with a proposal to change the TSD. This proposal differs from suggestions made by several authors to the extent that, in effect, not

---

1 Directive 94/47/EC of the European Parliament and the Council of 26 October 1994 on the protection of purchasers in respect of certain aspects of contracts relating to the purchase of the right to use immovable properties on a timeshare basis, OJ L 280, pp. 0083-0087.

2 Council Directive 86/653/EEC of 18 December 1986 on the coordination of the laws of the Member States relating to self-employed commercial agents, OJ L 382, pp. 0017-0021.

less but more information should be given. It will be suggested to give the key information first to sufficiently inform consumers in the first place, but, in addition, to oblige the vendor to seriously offer more detailed information. By this approach, the situation of consumers can be approximated to the situation of the parties of commercial agents' contracts.

The Directives

In the following, the information requirements contained in both directives will be outlined briefly.[3]

TSD

The TSD concerns contracts with consumers (purchasers) purchasing from a vendor the right to use one or more immovable properties on a timeshare basis. The goal of the TSD is consumer protection and approximation of laws.[4] According to Art. 11 TSD, the TSD provides for a minimum harmonization. Therefore, the Member States can provide for regulations that reach farther.

Apart from rights to withdraw from the contract under Art. 5 TSD, the TSD puts an emphasis on information requirements. According to Art. 8 TSD, information requirements are mandatory. Thus, the contract parties cannot stipulate to lessen them.

The information the vendor has to state in the contract is mentioned in Art. 4 TSD which refers to a list in the Annex.[5] The list in the Annex contains 13 items

---

3 Though EC-Directives usually have no direct effect but are directed to the Member States which have to implement them, in the following, for reasons of simplifying expression, the provisions the Member States are obliged to implement as national law will be referred to as contained in the Directives. This is no essential difference to the state of the law since the directives both contain full or minimum harmonizations with regard to these provisions.

4 Consideration nos. 2, 8, Art. 1 TSD.

5 Annex of the TSD:

Minimum list of items to be included in the contract referred to in Article 4

(a) The identities and domiciles of the parties, including specific information on the vendor's legal status at the time of the conclusion of the contract and the identity and domicile of the owner.

(b) The exact nature of the right which is the subject of the contract and a clause setting out the conditions governing the exercise of that right within the territory of the Member State(s) in which the property or properties concerned relates is or are situated and if those conditions have been fulfilled or, if they have not, what conditions remain to be fulfilled.

(c) When the property has been determined, an accurate description of that property and its location.

(d) Where the immovable property is under construction:

(1) the state of completion;

with many sub items. According to Art. 3 TSD, most of the necessary information must also be included in a brochure which must be made available to any person requesting information about the immovable property concerned, i.e. also to the purchaser on his or her request before conclusion of the contract. Altogether, the information required by both provisions amounts to approximately 90 individual items of information; according to the words of the TSD, they can be listed one after the other without any emphasis.[6]

For example, information regarding the exact nature of the right which is the subject of the contract has to be included as well as information on the principles on the basis of which the maintenance of and repairs to the immovable property

---

(2) a reasonable estimate of the deadline for completion of the immovable property;
(3) where it concerns a specific immovable property, the number of the building permit and the name(s) and full address(es) of the competent authority or authorities;
(4) the state of completion of the services rendering the immovable property fully operational (gas, electricity, water and telephone connections);
(5) a guarantee regarding completion of the immovable property or a guarantee regarding reimbursement of any payment made if the property is not completed and, where appropriate, the conditions governing the operation of those guarantees.

(e) The services (lighting, water, maintenance, refuse collection) to which the purchaser has or will have access and on what conditions.
(f) The common facilities, such as swimming pool, sauna, etc., to which the purchaser has or may have access, and, where appropriate, on what conditions.
(g) The principles on the basis of which the maintenance of and repairs to the immovable property and its administration and management will be arranged.
(h) The exact period within which the right which is the subject of the contract may be exercised and, if necessary, its duration; the date on which the purchaser may start to exercise the contractual right.
(i) The price to be paid by the purchaser to exercise the contractual right; an estimate of the amount to be paid by the purchaser for the use of common facilities and services; the basis for the calculation of the amount of charges relating to occupation of the property, the mandatory statutory charges (for example, taxes and fees) and the administrative overheads (for example, management, maintenance and repairs).
(j) A clause stating that acquisition will not result in costs, charges or obligations other than those specified in the contract.
(k) Whether or not it is possible to join a scheme for the exchange or resale of the contractual rights, and any costs involved should an exchange and/or resale scheme be organized by the vendor or by a third party designated by him in the contract.
(l) Information on the right to cancel or withdraw from the contract and indication of the person to whom any letter of cancellation or withdrawal should be sent, specifying also the arrangements under which such letters may be sent; precise indication of the nature and amount of the costs which the purchaser will be required to defray pursuant to Article 5 (3) if he exercises his right to withdraw; where appropriate, information on the arrangements for the cancellation of the credit agreement linked to the contract in the event of cancellation of the contract or withdrawal from it.
(m) The date and place of each party's signing of the contract.

6 Kind (1998), p. 80, for the German implementation of the TSD (*Teilzeitwohnrechtegesetz*).

and its administration and management will be arranged (Annex of the TSD (b) and (g)).

CAD

The CAD concerns relations between commercial agents and their principals. According to the legal definition of Art. 1 (2) CAD, commercial agents are self-employed intermediaries who have continuing authority to negotiate the sale or the purchase of goods on behalf of another person or to negotiate and conclude such transactions on behalf of and in the name of another person. This person is the principal.

The purpose of the CAD is the harmonization of national laws as well as protection of commercial agents[7] who usually are economically inferior to their principals. The CAD does not provide for a minimum harmonization but prohibits stricter national regulations as well as less severe ones.[8] Therefore, the law of commercial agents in the EU is largely harmonized.[9]

The information requirements contained in the CAD oblige and benefit the commercial agent as well as the principal. The information duties of both parties are listed as examples for their general obligation to act dutifully and in good faith (Art. 3 (1) CAD for the commercial agent, Art. 4 (1) CAD for the principal).

According to Art. 3 (2)(b) CAD, the commercial agent has to communicate to his principal all the necessary information available to him. In turn, according to Art. 4 (2) CAD, the principal has to provide his commercial agent with the necessary documentation relating to the goods concerned and to obtain for his commercial agent the information necessary for the performance of the agency contract, in particular notifying the commercial agent within a reasonable period once he anticipates that the volume of commercial transactions will be significantly lower than that which the commercial agent could normally have expected. In addition, according to Art. 4 (3) CAD, the principal must inform the commercial agent within a reasonable period of his acceptance, refusal, and of any non-execution of a commercial transaction which the commercial agent has procured for the principal. The principal's duty to inform the commercial agent regarding the non-conclusion of a transaction is important for the commercial agent's claim to a commission, which he can also be entitled to if the principal does not conclude that transaction.[10]

---

7 Recital 1 CAD.

8 Graf von Westphalen (1995), Chapter 4, no. 6.

9 Graf von Westphalen (1995), Chapter 4, no. 6. But see Fock (2001), pp. 258 *et seq.*, 266, doubting the CAD's success in legal harmonization, especially due to use of general clauses, however, not expressly with regard to information requirements, see also Fock (2001), pp. 275 *et seq.*, for open questions, which do not address the information requirements.

10 Eckert (1990), p. 384.

According to Art. 5 CAD, these duties have to be provided mandatorily by the national legislation. Thus, parties cannot be allowed to increase or lessen them.[11]

The commercial agent's contract is characterized by the commercial agent's claim to commission. This claim arises, basically, if the principal concludes a transaction as a result of the commercial agent's activities. The CAD regulates this claim in Arts. 6-12. For the commercial agent to check and enforce this claim, the principal has additional duties to disclose information. He is obliged to inform the commercial agent about circumstances from which the obligation to pay commission results.

According to Art. 12 (1) and (2) CAD, the principal is obliged to supply his commercial agent with a statement of the commission due, not later than the last day of the month following the quarter in which the commission has become due. This statement must set out the main components used in calculating the amount of commission. Moreover, a commercial agent is entitled to demand that he be provided with all the information and, in particular, an extract from the books, which is available to his principal and which he needs in order to check the amount of the commission due to him.

According to Art. 12 (3) CAD, these duties of the principal are semi-compelling in favour of the commercial agent, which means that the parties can stipulate stricter duties.

In contrast to the TSD, the CAD only vaguely describes the information to provide. The CAD contains a duty to communicate the 'necessary' information within a 'reasonable period'; the statement of the commission due has to set out the 'main components', and additional information has to embrace all which the commercial agent 'needs in order to check the amount of the commission due to him'. These are uncertain terms of law.[12] The actual content of an individual commercial agent's duty to communicate facts in a given situation depends on what the principal's interest objectively mandates with regard to speciality and urgency of the case.[13] 'Necessary' with regard to the principal's duty is, basically, everything suited to promote the commercial agent's activity for the principal as long as it is not the commercial agent's responsibility to obtain that information.[14]

Effects on Party Autonomy

In the following, it will be shown that the information requirements' effect on party autonomy (direct effect) is not the only measurement of legitimate criticism. In contrast, effects the *fulfilment* of information requirements has on party autonomy (indirect effects) can be essential for finding them appropriate or harmful.

---

11 Schmidt (1992), p. 518.

12 Westphal (1994), p. 75; Westphal (1996), p. 43.

13 See (regarding § 86 of the German *Handelsgesetzbuch* (*HGB*)) Baumbach and Hopt (2003), § 86 *HGB*, no. 42.

14 See (regarding § 86a *HGB*) Baumbach and Hopt (2003), § 86a *HGB*, no. 8.

Effects of the Information Requirement itself (Direct Effects)

The duties contained in both Directives are mandatory and cannot be excluded by the parties. Different scopes of the principal's duties can be stipulated with regard to information concerning the commission, but only in favour of the commercial agent.[15]

The creation of any mandatory information requirements has been seen as a restriction or restrictive modification of party autonomy.[16] The information requirements' direct effects on party autonomy will be discussed with regard to three aspects: the scope of the mandatory duty, the quality of the mandatory duty and the extent to which the mandatory duty deviates from the structure the contract would have were it not for the enactment of the Directive concerned.

Scope of the mandatory duty The principal's and the commercial agent's duties to report continually are part of their duty to act in good faith. The information requirements must be fulfilled during the whole run of the contract, but not before its conclusion. The CAD does not regulate pre-contractual obligations at all.[17]

In contrast, the TSD's duties to inform the prospective time-sharing purchaser have to be fulfilled before and when the contract is concluded. Even if the TSD ties consequences to later provision of the information,[18] this later activity has to be seen as poor fulfilment of a duty to inform beforehand. Moreover, the information still to be given is meant to influence the decision whether to withdraw from the contract and is thus, in a way, also provided in order to serve the decision whether effectively to conclude the contract in the first place.

Regarding the scope of information duties during the run of the contract, the CAD interferes with party autonomy much more than the TSD does.

Quality of the mandatory duty The finding that the CAD's impact on party autonomy is stronger than the TSD's is confirmed by a distinction made between information rules and substantive rules while assessing the impact on party autonomy:

While substantive rules reduce the range of options available to the parties for shaping their contract, information rules leave the choice of the content to the parties.[19] Even if mandatory, information requirements are meant to foster party

---

15 Kuther (1990), p. 304.

16 See Kind (1998), pp. 95, 97 *et seq.* with further references.

17 Riesenhuber (2003), no. 320.

18 According to Art. 5 (1) TSD, the period for a withdrawal of the contract is substantially prolonged if the contract does not contain certain information; however, this period is abbreviated if the information left out before is given later; in that case, the shorter period that would have started at the time of the conclusion of the contract now starts at the time the information is given.

19 Grundmann, Kerber and Weatherill (2001), p. 7; Grundmann (2000b), p. 1137. See also Hager (1995), p. 401, distinguishing between a regulation model that directly regulates an issue and an information model that leaves the power to decide with the consumer; Damm (1999), p. 137.

autonomy.[20] They interfere less with party autonomy than rules banning particular practices.[21]

Applying this distinction to the CAD's requirements, it becomes clear that they are substantive rules – the parties cannot conclude their commercial agent's contract with a different content.[22] The CAD's vague duties automatically and necessarily become an unchangeable part of the contract.

Only some of the principal's duties parallel the information model to a certain degree: According to Art. 4 (3) CAD, the principal is obliged to inform the commercial agent of his acceptance, refusal, and of any non-execution of a commercial transaction which the commercial agent has procured for him. Still, the principal can decide whether to accept and execute the contract concerned.[23] The same applies to his duty to notify the commercial agent once he anticipates that the volume of commercial transactions will be significantly lower than that which the commercial agent could normally have expected.

This is a substantial difference to the way the content of the time-sharing contract is influenced by the applicable directive. The TSD's information requirements do not interfere with the content of the contractual obligations:[24]

Even though the information given in the document before concluding the contract must become part of the contract (Art. 3 (2) TSD), the specific content of this document is also controlled by the vendor. Only the categories to fill in are prescribed, and the purchaser can choose whether to agree or to demand changes. The Directive does not automatically give the contract a certain content.

However, party autonomy is limited by the TSD's requirements to include information in the contract: If they are met and the contract is concluded, consent is reached regarding the items concerned. In order to fulfil the information requirement, the vendor must describe the object in detail. In accepting the offer to conclude the contract, the purchaser also accepts the properties described. Therefore, the contract must not proscribe that the determination of these properties is left to the vendor's discretion. Abstractly, by stating information requirements, the extent of precision of the contract itself is regulated.

Still, it has to be noted that, in effect, this form of content regulation is not mandatory according to the Directive. After all, omission of information in the contract merely prolongs the time for withdrawal (Art. 5, no. 1 TSD). It does not render the contract void.[25] Time-sharing contracts that do not contain specific

---

20 Grundmann, Kerber and Weatherill (2001), p. 7; Grundmann (2000b), pp. 1137 *et seq.*

21 Weatherill (2001), p. 181.

22 Cf. Fischer (2002), p. 150: a 'commercial agent's' contract for which many mandatory duties are excluded might be a contract of a different type.

23 See Fock (2001), p. 134, also for limits to this freedom of choice, pp. 134-138.

24 See Riesenhuber (2003), no. 284.

25 At least in this context, this chapter will not examine further whether the sanctions provided for failure to give information are adequate. Of primary interest is whether information requirements that are met actually benefit recipients. If information requirements are of no use, there is no justification to enforce them in the first place. But see *infra* at 'Enforcement of Information Requirements' (pp. 87 *et seq.*) for

terms on the topics of the information required are in no way prevented from becoming valid and enforced.[26] The TSD's information requirements are information rules.[27]

Deviation from the contract structure The finding that the CAD restricts party autonomy to a higher degree than the TSD does is limited somewhat if the information requirements are compared to the basic structure of the contract concerned.

Basically, the performance of the commercial agent's contract is rendered cooperatively. This cooperative element is only emphasized by the CAD's information requirements and their non-excludability. The mutual duties foster the mutual exchange as precondition for successful cooperation.[28] Moreover, the information requirements are based on the duties to act in good faith and only make them mandatory. Though a general duty to act in good faith has not been known in all Member States or in European law before,[29] with regard to the commercial agent, duties to serve the principal's interest have generally been recognized.[30] Also, duties of the principal to act in good faith have already been known.[31]

Altogether, the burden the CAD's information requirements impose on party autonomy consists solely of preventing the parties from derogating from duties that flow from the purpose of the contract itself. This comparably small burden on party autonomy is bearable in order to achieve the CAD's aim to ensure legal harmonization.

In contrast, in concluding the time-sharing contract, the parties' interests are basically antagonistic – at least while concluding the contract. After all, every party wants the exchange to be as profitable as possible. Usually, the burden of retrieving information that is needed to decide whether to conclude the contract rests on each party[32] (*caveat emptor*). The other party only must not provide false information.

All in all, the CAD's rules only emphasize the structure of the contracts concerned, while the TSD's rules profoundly change the usual distribution of

---

proposals in which ways the enforcement of information requirements contained in the TSD can be enhanced.

26 However, the laws of some Member States provide for harsher sanctions, e.g. invalidity of the contract according to French and Spanish law (see SEC (1999) 1795 (final), pp. 11, 14; Neises (1999a), p. 339 (regarding French law)) and Portuguese law (see Pöttler (2001), p. 164). Still, even void contracts are not contracts that automatically receive a certain content as the commercial agents' contract does.

27 Grundmann, Kerber and Weatherill (2001), pp. 33, 38.

28 Bacovsky (1995), p. 921, no. 94.

29 See Riesenhuber (2003), no. 571 *et seq.*

30 See Fock (2001), pp. 116 *et seq.*, 126 *et seq.*, concerning the law of Belgium, France, Germany and Great Britain (with the latter not recognizing such a general duty).

31 See Fock (2001), p. 133 *et seq.*, concerning the law of Belgium, France, Germany and Great Britain.

32 See Riesenhuber (2003), no. 299; Fleischer (2000), p. 791 *et seq.*

responsibility for obtaining information. With regard to their direct effects on party autonomy, the directives' information requirements are as diverse as apples and oranges.

Effects of Fulfilment of the Information Requirement (Indirect Effects)

Indirect effects of information requirements on party autonomy may occur in the form of effects of the information given.

Wanted effects of information given Information requirements can be a good means of ensuring that the contract is concluded voluntarily by creating the conditions for a thought-through and responsible decision.[33] An inseparable link has been noted between the proper use of freedom of decision-making with regard to conclusion of contracts and the level of information available to a party since the inferiority of one party in this respect can hamper actual freedom in contracting.[34] Information seems always useful for exercising party autonomy. This exercise is done by decision (even by a decision to do nothing). Decisions are usually made at least also after considering the effects of the action. Knowing these effects requires information. This notion is the very reason for requirements to provide information to consumers.

The enactment of information requirements is also motivated by the thought that information asymmetry causes market failure. If customers are not able to compare the goods offered to them due to lack of information, a 'market for lemons' evolves. If the main properties of good quality are not recognized, it pays off to offer cheaper goods of bad quality ('lemons').[35] Providing worse and, thus, cheaper quality earns the same revenue as providing good quality. Good quality providers are either driven out of the market or start providing bad quality, too. This process is also called 'adverse selection'.[36] Information given to consumers is meant to prevent this effect.

Unwanted effects of information given The TSD's information requirements are supposed to foster consumers' utilization of party autonomy. There is some consensus that this particular directive does not achieve this aim.[37] Information requirements meant to protect consumers are facing more and more criticism.[38] It is argued that information requirements do not guarantee that consumers understand the economic and legal range of the time-sharing contract; a bombardment with information does not equal transparency of contract.[39] It has been stated that, with

33 Fleischer (2001), p. 1.
34 Fleischer (2001), p. 571.
35 See Akerlof (1970).
36 See Wein (2001), p. 83 with further references.
37 But see Riesenhuber (2003), no. 284.
38 See, e.g., Schäfer (2000), p. 566; Haupt (2003), pp. 1142-1144 with further references.
39 See Martinek (1997), p. 1396; Mäsch (1995), pp. 11, 14; Kappus (1996), pp. 275, 277; see also Pöttler (2001), p. 173.

regard to information, 'more means less' because consumers only get confused by vast amounts of information.[40]

An impressive treatise by Kind (1998) applied results of consumer behaviour experiments to the information requirements contained in the *Teilzeitwohnrechtegesetz* (*TzWrG*), the former German implementation of the TSD (now §§ 481 *et seq. Bürgerliches Gesetzbuch* (*BGB*)). Since this law mainly just copied the words of the TSD, results can be transferred to the TSD itself.

There are natural limits of human capacity to perceive, process and remember information. On average, only seven items of information at once can be precisely recognized, stored and retrieved by the human brain.[41] In order to deal with more items, they must be organized in a way that one item stands for several of them. This method of organizing information is called 'chunking'; a 'chunk' is a condensed type of individual information that points to several items of sub-information[42] – but, on average, not to more than seven of them at once.[43] Moreover, only up to seven chunks at once can be processed. In addition, 'chunks' are created individually.[44] 'Chunks' actually useful for consumers in order to process information are called 'key information'.[45] In order to know which information can be used as key information, experience is necessary.[46]

If large amounts of unstructured information are provided, it is easily conceivable that either most of the information is not processed at all or the person supposed to deal with it employs chunking.[47] The results of this will vary greatly, depending on the person's ability to structure the information concerned due to different levels of experience and knowledge.[48] In general, if a certain amount of

---

40 See Kind (1998), pp. 530, 546; Martinek (2000), pp. 526 *et seq.*; see also Schäfer (2000), p. 566; Fleischer (2000), p. 798 (optimum, not maximum of information); Haupt (2003), p. 1142; see generally Diller (1978), pp. 30, 38 *et seq.*

41 Kuß and Tomczak (2000), p. 28; Miller (1956).

42 Kuß and Tomczak (2000), pp. 28, 117; Trommensdorf (2002), p. 87; Kroeber-Riel and Weinberg (2003), p. 284. See Behrens (1991), p. 157. The term 'chunk' with regard to limits of the human mind is also used: (a) for the information unit of which a person can remember only up to seven at once (see, e.g., Kuß and Tomczak (2000), p. 28; Hecker (1998), p. 37), (b) for a condensed information that stands for other information, and itself enables consumers to assess the product since this information is very important for them (see, e.g., Jacoby, Szybillo and Busato-Schach (1977), p. 210; Kroeber-Riel and Weinberg (2003), p. 284). In the following, the term will be used in the neutral sense described in the text above, which suggests that also bad chunks can be chosen which are not very helpful. Actually useful chunks will be referred to as 'key information'.

43 Kind (1998), pp. 453 *et seq.* with further references.

44 Trommensdorf (2002), p. 87.

45 Kroeber-Riel and Weinberg (2003), p. 286.

46 Kroeber-Riel and Weinberg (2003), p. 385.

47 Trommensdorf (2002), p. 268.

48 Kind (1998), pp. 467 *et seq.* with further references.

information is already available, adding more information does not improve the result of the decision based on that information anymore but even worsens it.[49]

Normally, individuals react to information overload by perceiving information only selectively and taking into consideration only key terms which are chosen by employing criteria that are not necessarily proper.[50] As if this was not bad enough, at the same time, the deciding person's subjective impression of the decision improves – the individual knows that there was so much information available, so, he or she concludes, the decision must have been good.[51] The level of the bearable amount of information varies, depending upon the individual's general abilities and his or her concrete situation.[52]

In a typical situation in which the consumer receives the information contained in the time-sharing contract, first, he or she is not able to process the great amount of information at once, and, second, he or she is emotionally tuned to a certain decision in a way that makes him or her perceive the information only selectively in order to confirm the decision already made.[53] Thus, the amount of mandatory information may hamper its positive effects in a way that the information might not be able to hinder the conclusion of the contract in situations where this might be desirable.[54]

This does not necessarily prevent the consumer from withdrawing from the contract.[55] However, after concluding the contract, consumers face emotional problems with admitting to themselves that they made a mistake which prevent them from correcting this mistake (overcoming of after-purchase-dissonance).[56]

Altogether, if information even petrifies the person concerned, the freedom of decision is impaired, and worse so, if the person continues to act and feels better with the result even though the quality of decision-making has, in fact, been diminished. Thus, too much unstructured information actually endangers use of consumers' party autonomy. Such information, however, fulfils the TSD's requirements verbatim.

In contrast, the fulfilment of information requirements contained in the CAD is not even fit to indirectly promote party autonomy. These duties arise only after conclusion of the contract and, thus, do not influence the use of party autonomy

---

49 See Jacoby, Speller and Kohn (1974), pp. 65 *et seq.*; Kroeber-Riel and Weinberg (2003), p. 381; Behrens (1991), pp. 153, 155; Hecker (1998), p. 42; Kind (1998), pp. 467 *et seq.* with further references; see also Wiedmann, Walsh and Polotzek (2000), pp. 57 *et seq.* with further references for descriptions and criticism of consumer behaviour experiments.

50 See Kind (1998), pp. 471 *et seq.* with further references.

51 See Jacoby, Speller and Kohn (1974), p. 67; Jacoby, Speller and Kohn-Berning (1974), p. 40; Behrens (1991), p. 155; Hecker (1998), p. 42; Kind (1998), p. 470 with further references; Berndt (1983), pp. 200 *et seq.*, p. 211.

52 Kind (1998), p. 468; Diller (1978), pp. 35 *et seq.*

53 Kind (1998), p. 513.

54 Kind (1998), p. 515 & n. 12.

55 Kind (1998), p. 515 & n. 12.

56 Kind (1998), p. 522 *et seq.*; Behrens (1991), pp. 107 *et seq.*; see Hecker (1998), pp. 45 *et seq.*

beforehand. At most, the information given can promote the readiness of a party to cancel the contract. This might be the case if the information reveals unsatisfactory behaviour of the other party.[57]

Moreover, counterproductive effects do not occur due to the wording of the duties. Only information actually needed must be given. There is no motivation of the parties to overwhelm the other party with information. In addition, even if, in an individual situation, the necessary information is very complex, the parties will usually be able to process it by doing chunking properly. After all, the information is vital for their business activity, and they will usually be sufficiently experienced. The core of the information overload problem is not amount, but structure.

Also with regard to their indirect effects on party autonomy, the information requirements contained in both directives are as diverse as apples and oranges.

Assessment of these effects Altogether, the information requirements contained in the CAD have no harmful indirect effects on party autonomy, while the requirements contained in the TSD are likely to have such effects.

This result is rather tragic since requirements to give information to consumers are supposed to *reduce* information asymmetries, not to create them. To neglect information asymmetries is considered a weakness in the unrealistic ideal of a perfectly informed consumer[58] as well as in the unrealistic ideal of a market in which competition necessarily works.[59]

Ironically, conclusions drawn from these findings with regard to information requirements turn out to be based on another unrealistic ideal:[60] the ideal of the informable consumer.[61] This consumer model has been promoted for a reason:

Information requirements as a means of consumer protection are typically preferred by a liberal view called 'market complementary'.[62] By the other view, which is called 'market corrective', such requirements are accepted but not seen as

---

57 For example, if the duty to inform regarding the commission is fulfilled, the commercial agent is able find out whether the principal has paid reasonable commission, see Baumbach and Hopt (2003), § 87c *HGB*, no. 3 (regarding § 87c *HGB*).

58 See, e.g., Grundmann, Kerber and Weatherill (2001), p. 13; Damm (1999), pp. 132, 136.

59 See, e.g., Simitis (1976), pp. 97-108; Weatherill (2001), p. 180. For a description of consumer information problems and conceivable market and public solutions, see, e.g., Wein (2001), pp. 80 *et seq.*

60 See Behrens (1991), p. 153; Kroeber-Riel and Weinberg (2003), pp. 380, 685; Martinek (2000), p. 529; Diller (1978), p. 25.

61 See Dreher (1997), pp. 171, 177, who advocates this ideal; for ways in which limits on human ability to process information prevent consumers from utilizing information to make rational choices, see Ulen (2001), pp. 98 *et seq.* with further references. See also Grundmann, Kerber and Weatherill (2001), pp. 13 *et seq.* with further references.

62 See, e.g., Schünemann (1996), p. 285 (proposing an information modell but not assuming that all consumers are actually capable of processing all information, see implicitly p. 284). See Kind (1998), p. 42 with further references; Damm (1999), p. 137; Simitis (1976), pp. 87-92; Fleischer (2001), p. 206.

the ultimate solution for market imbalances between consumers and entrepreneurs.[63]

According to the first view, indirectly, even mandatory information requirements are designed to promote party autonomy not only by optimizing consumers' choices but also by rendering interferences with the structure of the contract concluded superfluous because the information requirements pose a milder mean of consumer protection.[64]

This notion is visible in the ECJ's decision in *Cassis de Dijon*. The Court found that interferences with the content of the contract are only admissible if information requirements do not suffice to protect consumers.[65] If, to a certain degree, consumers are not able to be protected by means of information,[66] stronger interferences might be necessary.

The indirect effect of the TSD's information requirements on party autonomy justifies criticism. However, still, information requirements could suffice to protect time sharing purchasers, even if in a different form.

Consequences for Regulation of Time-Sharing Contracts

In the following, first, the question will be addressed briefly whether time-sharing contracts should be regulated in a way substantially different from the TSD, and, second, possible changes of the TSD's information requirements will be discussed.

Banning Time-Sharing Contracts?

Relying on information rules that do not necessarily work can be a method to avoid substantive rules. Moreover, behaviour experiments have shown that even if individuals understand the impact of their actions on an intellectual level, they cannot necessarily be expected to react rationally to their environment.[67]

However, in this respect, giving them understandable information does at least not harm them. This is the difference between providing information the implications of which consumers merely ignore and providing information that is

---

63 See Fleischer (2001), p. 206; Kind (1998), p. 46 with further references; Damm (1999), p. 137.

64 Grundmann (2000a), p. 18. Cf. Canaris (2000), pp. 303 *et seq.* After all, EC consumer protection is not in the first place meant to help consumers because they are inferior and, thus, in need of protection, but in order to enhance the internal market, see Heiderhoff (2002), p. 772.

65 ECJ C-120/78 *REWE-Zentral-AG* v. *Bundesmonopolverwaltung für Branntwein* [1979] ECR 649.

66 The ECJ supposes that consumers are able to properly process and use information available to them without inquiring whether this is actually the case, see Fleischer (2000), p. 781.

67 See Ulen (2001), pp. 105-127 with further references for an overview; for additional limits on rational choices see, e.g., Korobkin and Ulen (2000).

too complex and creates confusion and/or a false feeling of safety – information that turns to misinformation actually prevents proper use of party autonomy, understandable information might simply fail to guarantee such use.

Still, because consumers might merely not make use of the information provided to them, it could be asked whether time-sharing contracts should be regulated substantively or even banned instead of stating information requirements. The following paragraphs briefly address this question.

Time-sharing contracts are not considered to be dangerous and burdensome for consumers in general.[68] Comparisons of costs of time-sharing with costs of package-travel tours have not shown clear differences if all circumstances are taken into consideration. Compared to package-travel tours to a specific place, time-sharing has been found not to be necessarily more expensive if the costs are projected to a long enough time.[69] To the contrary, time-sharing has been found to be even cheaper if a right to use a place is concerned[70] and not much more expensive if a property right is concerned and if the safety of the investments in case of bankruptcy is taken into account.[71] According to some calculations, however, in effect, package tours are much cheaper than time-sharing,[72] and swap-exchanges are not very common.[73]

Condominiums are much cheaper if compared to time-sharing rights during the whole year.[74] However, the products are not comparable.[75] For most time-sharing customers, a purchase of condominiums is not an acceptable option so the comparison with the costs of this alternative is not useful.

In any event, apart from the price demanded, the very content of time-sharing contracts is not especially questionable.[76] The dubious sales practices usually employed in marketing time-sharing rights[77] can be sanctioned directly without banning time-sharing contracts as such.

Moreover, banning time-sharing contracts would be a drastic limitation on party autonomy. There might be persons who actually want to conclude such contracts even after thorough consideration – it may be that they can easily afford it, be it that they found opportunities for swap-exchanges. Moreover, the legal definition of prohibited time-sharing would either be too narrow or too wide, either failing to encompass every contract that would mandate the ban or applying also to harmless contracts. After all, the legal nature of a time-sharing contract is not specified in the TSD, and possible ways include a purchase of a property right or

68 See, e.g., Sousa (1998), pp. 31, 291.
69 See Tonner (1997), no. 49.
70 Kind (1998), pp. 254 *et seq.*
71 Kind (1998), pp. 260 *et seq.*
72 Grundmann (1999), p. 634, no. 3; Mäsch (1995), p. 9.
73 Grundmann (1999), p. 643, no. 2 & n. 11 with further references.
74 Kind (1998), p. 244.
75 Kind (1998), pp. 253 *et seq.*
76 See Martinek (1994), p. 477.
77 See Kind (1998), pp. 230-238, for a description of such sales methods, e.g. luring consumers by pretending they have won a prize.

any other right to use a building, e.g., also in the form of a membership of a corporation.[78]

Altogether, banning time-sharing contracts is not an alternative to protecting consumers by other means. Such means other than information requirements – e.g., a vendor's duty to guarantee the administration and maintenance of the property and a rule for calculating the annual costs[79] or a different structure of the right to withdraw from the contract[80] – are not the subject of this chapter. In any event, they would not render information requirements useless. Even if the content of the time-sharing contract would be made to take a shape that meets consumers' interests better than now, they still are long-term contracts concerning a legal product which consumers should be sufficiently informed about in order to make proper use of their party autonomy.

Changing the TSD

Now I will turn to conclusions that can be drawn from the CAD and results of consumer behaviour experiments for a proposal to change the TSD's information requirements in order to prevent information overload and to make them work the way they were designed to.

Conclusions to draw from the CAD To model the TSD's information requirements after the duties contained in the CAD is not an option. Vague duties do not help consumers. With regard to commercial agents' contracts, since the content of information can vary greatly in different situations, it can be decided only with respect to the individual case which information is actually 'necessary' for the other party, which can and must be done by national courts.[81] This is not the case with time-sharing contracts. The 'necessary' information can and should be stated once for all cases, as the TSD tries to do.

Still, other useful conclusions can be drawn from the CAD for information requirements fit to protect consumers.

Instead of approximating the information, another approach can be to approximate the receiver of the information. Commercial agents and principals might also receive very detailed information. However, it can be assumed that they are able to process it. Biological limits on information processing do not change all of a sudden as soon as a person becomes party of a commercial agent's contract.

---

78 See Kind (1998), p. 108.

79 Sousa (1998), p. 289.

80 e.g., a construction under which the contract does not have to be revoked but a written later confirmation is necessary to conclude the contract in the first place (Kind (1998), pp. 534 *et seq.*) or a duty to provide a revocation form the purchaser has only to mail to the vendor (Kind (1998), pp. 533 *et seq.*, referring to French and Swedish law). Moreover, generally, the duration of the withdrawal period is considered too short, *see* Pöttler (2001), p. 174; Martinek (1997), p. 1397 with further references.

81 Westphal (1994), pp. 76 *et seq.*

There are several reasons why they can cope with the information provided to them.

First, they are in a calmer situation than time-sharing purchasers who are usually urged to conclude the contact by the vendor. Second, since commercial agents and principals need the information provided to them for their work, they are highly motivated to properly process it.

Third, since they act in their area of business, they are able to structure the information due to their pre-existing knowledge. They can be expected to have received enough other information regarding the meaning of the information concerned by the CAD long ago before receiving the latter.[82]

Of course, the situation of time-sharing purchasers cannot be modelled closely along these lines. That would require broadening their horizon on a fundamental level. They would have to be made time-sharing experts. It would be unreasonable to demand that the vendor give a crash-course in time-sharing and its alternatives like condominiums and package-travel-tours. After all, consumers might pay no attention in this case and not process this information, either.

However, at least the necessary structuring of information can be done for the consumers. Only understandable and prominent information should be given to them, putting them into the position that the parties of a commercial agent's contract are in due to their own knowledge. This is the main proposal made in order to improve the TSD's information requirements: Information must be limited to core information, enhancing comprehensibility.[83] This method of giving consumers few useful items of key information which they can remember is called 'pre-chunking'.[84] Giving key information can avoid information overload[85] by replacing individual information, helping consumers to make decisions without doing individual testing processes.[86]

Conclusions to draw from consumer behaviour experiments Still, the finding that it is necessary to give key information need not mean vendors should not be obliged to give more information. First, there might be consumers who are actually

---

82 This might not apply to parties who are new in their profession. Still, unlike with consumers, on average, they are sufficiently experienced. For those who are not, it could be argued that they voluntarily entered the market and assumed a position in which said experience can be expected from them. In this case, their actual abilities can be ignored for policy reasons. This is different as with consumers, who, even on average, are not able to deal with the information provided to them and, thus, whose limited abilities are not taken into account at all while formulating information requirements.

83 Kind (1998), p. 531 with further references; Martinek (2000), p. 529. Cf. generally Grundmann (2000a), p. 18.

84 Berndt (1983), p. 140.

85 Behrens (1991), p. 157.

86 Kroeber-Riel and Weinberg (2003), p. 284.

capable of processing the information. Consumers should be allowed to choose whether they want more than key information.[87]

Second, the structure of information processing gives rise to hope in this respect: less but still sufficient information enables better decision-making than more information.[88] According to consumers' behaviour experiments, at the same time, consumers become less satisfied with their decision[89] and ask for more information, which then has a good chance of being processed properly.[90]

If information exceeding the necessary minimum is given only if consumers demand it, there is a greater chance that this information will be processed properly than if all information is given from the beginning. Moreover, if useful key information is given to consumers, their demand for more information decreases.[91] Thus, if the key information provided is sufficiently useful to them, there is no likelihood that they will demand more information than they can bear.

In effect, the information requirements should not be lessened but increased. However, this has to be done in a way that lets the consumers' situation approach the situation of the parties of the commercial agent's contract.

Chunking – the mental process that has been described before – has to be done for consumers so they are faced with usable information like commercial agents are due to their own ability. After all, chunks are meta-information that can be given *in addition* to the information it structures. Thus, the material processed by means of chunking is not necessarily limited to the key terms *themselves*. If chunking is done properly, a mental tree-structure is built the branches of which split up in only up to seven arms at once but whose arms split up again, so, actually, vast amounts of information can be stored.[92] The way chunking works has been described as the short-term-memory being a machine with only seven slots, in which, however, cents can be inserted as well as euros – but only seven at a time.[93]

By giving only key information first, a demand for further information might be created. If it arises, vendors should be obliged to satisfy it. The main requirement is that an actual demand is felt by the consumers. If it does not arise, the items of key information are still fit to enable a better decision than consumers are making now based on information overload. In order to guarantee that this happens, either key information can be provided as an outline to the content presently required by the TSD or consumers should receive only the outline first and then be asked with regard to what topics they would like to have more information. The TSD even starts with this demand-orientated approach in the way

87 See Haupt (2003), p. 1144: Consumers should not have to receive information they do not really want but should have the right to choose whether they are satisfied with the information already provided.

88 Berndt (1983), p. 216.

89 Berndt (1983), pp. 215, 217; Scammon (1977), p. 148.

90 Martinek (2000), p. 529.

91 Kuß and Tomczak (2000), p. 118; Kroeber-Riel and Weinberg (2003), p. 385; Jacoby, Szybillo and Busato-Schach (1977), pp. 212, 214; cf. Scammon (1977), p. 154.

92 See Felser (2001), p. 157; Miller (1956).

93 See Kind (1998), p. 454 with further references.

that, before contract negotiations start, the brochure must be given to the consumer only on his express request.[94]

Existing duty to give (additional) key information? There might already be a duty to create and provide such meta-information. First, it has been argued that, under the TSD, a duty exists to keep the information brief and accurate which is violated by providing very long documents or documents which are not clearly arranged.[95] However, Art. 3 TSD requires giving only 'at least' 'brief and accurate information' concerning most of the items of information mentioned in the Annex. Therefore, it is not prohibited to 'enrich' the document with even more information which might confuse consumers solely by means of their multitude[96] – after all, they might be 'brief and accurate' with respect to their concrete content.

Moreover, the information requirement provided for in Art. 4 (1) TSD concerning the contract itself does not even restrict the information to 'brief and accurate information' but requires only 'at least' the statements listed in the Annex. Therefore, the clarity of the text is not provided for in the TSD, which leads to possible incomprehensibility since the vendor has no reason to make the information clearer than he has to.[97]

Altogether, a duty to create and provide structuring meta-information concerning the information required by the TSD cannot be found in the TSD itself. Instead, the elements of a demand-oriented approach contained in Art. 3 (1) TSD leads to the consumers having only the choice to receive either no information or information that might be too detailed and too unstructured.

Second, it has also been argued that the duty to keep contract terms transparent contained in Art. 5 of the Unfair Contract Term Directive (UCTD)[98] encompasses the duty to properly structure the information required by the TSD since this information is often part of pre-formulated contract terms.[99] However, the information concerned is legally required. This does not prevent the controlling of the clause with regard to Art. 1 (2) UCTD as being dispositive law. After all, if not the categories, but the specific content of the information is chosen by the vendor. Also, basically, giving information and making clauses transparent are different duties that might be governed by different legal requirements. Still, if

94 Van den Bergh (1997), p. 85, presumes the duty to hand out the brochure first equals a duty to give consumers only as much information as they actually want. However, since the duty to include all information in the contract is mandatory, the TSD does not protect consumers from receiving more information. Even with regard to the brochure itself, it is not guaranteed that consumers receive only a moderate amount of information: If the request for the brochure is made, *all* information provided for in Art. 4 TSD and the Annex must be given.

95 See, e.g., Fleischer (2000), p. 787; Grundmann (1999), pp. 639 *et seq.*, no. 14; Grundmann (2000b), p. 1140 & n. 59; see also Van den Bergh (1997), p. 85.

96 Mäsch (1995), pp. 11, 14; Kappus (1996), pp. 275, 277; Martinek (2000), p. 521.

97 Kind (1998), p. 517.

98 Council Directive 93/13/EEC of 5 April 1993.

99 See Grundmann, Kerber and Weatherill (2001), p. 27 & n. 47; Grundmann (2000b), p. 1140 & n. 59.

information requirements are stated, it should be presumed that the law requiring the information regulates the issue completely. This can be shown by the fact that the TSD also concerns the way information is supposed to be given. For example, the TSD requires the contract to be in writing and drawn up in certain languages (Art. 4 TSD) and most of the information being given also in a document apart from the contract (Art. 3 (1) TSD). It has also been argued that the duty to keep contract terms transparent and comprehensible prevents vendors from providing the required information scattered throughout the contract, but that the Annex of the TSD must be used as a form.[100]

Moreover, from a practical point of view, since the requirement to provide certain information is created legally, it should not be left to the vendors to structure the information.[101] It seems unnecessary to burden them with this responsibility and the risk of the contract terms being void under laws that implement the UCTD. To do this would also not benefit consumers: If vendors have to select key information themselves, they will less easily do this than simply abide to the law if the key information is stated there. Moreover, simply to copy and fill in the properties of the own offer is cheaper for vendors than to create their very own information pamphlet, and additional costs of consumers' protection means are usually transferred to consumers. Also, comparability of different offers is enhanced.

Therefore, a duty to provide structuring meta-information concerning the information required by the TSD can also not be found in the UCTD. Such a duty still has to be enacted.

Proposal: content and form of information This chapter will now turn to a proposal for a change of the TSD's information requirements.

Key information considered actually useful for consumption decisions in general are the price, the trademark and the origin of the product and results from grading organizations.[102] However, with time-sharing contracts, due to the structure of the market, no such usable chunks exist so far.[103]

Key terms proposed by authors to be included are the statement of the total purchase price plus the total annual cost (comprising of the cost of use and the fee for swap-exchanges).[104] Moreover, because property rights and other rights to use are treated differently in case of the vendor's bankruptcy,[105] the consumers should be told not only whether they receive property rights but also what consequences this might have.[106] Also considered important is the quality of the building and the

---

100 Kappus (1996), p. 277. See also Bütter (1999), pp. 78 *et seq.*, finding conceivable transparency problems in many respects but not with regard to contracts that abide by the information duties.

101 But see Van den Bergh (1997), p. 85, presuming that entrepreneurs as the cheapest-cost-avoiders should decide how to structure information.

102 Kuß and Tomczak (2000), pp. 28, 117; Trommensdorf (2002), p. 87.

103 Kind (1998), p. 514; Martinek (2000), p. 526.

104 Kind (1998), p. 441; Martinek (2000), p. 529.

105 Tonner (1997), no. 49.

106 Kind (1998), pp. 436, 438, 441; see also Martinek (2000), p. 529.

limits on swap possibilities.[107] In addition and apart from the information regarding the material content of the contract, information on the right to cancel or withdraw from the contract must be provided.

In enacting an information requirement concerning key-information, it would be advisable to legally provide a form of information.[108] The information requirement should be different for the brochure and the contract. The brochure should include only key information and a serious offer to provide more information if specifically demanded. Moreover, the vendor should be obliged to hand out the brochure not only on express request but to anybody showing interest in the product (not necessarily in the information).[109] The contract should include all information required now. In this case, consumers are also protected since the vendor must specifically state certain terms instead of leaving them to his own discretion.[110] However, the contract should state the key information first on a separate sheet and provide a clear outline for the rest of the information.

Moreover, a third information requirement seems to be advisable. The brochure can be given at any time or not at all if the consumer does not demand it (or shows no interest in the product before negotiations commence). The contract should contain all information, properly structured. Thus, a step-by-step information and understanding of information is only guaranteed if, in addition, the vendor is obliged to give key information first and let the consumer ask questions regarding this or other information before concluding the contract. This third duty can be enacted as a modification of the duty to provide the brochure – even if the consumer shows up for contract negotiations, the brochure containing only key information must be handed out and then the consumer must be asked what additional information he or she would like to receive.[111]

In effect, the vendor would have a (reduced) duty to advise the purchaser. This is also an alternative to another proposal made for a change of the information requirements. It has been suggested to require the contract to be certified by a public notary in order to ensure the warning effect[112] of this

---

107 See Kind (1998), p. 433.

108 As it has been done for the notice of the right of withdrawal in Annex 2 *Informationsverordnung* zu § 355 *BGB*. But see Kind (1998), p. 533, considering information form as too great a limitation on party autonomy. At least, mandatory information should be made recognizable, see Kind (1998), p. 533; Martinek (2000), p. 530.

109 As provided for in the German implementation (which is admissible since the TSD provides only for a minimum harmonization).

110 For this aspect of the duty to state certain terms, see *supra* 'Effects of the Information Requirement itself (Direct Effects)' (pp. 72 et *seq.*).

111 Providing for, in addition, a cooling-off period between receiving such information and conclusion of the contract would guarantee that the consumer does not only understand the impact of the transaction but has the opportunity to consider it in relation to his or her needs and resources even before concluding the contract, see, e.g., Pöttler (2001), p. 174.

112 Kind (1998), p. 536.

requirement and the advice[113] which notaries are obliged to give. To have information explained by a person might enhance comprehensibility and diminish the chances that consumers mentally 'escape' the information as they might while reading a long document. Also, a notary as an impartial third party might fulfil the function to inform the consumer better than a vendor. Drawbacks of this proposal are the additional costs of this requirement and the language problem which also creates costs. After all, it has been stated that costly consumer protection measurements raise prices and drive those consumers out of the market who are not well-off enough to pay them.[114] In contrast, filling in an information form and reading it to the consumer step-by-step, asking what more information he or she would like to receive is also a comparable small and cheap effort if the usual sale efforts are considered which vendors are making in marketing time-sharing rights anyway.

Enforcement of Information Requirements

Altogether, information requirements contained in the TSD might be helpful at least if modified. Therefore, in the following, it will be discussed briefly whether the way in which they are enforced should be changed.

The CAD's information requirements cannot be a model for the TSD's information requirements with regard to their enforcement. First, the CAD does not even provide for sanctions in case of non-compliance with the information requirements; these are left to the Member States.[115] For example, in German law, sanctions consist of actions to seek compliance and, in case of violation, claims for monetary relief because of non-compliance and also a right to terminate the contract in case of substantial breach.[116]

Second, any such sanctions are only of use if the party entitled to receive the information is capable of recognizing the lack of important information because he or she is sufficiently involved in the transaction concerned. In this case he or she knows best whether to sue for compliance or relief because of omitted information. This is shown by the fact that without enforcing the information requirements – be it by suing for performance or for compensation or cancelling the contract – the obliged party's failure to comply has no actual effect, and enforcing a right requires to know there is a right. This applies also to the content of the right. Since hardly any party under an obligation will resort to absolute refusal to give any information, the party entitled to receive all necessary information has to notice or suspect first that there is something missing before he or she can take further steps to enforcement. The CAD's information requirements are designed to benefit parties who might need certain information but at least know that they need it – they know that they don't know!

---

113 Kind (1998), p. 536; Martinek (1997), p. 1396.
114 Schäfer (2000), p. 563; Calliess (2003), p. 585.
115 Fischer (2002), p. 145.
116 See (regarding § 86 *HGB*) Baumbach and Hopt (2003), § 86 *HGB*, no. 47.

Failure to comply with the TSD's information requirements, in contrast, has results a court will take into consideration in lawsuits concerning other issues. For example, if the vendor demands performance, the court will regard a withdrawal as valid if the duration of the period has been prolonged due to the vendor's failure to provide information.

Information requirements can be enforced by providing incentives for the vendors to abide by them, at least later. Moreover, informing consumers after conclusion of the contract with regard to its content is only useful if this information can still influence their decision to be bound by the contract. Thus, apart from the cases referred to in Art. 5 (1) TSD in which the contract lacks certain information, the withdrawal period should also be prolonged if other (new and modified) information requirements are not met that are also meant to optimize the decision whether to conclude the contract, and this longer period should also be abbreviated to the usual period if the information is given later, starting from when it is given. For example, if the brochure is not handed out or if the brochure or the contract does not contain the necessary information, arranged in a way provided for in an information form, the period for withdrawal should be prolonged. Moreover, it has been proposed to provide for the contract being void if the information requirements are not met with respect to items of information that are especially important.[117] Such items would be the key information described before which the consumer has to receive in any event.

In addition, since consumers hardly know what they do not know, enforcement of information requirements by third parties seems useful. This can be done by organizations designed to protect consumers' interests. Such bodies or organizations already exist in the Member States and have rights to protect consumers according to national legislation implementing the Directive on injunctions for the protection of consumers' interests.[118] According to Art. 1 (2), Annex no. 8 of this Directive, they also enforce the TSD's information requirements by reacting to infringements. In this regard, it seems that enforcement is sufficiently provided for.

In some Member States, violation of the TSD's information requirements is also sanctioned by fines, e.g., under Italian law.[119] Since this area belongs to punitive law, the EC cannot regulate this area. Therefore, with regard to third party enforcement, it must be considered sufficient if the TSD – as it does in Art. 3 (1) and Art. 4 – provides that the Member States shall make provision in their legislation for measures to ensure that the information requirements are met.

Altogether, enforcement of the TSD's information requirements should be enhanced in the way that:

---

117 Kind (1998), p. 536.

118 Directive 98/27/EC of the European Parliament and of the Council of 19 May 1998 on injunctions for the protection of consumers' interests, OJ L 166, 11/06/1998, pp. 0051 - 0055.

119 See Neises (1999b), p. 1080.

- the withdrawal period should be prolonged if the information requirements other than those concerning the text of the contract are not met, and
- the contract should be void if key information is not included in the contract.

Summary

Different information requirements must be seen very differently. As in the CAD, information requirements might, in fact, be substantive provisions regulating the very content of the contract. However, the extent of formal limitations on party autonomy is not the only criterion to judge them by. It is also necessary to look to the degree of deviation from the 'natural' contract structure and, moreover, to indirect effects of the fulfilment of information requirements on party autonomy.

The information requirements contained in the TSD, however, are of little formal effect on party autonomy, but may have harmful counterproductive effects. The ability of the human mind to process information is very limited. Duties to provide much detailed and unstructured information are therefore controversial. The duties contained in the CAD, by contrast, require information to be provided which the receivers do not only actually need, but know that they need it and can handle it.

Changes in the TSD are thought to be necessary. Most commentators propose a mere reduction of information to meaningful key terms. This contribution instead proposes that vendors should be required to give those key terms first and then, in addition, provide the information now stated in the TSD, if actual demand for it arises. By this method, the consumers' ability to actually use the information provided can be assimilated somewhat to the ability of parties of the commercial agents' contract. Hopefully, by comparing apples and oranges, I have come closer to the core of the information overload problem – and to its solution.

References

Akerlof, G.A. (1970), 'The Market for "Lemons": Qualitative Uncertainty and the Market Mechanism', 84 , *Quarterly Journal of Economics*, pp. 488-500.

Bacovsky, G. (1995), 'Österreich', in Westphalen, Graf von, F. (ed.), *Handbuch des Handelsvertreterrechts in EU-Staaten und der Schweiz* (Cologne: O. Schmidt), pp. 889-974.

Baumbach, A. and Hopt, K.J. (2003), *Handelsgesetzbuch*, 31st edn. (Munich: Beck).

Behrens, G. (1991), *Konsumentenverhalten*, 2nd edn. (Heidelberg: Physica).

Berndt, H. (1983), *Konsumentscheidung und Informationsüberlastung* (Munich: GBI).

Bütter, M. (1999), 'Vorvertragliches Aufklärungsverschulden und AGB-Kontrolle bei Time-Sharing-Verträgen nach Inkrafttreten des TzWrG', *Zeitschrift für Miet- und Raumrecht*, pp. 73-83.

Calliess, G.-P. (2003), 'Nach der Schuldrechtsreform: Perspektiven des deutschen, europäischen und internationalen Verbrauchervertragsrechts', 203, *Archiv für die civilistische Praxis*, pp. 575-602.

Canaris, C.-W. (2000), 'Wandlungen des Schuldvertragsrechts – Tendenzen zu seiner „Materialisierung"', 200, *Archiv für die civilistische Praxis*, pp. 273-364.

Damm, R. (1999), 'Privatautonomie und Verbraucherschutz – Legalstruktur und Realstruktur von Autonomiekonzepten', *Versicherungsrecht, Haftungs- und Schadensrecht*, pp. 130-141.

Diller, H. (1978), 'Verbesserungsmöglichkeiten der Verbraucherinformation durch Berücksichtigung verhaltenstheoretischer Erkenntnisse', *Journal of Consumer Policy*, pp. 24-41.

Dreher, M. (1997), 'Der Verbraucher – Das Phantom in den opera des europäischen und deutschen Rechts?', *Juristenzeitung*, pp. 167-178.

Eckert, H.W. (1990), 'Das neue Recht der Handelsvertreter – Die Umsetzung der EG-Richtlinie in deutsches Recht', *Neue Zeitschrift für Arbeitsrecht*, pp. 384-386.

Felser, G. (2001), *Werbe- und Konsumentenpsychologie*, 2nd edn. (Stuttgart: Schäffer-Poeschel).

Fischer, M. (2002), 'Der Handelsvertreter im deutschen und europäischen Recht', 101, *Zeitschrift für Vergleichende Rechtswissenschaft*, pp. 143-157.

Fleischer, H. (2000), 'Vertragsschlussbezogene Informationspflichten im Gemeinschaftsinformationsrecht', *Zeitschrift für Europäisches Privatrecht*, pp. 772-798.

Fleischer, H. (2001), *Informationsasymmetrie im Vertragsrecht*, habil. Cologne (Munich: Beck).

Fock, T. (2001), *Die europäische Handelsvertreter-Richtlinie*, diss. Berlin (Baden-Baden: Nomos).

Grundmann, S. (1999), *Europäisches Schuldvertragsrecht* (Berlin: de Gruyter).

Grundmann, S. (2000a), 'Europäisches Schuldvertragsrecht – Struktur und Bestand', *Neue Juristische Wochenschrift*, pp. 14-23.

Grundmann, S. (2000b), 'Privatautonomie im Binnenmarkt – Informationsregeln als Instrument', *Juristenzeitung*, pp. 1133-1143.

Grundmann, S., Kerber, W. and Weatherill, S. (2001), 'Party Autonomy and the Role of Information – an Overview', in Grundmann, S., Kerber, W. and Weatherill, S. (eds.), *Party Autonomy and the Role of Information in the Internal Market* (Berlin: de Gruyter), pp. 2-38.

Hager, G. (1995), 'Ökologisierung des Verbraucherschutzrechtes', *Umwelt- und Planungsrecht*, pp. 401-407.

Haupt, S. (2003), 'An Economic Analysis of Consumer Protection in Contract Law', Vol. 4, no. 11, *German Law Journal*, pp. 1137-1164.

Hecker, M. (1998), *Informationsüberflutung und deren Vermeidung* (Lüneburg: Kovac).

Heiderhoff, B. (2002), 'Vertrauen versus Vertragsfreiheit im europäischen Verbrauchervertragsrecht', *Zeitschrift für Europäisches Privatrecht*, pp. 769-788.

Jacoby, J., Speller, D.E. and Kohn, C.A. (1974), 'Brand Choice Behavior as a Function of Information Load', 11, *Journal of Marketing Research*, pp. 63-69.

Jacoby, J., Speller, D.E. and Kohn-Berning, C. (1974), 'Brand Choice Behavior as a Function of Information Load-Replication and Extension', 1, *Journal of Consumer Research*, pp. 33-41.

Jacoby, J., Szybillo, G.J. and Busato-Schach, J. (1977), 'Information Acquisition Behavior in Brand Choice Situations', 3, *Journal of Consumer Research*, pp. 209-216.

Kappus, A. (1996), 'EU-Time-Sharing-Richtlinie und deutsche Umsetzungsgesetzgebung', *Europäisches Wirtschafts- und Steuerrecht*, pp. 273-277.

Kind, S. (1998), *Die Grenzen des Verbraucherschutzes durch Information – aufgezeigt am Teilzeitwohnrechtegesetz*, diss. Mainz (Berlin: Duncker & Humblot).

Korobkin, R.B. and Ulen, T.S. (2000), 'Law and Behavioural Science: Removing the Rationality Assumption from Law and Economics', 88, *California Law Review*, pp. 1051-1119.

Kroeber-Riel, W. and Weinberg, P. (2003), *Konsumentenverhalten*, 8th edn. (Munich: Vahlen).

Kuß, A. and Tomczak, T. (2000), *Käuferverhalten*, 2nd edn. (Stuttgart: Lucius & Lucius).

Kuther, H. (1990), 'Die neuen Handelsvertretervorschriften im HGB', *Neue Juristische Wochenschrift*, pp. 304-305.

Martinek, M. (1994), 'Das Teilzeiteigentum an Immobilien in der Europäischen Union – Kritik des Timesharing-Richtlinienvorschlags der Europäischen Kommission', *Zeitschrift für Europäisches Privatrecht*, pp. 470-492.

Martinek, M. (1997), 'Das neue Teilzeit-Wohnrechtegesetz – mißratener Verbraucherschutz bei Time-Sharing-Verträgen', *Neue Juristische Wochenschrift*, pp. 1393-1399.

Martinek, M. (2000), 'Unsystematische Überregulierung und kontraintentionale Effekte in Europäischen Verbraucherschutzrecht oder: Weniger wäre mehr', in Grundmann, S. (ed.), *Systembildung und Systemlücken in Kerngebieten des Europäischen Privatrechts* (Tübingen: Mohr Siebeck), pp. 511-557.

Mäsch, G. (1995), 'Die Time-Sharing-Richtlinie – Licht und Schatten im Europäischen Verbraucherschutzrecht', *Europäische Zeitschrift für Wirtschaftsrecht*, pp. 8-14.

Miller, G.A. (1956), 'The Magical Number Seven, Plus or Minus Two: Some Limits on Our Capacity for Processing Information', *The Psychological Review*, pp. 81-97, reproduced at http://www.well.com/user/smalin/miller.html.

Neises, R. (1999a), 'Zur Umsetzung der Time-Sharing-Richtlinie in Frankreich', *Neue Zeitschrift für Miet- und Wohnungsrecht*, pp. 338-341.

Neises, R. (1999b), 'Zur Umsetzung der Time-Sharing-Richtlinie in Italien', *Neue Zeitschrift für Miet- und Wohnungsrecht*, pp. 1078-1081.

Pöttler, G. (2001), *Vergleichende Verbraucherschutzrichtlinienumsetzung in europäischen Mitgliedstaaten*, diss. Salzburg (Frankfurt am Main: Peter Lang).

Riesenhuber, K. (2003), *Europäisches Vertragsrecht* (Berlin: de Gruyter).

Scammon, D.L. (1977), '"Information Load" and Consumers', 4, *Journal of Consumer Research*, pp. 148-155.

Schäfer, H.-B. (2000), 'Grenzen des Verbraucherschutzes und adverse Effekte des Europäischen Verbraucherrechts', in Grundmann, S. (ed.), *Systembildung und Systemlücken in Kerngebieten des Europäischen Privatrechts* (Tübingen: Mohr Siebeck), pp. 559-568.

Schmidt, J. (1992), 'Vertragsfreiheit und EG-Handelsvertreterrichtlinie', 156, *Zeitschrift für das gesamte Handelsrecht und Wirtschaftsrecht*, pp. 512-520.

Schünemann, W. (1996), 'Mündigkeit versus Schutzbedürftigkeit – Legitimationsprobleme des Verbraucher-Leitbildes', in Pfeiffer, G., Kummer, J. and Scheuch, S. (eds.), *Festschrift für Hans Erich Brandner zum 70. Geburtstag* (Cologne: O. Schmidt), pp. 279-298.

Simitis, K. (1976), *Verbraucherschutz, Schlagwort oder Rechtsprinzip?* (Baden-Baden: Nomos).

Sousa, M.C.D.U. (1998), *Das Timesharing an Ferienimmobilien in der EU – eine rechtsvergleichende Studie unter Berücksichtigung der Timesharing-Richtlinie (94/47/EG)*, diss. Saarbrücken (Baden-Baden: Nomos).

Tonner, K. (1997), *Das Recht des Time-sharing an Ferienimmobilien* (Munich: Beck).

Trommensdorf, V. (2002), *Konsumentenverhalten*, 4th edn. (Stuttgart: Kohlhammer).

Ulen, T.S. (2001), 'Information in the Market Economy – Cognitive Errors and Legal Correctives' in Grundmann, S., Kerber, W. and Weatherill, S. (eds.), *Party Autonomy and the Role of Information in the Internal Market* (Berlin: de Gruyter), pp. 98-129.

Van den Bergh, R. (1997), 'Wer schützt die europäischen Verbraucher vor dem Brüsseler Verbraucherschutz? Zu den möglichen adversen Effekten der europäischen Richtlinien zum Schutze des Verbrauchers', in Ott, C. and Schäfer, H.-B. (eds.), *Effiziente Verhaltenssteuerung und Kooperation im Zivilrecht, Beiträge zum V. Travemünder Symposium zur Ökonomischen Analyse des Rechts, 27.-30. März 1996* (Tübingen: Mohr Siebeck), pp. 77-102.

Weatherill, S. (2001), 'Justifying Limits to Party Autonomy in the Internal Market', in Grundmann, S., Kerber, W. and Weatherill, S. (eds.), *Party Autonomy and the Role of Information in the Internal Market* (Berlin: de Gruyter), pp. 173-196.

Wein, T. (2001), 'Consumer Information Problems – Causes and Consequences' in Grundmann, S., Kerber, W. and Weatherill, S. (eds.), *Party Autonomy and the Role of Information in the Internal Market* (Berlin: de Gruyter), pp. 80-97.

Westphal, B. (1994), *Die Handelsvertreterrichtlinie und deren Umsetzung in den Mitgliedstaaten der Europäischen Union*, diss. Münster (no publisher).

Westphal, B. (1996), 'Neues Handelsvertreterrecht in der Europäischen Union', *Europäisches Wirtschafts- und Steuerrecht*, pp. 43-49.

Westphalen, Graf von, F. (1995), 'Die EG-Handelsvertreterrichtlinie und kartellrechtliche Erwägungen' in Westphalen, Graf von, F. (ed.), *Handbuch des Handelsvertreterrechts* (Cologne: O. Schmidt), pp. 1-8.

Wiedmann, K.-P., Walsh, G. and Polotzek, D. (2000), *Informationsüberlastung des Konsumenten – Stand der Forschung, Konzept und Messung* (Hannover: Lehrstuhl für Marketing II, Univ. Hannover).

Chapter 6

Information Requirements in the E-Commerce Directive and the Proposed Directive on Unfair Commercial Practices

Annette Nordhausen

Introduction

Information obligations become a more and more central element of European consumer protection regulation. The amount of information which has to be provided is constantly increasing. This is a quite demanding task for service providers. On one hand the European harmonization gives service providers some guidelines which they can rely on in the whole Community, on the other hand exactly this regulation gets – following Internal Market principles[1] and aiming to increase consumer protection – more and more elaborated and demanding for service providers. The question of whether the existing regulation in fact increases consumer protection and enables the consumer to make an informed choice shall not be looked at in detail in this chapter. Surveys[2] show that consumers can only deal with a limited amount of information at a time. More information will not be taken into account and might even tempt the consumer not to deal with the information at all – which, as a result would mean that too much information means effectively less information (if any at all). As this cannot fulfil the aims of consumer protection nor a functioning Internal Market the question arises if the information given to the consumer can be prioritized in a way that ensures that the consumer gets the most important information and will be able to take this information into account for his or her decision. One recent example of a different approach to information obligations is the proposed Directive on Unfair

1 Following the Cardiff reports *Economic Reform: report on the functioning of Community product and capital markets*, COM (2002) 743 final and the previous COM (2001) 736 final, cross border shopping has a role to play in achieving further integration and efficient functioning of the market.

2 See Wendlandt, Chapter 5 of this volume.

Commercial Practices.[3] This chapter will examine if this approach can be used to prioritize information obligations in general.

Proposed Directive – Overview

Background

On 18 June 2003 the Commission presented a proposal for the Directive on Unfair Commercial Practices.[4] The Green Paper on EC Consumer Protection from 2001[5] was the first incentive for a directive on unfair commercial practices. The Green Paper already suggested the two main fundamentals of the proposed directive, regulation by framework directive and a general clause to trade fairly. This was confirmed and specified in the Follow-up Communication to the Green Paper[6] and finally prioritized in the Council resolution on the Commission's consumer strategy 2002-2006.[7] Although the Commission starts from the fact that unfair commercial practices are not the only barriers[8] to trade this is one issue to be addressed as it can undermine consumer confidence. Other barriers – like tax (VAT), language and distance – are recognized as well. These can be addressed in different ways but are not very interdependent to unfair commercial practices and therefore unfair commercial practices can be regulated on their own.

Framework Directive

The Commission proposes regulation by a framework directive. The main reason behind this is the fear that a specific directive without a general framework would lack harmonization of existing national general clauses and legal principles. This also requires the maximum harmonization approach to achieve clarity and legal certainty. The proposed Directive shall be supplemented if necessary by sector specific legislation. This legislation is already in force for electronic commerce[9] as the E-Commerce Directive also regulates commercial communications[10] and in particular unsolicited commercial communications.[11] According to the

3 Proposal for a Directive of the European Parliament and of the Council concerning unfair business-to-consumer commercial practices in the Internal Market and amending directives 84/450/EEC, 97/7/EC and 98/27/EC, presented on 18 June 2003, COM (2003) 356 final.

4 COM (2003) 356 final.

5 COM (2001) 531 final.

6 COM (2002) 289 final.

7 Of 2 December 2002.

8 Others including tax (VAT), language, distance.

9 Directive 2000/31 of 8 June 2000 on certain legal aspects of information society services, in particular electronic commerce, in the Internal Market, OJ L 178 of 17 July 2000.

10 Art. 6.

11 Art. 7.

Commission this approach will increase consumer confidence in cross-border consumer protection. For businesses market-entry, transaction and marketing costs will decrease through harmonization. As a framework directive, the proposed Directive applies where there are no specific provisions regulating unfair commercial practices in sectoral legislation, if such sector specific provisions exist, they will take precedence over the framework directive. General references to principles in sector specific directives, however, will not be sufficient and the framework directive will apply in these cases.

Benchmark Consumer

The proposed Directive defines the term 'consumer' as well as introducing a new criterion as a benchmark, the 'average consumer'.

The consumer definition in Art. 2 (a) of the proposed Directive follows the standard definition known from other consumer protection directives like the Financial Services Directive,[12] E-Commerce Directive,[13] Sale of Goods Directive,[14] Distance Selling Directive,[15] Unfair Contract Terms Directive[16] or the Doorstep Selling Directive.[17] The consumer is defined as 'any natural person who [...] is acting for purposes which are outside his trade, business or profession'.[18] This definition shall only apply to the proposed Directive on Unfair Commercial Practices but it is unlikely (and would also cause unnecessary confusion) if this definition were to be interpreted differently from other directives.

In addition, the proposed Directive on Unfair Commercial Practices uses the term 'average consumer' which is the benchmark consumer with regard to this proposed Directive. The average consumer is defined in Art. 2 (b) as being reasonably well informed and reasonably observant and circumspect. This definition follows the rulings of the European Court of Justice and incorporates

---

12 2002/65/EC concerning the distance marketing of consumer financial services and amending Council Directive 1990/619/EEC and Directives 1997/7/EC and 1998/27/EC of 23 September 2002, OJ L 271 of 9 October 2002.

13 2000/31/EC on certain legal aspects of information society services, in particular electronic commerce, in the Internal Market of 8 June 2000, OJ L 178 of 17 July 2000.

14 1999/44/EC on certain aspects of the sale of consumer goods and associated guarantees of 25 May 1999, OJ L 299 of 12 December 1999.

15 1997/7/EC on the protection of consumers in respect of distance contracts of 20 May 1997, OJ L 144 of 4 June 1997.

16 1993/13/EEC on unfair terms in consumer contracts of 5 April 1993, OJ L 95/29.

17 1985/577/EEC to protect consumers in respect of contracts negotiated away from business premises – door to door selling – of 20 December 1985, OJ L 372 of 31 December 1985.

18 Art. 2 (a).

them into the statutory law.[19] This average consumer test also takes social cultural or linguistic factors into account.[20]

General Clause

Resulting from the regulation by framework directive, the proposed Directive on Unfair Commercial Practices uses a general clause to define the duty to trade fairly. The proposed Directive defines rules determining whether a commercial practice is unfair. From this definition of unfairness it follows that generally unfairness (not fairness) has to be proved and ensures proportionality. The proposed Directive generally prohibits the use of unfair commercial practices. This general clause is specified by further definitions of two types of unfair commercial practices, 'misleading' and 'aggressive' practices and a blacklist in Annex 1 of the proposed Directive. From the nature of a general clause it follows that whenever commercial practices are named in the Annex or fall under one of the definitions of 'misleading' or 'aggressive' they are automatically regarded as unfair. If a practice does not fall under any of these categories the general clause will determine if the practice is unfair.

The use of general clauses as a regulative technique in directives is not regarded as problematic in all Member States where this technique is used in the national law as well and general clauses exist in the national law as well.[21] In Member States however, in which the use of general clauses is not common or not known at all in national legislation[22] the regulation by general clause is regarded as problematic[23] and contrary to transparency and certainty. Their introduction by directive has led to intensive discussions whenever European Law introduces general clauses.[24] In my opinion the introduction of general principles is unlikely to change the structure of the law in these countries where the use of general clauses is not common. In most areas similar principles exist developed through case law and it seems very foreign to the legal system to introduce these by a legislative act

19 e.g. C-315/92 *Verband Sozialer Wettbewerb e.V.* v. *Clinique Laboratories SNC and Estée Lauder Cosmetics GmbH* (1994) ECR-I-317; C-210/96 *Gut Springheide GmbH* v. *Oberkreisdirektor des Landkreises Steinfurt* (1998) ECR-I-4657.

20 Recital 13: 'This Directive codifies the average consumer test elaborated by the European Court of Justice. Pursuant to the Court of Justice case law national courts will in applying the test also take social, cultural or linguistic factors into account. Where a commercial practice is specifically aimed at a particular group of consumers, such as children, it is desirable that the impact of the commercial practice is assessed from the perspective of the average member of that group.'

21 Most continental jurisdictions like France and Germany are familiar with general clauses in the national laws.

22 As in the United Kingdom.

23 Problems very clearly outlined in the consultation process before the presentation of the proposed directive by the commission; very detailed and differentiated: Bradgate, Brownsword, Twigg-Flesner (July 2003).

24 i.e. Unfair Contract Terms Directive – Directive 1993/13/EEC on unfair terms in consumer contracts of 5 April 1993, OJ L 95/29.

rather than through case law, but looked at from the perspective of the results rather than the means the difference seems less important. As European law introduces a codified legislation for all areas regulated by European law also to common law jurisdictions legal certainty is guaranteed – although not in the same way as known from some national jurisdictions.

Country of Origin Principle

The country of origin principle or Internal Market clause is becoming one of the principles for consumer protection legislation in the Community. It ensures that traders only have to comply with their own national provisions and the Member States have to ensure providers established in their territory comply with their laws. Although this is not necessary suitable to increase consumer confidence in this proposed Directive it is accompanied by full harmonization. The proposed Directive aims for full harmonization of requirements relating to unfair business-to-consumer commercial practices to ensure a high level of consumer protection and consumer confidence while allowing the application of the principle of origin.

The Commission adds further explanation:

> The convergence brought about by the proposed Directive creates the conditions for introducing the principle of mutual recognition of laws relating to unfair commercial practices. Thus Article 4 provides that traders are required to comply only with the laws of the Member State where they are established and prohibits other Member States from imposing additional requirements on such traders within the field co-ordinated by the Directive or from restricting the free movement of goods and services where the trader has complied with the laws of the Member State of Establishment.[25]

The main objective of the proposed Directive is a high level of consumer protection and the functioning of the Internal Market.[26] The rights for consumers shall be clearer which will allow the consumers to develop confidence in cross-border trade. This is also advantageous for businesses, as cross-border trade gets less complicated.[27]

The single, common, general prohibition of unfair commercial practices shall replace the existing multiple volumes of national rules and court rulings on commercial practices.

Unfair Commercial Practices

As Art. 1 outlines, the proposed Directive is only concerned with matters affecting economic interests of consumers. All other matters, like taste, decency and social responsibility are outside the scope of the proposed Directive. Also, the proposed

25 Explanatory memorandum, no. 47.

26 Art. 1.

27 Creating 'a triple-win situation: consumers, businesses and Europe's economy' (Byrne (2003)).

Directive does not regulate competition or unfair competition. In some Member States unfair commercial practices are regarded as unfair competition.[28] The proposed Directive does not interfere with this approach generally as competition law remains outside the scope of application. Accordingly the Member States can maintain their general competition rules as well as competition rules on unfair commercial practices as long as these are generally consistent with the proposed Directive and other European Law. This might lead to different interpretations of unfair commercial practices in these Member States with regard to the proposed Directive and to competition law. In practice however, it is unlikely that the Member States and the national courts will develop and apply different standards for unfair commercial practices as these issues will in most Member States be dealt with by the same courts and public authorities.

Commercial Practices

The term 'commercial practices' is defined in Art. 2 (e) of the proposed Directive. Commercial practices include commercial communications as known from and defined in other directives,[29] especially the E-Commerce Directive, but the term commercial practices has to have a wider understanding.

Art. 2 (e) defines commercial practices as:

> any act, omission, course of conduct or representation, commercial communication including advertising and marketing, by a trader, directly connected with the promotion, sale or supply of a product to consumers.

This definition of commercial practices is not restricted to the pre-contractual stage – like commercial communications in the E-Commerce Directive – but also includes contractual information.

General Prohibition of Unfair Commercial Practices

Art. 5 (1) generally prohibits unfair commercial practices. This provision shall replace the existing general clauses in the national regulation and establish a European general clause. This general clause will have to be interpreted primarily by the European Court of Justice.

As the proposed Directive also introduces the internal market clause[30] a practice judged as unfair in one Member State will have to be regarded as unfair in all other Member States and a practice not seen as unfair in the Member State of establishment cannot be regarded as unfair in any other Member State.

The general prohibition of unfair commercial practices established in Art. 5 (2) three conditions to test whether a practice is unfair:

---

28 i.e. in Germany §§ 1, 3 *Gesetz gegen den unlauteren Wettbewerb* (*UWG*).

29 Explanatory memorandum, no. 36.

30 Art. 4.

1. The practice must be contrary to the requirements of professional diligence.
2. The practice must materially distort or be likely to materially distort consumers' economic behaviour.
3. The practice has to be assessed by considering the benchmark consumer, which is the 'average' consumer, established by the rulings of the European Court of Justice.

The general clause is specified in Art. 5 (3) where particularly misleading or aggressive commercial practices are regarded as unfair. In Arts. 6, 7 and 8 the proposed Directive specifies the terms misleading actions and omissions as well as aggressive practices. Some misleading practices are blacklisted as misleading and aggressive in Annex 1 of the proposed Directive. The listing in Annex 1 means that a practice listed in the Annex shall be in any event be regarded as a misleading or an aggressive commercial practice. Only if a practice is not mentioned in Annex 1, do Arts. 5-8 of the proposed Directive have to be considered.

Misleading Actions

Art. 6 of the proposed Directive defines misleading actions and mentions a number of typically misleading actions which will or are likely to deceive the consumer. These issues include the main characteristics of the product, symbols used, price calculation, need for service or repair, issues concerning the trader or agent, unsubstantiated claims and consumer's rights or risks as well as marketing methods, non-compliance with codes of conduct or non-compliance with a commitment given to a public authority. Mainly, all statements shall be true and be presented in a way that cannot be misleading.

Misleading Omissions

Art. 7 deals with misleading omissions and is therefore of particular importance for information obligations. Following the general rule in Art. 7 (1) a commercial practice shall be regarded as misleading if any material information that an average consumer needs to take an informed decision is missing and this causes or is likely to cause the average consumer to take a decision he would not have taken if these information had been provided correctly. The proposed Directive introduces explicitly some information obligations as material, but some of the information obligations arising from other directives are also regarded as material. All information requirements introduced by the proposed Directive shall be established in addition to other information requirements established by Community Law.

This means that at least for some of the information obligations arising from other directives the non-fulfilment or improper fulfilment of these duties will have to be regarded as a misleading omission and therefore an unfair commercial practice. In Art. 7 (2) the proposed Directive states that material information given in an unclear, unintelligible, ambiguous or untimely manner shall also be regarded as misleading omission, likewise where a trader hides such information or fails to identify their commercial intent.

However, a commercial transaction based on a misleading omission may only occur if the trader makes an invitation to purchase. This means that general advertisements which do not include an invitation to purchase do not have to contain all material information. This is generally appropriate as the consumer should be used to advertisements and will usually not buy the advertised product straight away and without any further thought. For electronic commercial communications the situation is slightly different. As the consumer is very often using the distance communication at the very moment he receives the commercial communication[31] the consumer is very much more likely to enter into a contract immediately. In addition, in the offline environment it is rather easy to distinguish between advertisements without an invitation to purchase and commercial communication including an invitation to purchase. Mostly advertisement and purchase will be at a different time or location. In the online environment the advertisement and the invitation to purchase may be located on a different website with a different address, but this can technically be designed in a way that it may only be one mouse-click – and this means not only hardly any effort but also almost no time – from the advertisement to the ordering process. The consumer may not be aware about the change of the quality of the transactions at all. The consumer is therefore in the online environment more likely to enter into a contract following an advertisement (straightaway). The requirement of an invitation to purchase should – like misleading omissions under Art. 7 (1) and (2) – be considered with regard to the perception of the average consumer and not be related to the technical background.

Material Information

The proposed Directive regards some information as material. Material information are according to Art. 7 (3) of the proposed Directive:

a. The main characteristics of the product;
b. The trading name of the trader and, where applicable, the name of the trader on whose behalf he is acting;
c. The price inclusive of taxes, as well as, where appropriate, all additional freight, delivery or postal charges or, where these charges cannot reasonably be calculated in advance, the fact that additional charges may be payable;
d. arrangements for payment, delivery, performance and the complaint handling policy, if they depart from the requirements of professional diligence;
e. for products and transactions involving a right of withdrawal or cancellation the existence of such a right.

In addition, information requirements in relation to advertising, commercial communication or marketing established by Community Law shall be regarded as material.[32] This means that the information requirements arising i.e. from Art. 6[33]

31 i.e. telephone communication or online transactions over the Internet.
32 Art. 7, no. 4.
33 And Art. 7 as far as this is applicable.

of the E-Commerce Directive are regarded as material information and their omission will be a misleading omission and therefore an unfair commercial practice. The proposed Directive contains in Annex 2 a non-exhaustive list of Community Law provisions setting out information requirements in relation to commercial communication, advertising or marketing. Infringement of any of these provisions shall be regarded as non-fulfilment of material information and hence as a misleading omission and unfair commercial practice. Regarding the E-Commerce Directive, Annex 2 mentions Art. 6 which specifically deals with information requirements in commercial communications as material information but as electronic communication is also distance communication the Distance Selling Directive is also applicable and Annex 2 regards Arts. 4 and 5 of the Distance Selling Directive as material. These articles include all pre-contractual information and the written confirmation.

Incomplete or incorrect information on any of the pre-contractual information obligations should be regarded as an unfair practice and sanctioned accordingly. This stresses the importance information requirements are given by Community Law and will ensure that the infringement of information obligations regarded as absolutely essential will be sanctioned. The Member States as well as the Community so far regarded information obligations as an important measure to achieve efficient consumer protection, but enforcement and sanctions for infringements were rather unclear, lacked harmonization and efficiency.[34] More or less through the back door by reference to unfair commercial practices this shall be altered. For a number of Member States this reference to commercial practices is a reference to commercial law in general and in many cases to competition law. The general implications of this way of referencing shall not be examined here. For electronic commercial communications, however, it follows that some of the information obligations have to be regarded as material information in general and will be sanctioned differently. By reference to all information requirements of the Distance Selling Directive and only the information obligations for commercial communications of the E-Commerce Directive, some other information obligations arising from the E-Commerce Directive will – in case of their infringement – be treated differently. This different treatment leads to the question if these are of different importance generally. Another problem is that, as far as the materials show, these implications were not intended by the Commission. The differentiation means, however, significant changes not only to the sanctions, but also to information requirements in general and should therefore get more attention from the legislator and be altered by a conscious decision rather than by accident and through the back door.

---

34 For German Law see the comprehensive analysis of Janal (2003).

Current Information Obligations in Electronic Commerce Contracts

Currently, a number of directives introduce information obligations with the aim of increasing consumer protection and enabling the consumer to an informed choice and interfering with the free market and the freedom of choice as little as possible. As the consumer shall be enabled to take a free and informed choice, the consumer shall be provided with all necessary information. This information is distinguished as to the time they have to be given and their connection to contractual relationships. Generally, the information requirements can be distinguished into pre-contractual and contractual information obligations.

The relevant directives all use a slightly different terminology. The Distance Selling Directive uses the term 'prior information'[35] and the Financial Services Directive 'prior to the conclusion of the distance contract'[36] whereas the E-Commerce Directive uses 'general information'.[37] All directives define the latest possible time for the provision of the required information slightly differently, but in any case the information must be provided before the conclusion of a contract. The E-Commerce Directive requires the general information in any case and not only in the process of concluding a contract.

The contractual information obligations require in all directives a confirmation in writing or on a durable medium; the amount of information to be given varies. The latest possible time is the fulfilment of the contract.

The situation for commercial communications is similar, but slightly less problematic. The time the information has to be provided is the same as the commercial communication; the commercial communication itself and the information obligations have to be given together. As mentioned earlier, the term 'commercial practices' as used in the proposed Directive on Unfair Commercial Practices is to be understood in a wider sense than the term 'commercial communications' used in other directives but commercial communications are explicitly included in commercial practices.

The existing information obligations will be examined in more detail in the following sections. As Financial Services are of a different nature and therefore would require a separate discussion the following discussion will be restricted to the obligations arising from the E-Commerce Directive and the Distance Selling Directive.

E-Commerce Directive

All information obligations in the E-Commerce Directive have to be given in addition to other information obligations arising from Community law. For electronic commerce this means in particular information obligations arising from the Distance Selling Directive as all contracts concluded by way of electronic

---

35 Art. 4.
36 Art. 3.
37 Art. 5.

commerce are also distance contracts. Of all directives discussed here only the E-Commerce Directive requires general information obligations.

These general information obligations as well as the pre-contractual and contractual information obligations are not regarded as material information in the proposed Directive on Unfair Commercial Practices and their omission will not be regarded as an unfair commercial practice automatically,[38] but will have to be examined and judged under the general clause. This leads to the result that especially the general information obligations in the E-Commerce Directive are regarded and treated in very different ways. Whereas the E-Commerce Directive treats them as material information that has to be given in any event and regardless of any contractual relationship, both in business-to-consumer contracts and business-to-business contracts they are not (automatically) regarded as material information in the proposed Directive on Unfair Commercial Practices. Their omission will only be regarded as unfair if the individual presentation is regarded as misleading under the general clause.

The practical implications, however, will not be as severe as the dogmatic analysis may suggest. As many of the general information requirements of the E-Commerce Directive are also part of the information required under the Distance Selling Directive – and these are all regarded as material information under the proposed Directive on Unfair Commercial Practices – most of this information will in practice be regarded as material information. Therefore their omission will also be regarded as unfair commercial practice. In some cases, however, the dogmatic differentiation will have practical implications.

General Information Obligations

According to Art. 5 of the E-Commerce Directive this information has to be given in any case, regardless of whether the customer is actually ordering or considering whether to conclude a contract or not. This shall give the user (not only the consumer) essential information at a very early stage. This general information is obligatory for business-to-business transactions as well.

The general information obligations include the name of the service provider and their geographic address. PO Box addresses are not sufficient. The user shall have the opportunity to see with whom he is dealing or find out more about the service provider. In addition, details about means for rapid contact and communication, including an e-mail address, must be provided. This shall ensure that the user can communicate with the service provider directly and effectively. The requirement to provide an e-mail address causes the service provider to incur no additional costs and it ensures that the user can communicate with the provider through the same medium he has chosen for offering his products or services. The service provider also has to inform about any details of trade registry entries, professional details and VAT details. Any indication of price should be clear and unambiguous and state whether tax and delivery costs are included.

---

38 As not mentioned in Annex 2.

Pre-Contractual Information Obligations

In addition to the general information obligations in Art. 5, the E-Commerce Directive requires pre-contractual information in Art. 10. The obligations arising from Art. 10 of the E-Commerce Directive are generally applicable for business-to-consumer as well as business-to-business transactions, although in business-to-business transactions the parties can agree to exclude all or certain information obligations. In business-to-consumer transactions an exemption exists for e-mail or equivalent individual communication. The case of individual communication between the business and the consumer is viewed as equivalent to individual negotiations in the offline world. The consumer will either have some knowledge about the business or be more likely to inquire.

Information must be provided on:

1. The different technical steps to conclude a contract.
   This requirement is not only an information obligation, but also of a completely new nature. In contrast to the offline environment this requires the supplier to explain not only the technical steps, but their legal implications as they relate to the process of contract formation. Although the consumer will generally be more familiar with the mechanisms of the conclusion of contracts in the offline environment, this is not true for all consumers and is certainly not usually the position in international consumer contracts where an equivalent requirement does not exist.
2. Whether the concluded contract is filed and accessible for the consumer.
3. Technical means for identification and correction of input errors.
4. The languages offered for the conclusion of a contract.
5. Relevant codes of practice and their electronic accessibility.
6. Contract terms and general conditions have to be available and storable.
   This will also include allowing the consumer to print the terms and conditions.

The service provider has furthermore to provide the consumer with 'appropriate, effective and accessible means allowing the consumer to identify and correct input errors prior to the placing of the order'.[39] This provision is not explicitly phrased as an information obligation but the provision of means to correct input errors becomes only an effective instrument for the consumer if the consumer knows about it. It must therefore be understood as an implied information obligation.

All this information has to be given in addition to other information requirements arising from Community law. In the context of E-Commerce transactions this refers first of all to information obligations arising from the Distance Selling Directive.[40]

Again, only the information obligations arising from the Distance Selling Directive are automatically regarded as material and their omission as unfair commercial practice under the proposed Directive on Unfair Commercial Practices.

---

39 Art. 11, no. 2.

40 But also other specific sectoral directives.

All pre-contractual information obligations under the E-Commerce Directive are only automatically regarded as material (and their omission as unfair) as long as they are covered in the Distance Selling Directive, others are only unfair if they are judged as unfair under the general clause.

Contractual Information

Apart from general information and pre-contractual information the E-Commerce Directive also requires some contractual information. These are information to be given in addition to the contractual information obligations arising from the Distance Selling Directive. The E-Commerce Directive requires the service provider[41] to acknowledge the receipt of the recipient's order without undue delay and by electronic means. This is a special regulation for contracts concluded by electronic means and has no equivalent for offline-contracts. The regulative approach of the first proposals[42] of the E-Commerce Directive suggested introducing an exchange of more information in the process of the conclusion of a contract,[43] but this was changed during the legislative process. The regulation in Art. 11 deals with 'placing the order' and does not appear as an information obligation. It must, however, be understood as an information requirement. As this provision is also not mentioned in Annex 2 of the proposed Directive on Unfair Commercial Practices it is not regarded as material information for the purposes of this proposed Directive and an infringement will not automatically be regarded as unfair. As a non-fulfilment of this obligation is unlikely to influence the consumer's decision it will usually not fulfil the requirements of the general clause and sanctions will have to follow from the national laws. This seems a fair result as this information only can show that the electronic transmission was successful. The acknowledgement cannot generally be understood as an acceptance[44] and should not have any relevance for the contract.

Commercial Communications

The E-Commerce Directive uses a different terminology than the proposed Directive on Unfair Commercial Practices. Whereas the latter uses the term 'commercial practices' the E-Commerce Directive uses the term 'commercial communications'. The explanatory memorandum to the proposed Directive on Unfair Commercial Practices clarifies[45] that the term 'commercial practices' includes commercial communication. Hence the definition in the framework directive is wider but includes the definition in the sector specific directive.

---

41 In Art. 11, no. 1.

42 COM 98/586 final.

43 Requiring order, acknowledgement, confirmation and acceptance.

44 Although in some cases the acceptance may be communicated together with the acknowledgement.

45 Explanatory memorandum, no. 36.

Commercial communication is defined as 'any form of communication designed to promote, directly or indirectly, the goods, services or image of a company, organization or person pursuing a commercial, industrial or craft activity or exercising a regulated profession'.[46] Excluded is the communication of a domain name or an e-mail address. Although this communication may have a commercial background it would be inappropriate to regard this already as a commercial communication.[47]

According to Art. 6 of the E-Commerce Directive all commercial communications have to be clearly identifiable as such and the person on whose behalf the commercial communications are made has to be identified. Special requirements exist for promotional offers, competitions and games. These have to be clearly identifiable and the conditions have to be easily accessible and clearly and unambiguously presented.

The E-Commerce Directive generally permits unsolicited commercial communications, but the Member States have to ensure that opt-out registers exist and are respected. As the directive follows the minimum harmonization approach the Member States can also forbid the use of unsolicited e-mails completely, both by introducing or maintaining such a prohibition. Following the internal market clause,[48] however, the Member States can only regulate the service providers established in their territory and not prohibit the use of unsolicited commercial communications completely. The E-Commerce Directive requires that all unsolicited commercial communications have to be clearly identifiable as soon as the user receives them. For the most common unsolicited communications – e-mail Spam – this means that the identification as Spam must be obvious in the heading. The user can then decide if he wants to download the message or could also introduce a Spam-filter and avoid unsolicited commercial communications completely. In practice this quite often causes problems, as some desired e-mails get blocked or deleted whereas other Spam still reaches the user's mailbox. The Directive on Privacy in Electronic Communications[49] has now imposed a requirement of prior consent for e-mail commercial communications.

Distance Selling Directive

The Distance Selling Directive requires pre-contractual information and a written confirmation as contractual information. Although the written confirmation is not explicitly described as contractual information, due to the nature and the latest possible time for fulfilment of this obligation, they are in practice contractual information obligations.

46 Art. 2 (f).

47 Also a number of other problems would follow as these information are often only communicated as information with other contact details.

48 Art. 3.

49 Art. 13, Directive 2002/58/EC of 12 July 2002 concerning the processing of personal data and the protection of privacy in the electronic communications sector, OJ L 201 of 31 July 2002.

Pre-Contractual Information

The pre-contractual information must be given 'in good time prior to the conclusion of any distance contract'.[50] This means that the latest possible point of time for providing this information is just before the last step necessary for the binding conclusion of the contract. When this point of time is exactly reached depends on the national laws.

The information required is the following:

The identity of the supplier (and additionally the address if prior payment is required) This is particular important for contracts concluded over the Internet. Unfortunately the address is only required if prior payment is required and not in all cases. For contracts concluded over the Internet usually payment by credit card is offered (or required). Even if the supplier promises to charge the amount only after delivery, this should be considered as prior payment as it is completely at the discretion of the supplier.

The main characteristics of the goods or services This requirement is fairly obvious and will in most Member States be essential for the contract (*essentialia negotii*), but it is important that this information has also to be given prior to the conclusion of the contract.

The price of the goods or services including all taxes The price is also an essential issue for the consumer and needs to be as detailed as possible. As the price has to be mentioned including all taxes, the taxes have to be added to the price of the goods or services and cannot be noted separately or as a percentage rate. If a supplier is contracting with businesses as well as consumers he may show the taxes separately.

Delivery costs Delivery costs are another crucial issue in distance contracts and depending on the goods or services (and their origin) may be a high percentage of cost of the goods or even higher.

The arrangement for payment, delivery or performance Payment and delivery arrangements are also important at the pre-contractual stage. In an extreme case an arrangement for delivery could be that the consumer has to collect the goods at the supplier's premises – and the consumer ought to be informed about this before he enters into a contract.

The existence of a right of withdrawal The right of withdrawal is one of the main issues of the Directive and the consumer has to be informed about the existence prior to the conclusion of the contract. The information about the existence does not include the information about the details of the right and also not the

---

50 Art. 4.

information that a right of withdrawal does not exist for the particular contract. Exempt are cases in which the consumer may not exercise the right of withdrawal, unless the parties have agreed otherwise, and cover situations like goods made to the consumer's specification, products dependant on fluctuations in the financial market or where performance of a service contract has begun with the consumer's consent.

The cost of using the means of distance communication, where it is calculated other than at the basic rate The normal communication costs (i.e. telephone) are foreseeable for the consumer and beyond the supplier's knowledge and control, whereas concerning other costs (i.e. special phone numbers or costs for using databases which will be charged through the telephone companies) the consumer needs information to enable him to decide if he wants to enter in the contract in question.

Where appropriate, the minimum duration of the contract in the case of contracts for the supply of products or services to be performed permanently or recurrently This ensures that the consumer is informed about the fact that the contract runs over a long period as well as the length of that period. Where other provisions exist (i.e. for standard contract terms) and the minimum length is generally restricted, these provisions remain in force. The notice period does not necessarily have to be mentioned at the pre-contractual stage.

All information has – according to Art. 4 (2) – to be given in a clear and comprehensible manner, appropriate according to the means of distance communication used. This means that the information can – and shall – be given differently on a website, for instance, as compared to during a telephone conversation. The language in which these information have to be given is not specified and therefore it must not necessarily be the first language of the consumer, but the information must also be given with due regard to the principles of good faith in commercial transactions.[51] Information given in a language other than the first language of the consumer (or his country of residence), the language of the origin of the supplier, a commonly understood language or the language of the advertisement or the contract will be against these principles.[52]

The proposed Directive on Unfair Commercial Practices mentions Art. 4 of the Distance Selling Directive in its Annex 2. Therefore all the information required as pre-contractual information in distance contracts are regarded as material information for the proposed Directive on Unfair Commercial Practices and incorrect or incomplete fulfilment of these information requirements will automatically be regarded as unfair commercial practice.

---

51 Mankowski (2001).

52 Reich in Reich and Nordhausen (2000), nos. 112 *et seq.*; Mankowski (2001).

Contractual Information

Art. 5 of the Distance Selling Directive requires that a written confirmation of the information has to be provided to the consumer.[53] In all cases, all information except the right of withdrawal is not restricted to writing, but can either be given in writing or on another durable medium available and accessible to the consumer. This term includes other forms than writing on paper, and nowadays certainly covers floppy or compact discs. At the time the Directive was introduced the compact disc was not standard in personal computers and therefore it was argued that any medium might only be used if the consumer is able to use the medium. The wording of the Directive 'accessible to the consumer' also covers this requirement. The wording of the Directive 'the consumer must receive' should be interpreted as it being the supplier's duty to ensure that the consumer receives the information. The provider may have to ask the consumer about the preferred technical means to communicate this.

The Financial Services Directive is more precise and defines the term 'durable medium'. Recital 20 makes it clear that durable medium includes floppy discs, CDs, DVDs and the hard drive of the consumer's computer, but Internet websites are explicitly excluded although some definitions of writing in the national laws are very broad and do consider representation on a web-site as writing.[54]

The time for the written confirmation is the time of delivery at the latest. Again, the language is not regulated but following the general rules it should be the language of the language of the negotiations.[55]

The information to be provided is the pre-contractual information required in Art. 4 (1)(a)-(f) and in addition:

1. The conditions and procedures for exercising the right of withdrawal, including possible exemptions.
2. The geographical address of the place of business of the supplier to which the consumer may address any complaints.
3. Information on after-sales services and existing guarantees.
4. The notice period for contracts for unspecified duration or a duration exceeding one year.

Excluded are services supplied on only one occasion which are performed through a means of distance communication and invoiced by the operator of the communication means, but the consumer must still be able to obtain the geographical address of the place of business to which he can address any complaints. This information shall enable the consumer to exercise the right of withdrawal without further investigation.

All information, the pre-contractual information as well as the written confirmation (in writing or on a durable medium) has to be provided in good time

53 Madden (2002).

54 See for the UK Law Commission (December 2001), p. 8.

55 Nordhausen in Reich and Nordhausen (2000), nos. 37-42.

during the performance of the contract, and at the latest at the time of delivery. They have to be presented in a clear and comprehensible way that is appropriate to the means.

The Directive regulates one method of distance communication explicitly. For telephony communication the commercial purpose of the call has to be made explicitly clear at the beginning of any telephony communication. Prior consent of the consumer is required for the use of automated calling machines and fax. For all other means of distance communication the use is only permitted where there is no clear objection from the consumer. This allows the consumer to opt-out, but generally permits the use of distance communication for commercial purposes.

Although this contractual information seems very unlikely to influence the consumer's decision it is regarded as material information in the proposed Directive on Unfair Commercial Practices and the improper fulfilment results in it being treated as unfair commercial practice. As this information only has to be provided on delivery at the latest, any of the information not provided or not provided in time cannot possibly influence the consumer's decision about entering into a transaction. But they can and do influence the consumer's decision how to proceed. Without explicit information and written confirmation about the right of withdrawal the consumer is less likely to withdraw. The proposed Directive on Unfair Commercial Practices therefore stresses the importance of the right of withdrawal by regarding the lack of information as unfair commercial practice.

Electronic Commercial Communications

For electronic commercial communication several laws apply at the EU level. The proposed Directive on Unfair Commercial Practices regulates, amongst other commercial practices, also electronic commercial communication. As the proposed Directive on Unfair Commercial Practices is a framework directive this proposed Directive only applies in the absence of other special community regulation. But as the proposed Directive on Unfair Commercial Practices follows also the maximum harmonization (full harmonization) approach, there is little scope for implementation for the Member States. Apart from the proposed Directive on Unfair Commercial Practices, for electronic commercial communication the E-Commerce Directive and the Distance Selling Directive are applicable. The Distance Selling Directive does not explicitly deal with electronic communication or commercial communication, but the E-Commerce Directive regulates commercial communications specifically. As these directives are already in force for some time whereas the proposed Directive on Unfair Commercial Practices has been proposed recently the question arises if the relevant provisions in these directives supplement each other correspondingly or if they contain conflicting rules. The E-Commerce and Distance Selling Directives, contrary to the proposed Directive on Unfair Commercial Practices, follow the minimum harmonization approach and therefore allow the Member States a greater scope for implementation. The directives use a different terminology. The proposed

Directive on Unfair Commercial Practices uses the term 'commercial practice', defined as 'any act, omission, course of conduct or representation, commercial communication including advertising and marketing, by a trader, directly connected with the promotion, sale or supply of a product to consumers'.[56] The E-Commerce Directive defines and uses only the term 'commercial communication' as

> any form of communication designed to promote, directly or indirectly, the goods, services or image of a company, organization or person pursuing a commercial, industrial or craft activity or exercising a regulated profession. The following do not in themselves constitute commercial communications:
>
> - information allowing direct access to the activity of the company, organization or person, in particular a domain name or an electronic-mail address,
> - communications relating to the goods, services or images of the company, organization or person compiled in an independent manner, particularly when this is without financial consideration.[57]

The comparison shows that the term 'commercial practices' as used in the proposed Directive on Unfair Commercial Practices is wider than the term 'commercial communications' as used in the E-Commerce Directive. The explanatory memorandum of the Unfair Commercial Practices Proposal refers to the connection with and incorporation of provisions from the Misleading Advertising Directive[58] but does not mention other relevant directives like the E-Commerce Directive.[59] As commercial communications are explicitly included in the wider definition of commercial practices and the E-Commerce Directive regulates electronic commercial communications in Arts. 6 and 7, the new framework regulation in the proposed Directive on Unfair Commercial Practices does not cause any conflicts. The more specific regulations arising from the E-Commerce Directive will be applicable. These acknowledge the importance of commercial communications for electronic commerce generally[60] and distinguish between commercial communications generally and unsolicited commercial communications.

---

56 Art. 2 (e) Proposed Directive on Unfair Commercial Practices.

57 Art. 2 (f) E-Commerce Directive.

58 Directive 84/450/EEC, OJ L 250, 19 September 1984, as amended by Directive 97/55/EC.

59 Recital 36.

60 Recital 29 E-Commerce Directive:
'Commercial communications are essential for the financing of information society services and for developing a wide variety of new, charge-free services; in the interests of consumer protection and fair trading, commercial communications, including discounts, promotional offers and promotional competitions or games, must meet a number of transparency requirements; these requirements are without prejudice to Directive 97/7/EC; this Directive should not affect existing Directives on commercial communications, in particular Directive 98/43/EC.'

As the proposed Directive also follows the internal market principle,[61] exclusions only in some member states are not very efficient. Traders can easily circumvent prohibitions of unsolicited commercial communications in some member states.[62]

Any conflicts between provisions of the proposed Directive on Unfair Commercial Practices and any other directive governing specific aspects of unfair commercial practices[63] are regulated by Art. 3 (5) of the proposed Directive on Unfair Commercial Practices which gives precedence to the specific regulation.[64] This means that a specific sectoral directive is generally applicable in any conflict or may be applicable in addition to the framework directive. The framework directive however, will come into play for other elements such as the question of whether a practice is misleading.[65] As the proposed Directive on Unfair Commercial Practices follows the principle of maximum harmonization, whereas most of the other directives follow the minimum harmonization approach[66] this might lead to conflicts between different ways of implementation in the Member States and the framework directive which may in practice either obstruct the minimum harmonization approach of these directives or hinder the effectiveness of the framework directive and full harmonization.

Conclusion

The proposed Directive on Unfair Commercial Practices can as a framework directive and following the maximum harmonization approach reach its aims, a high degree of consumer protection and the functioning of the Internal Market. The proposed Directive can be a framework for other European directives as well as national legislation.

The introduction of a general clause prohibiting unfair commercial practices is an effective way to regulate commercial practices and also follows principles of legal certainty and transparency. The definition of the 'average consumer' as the

---

61 Art. 3.

62 As Recital 30 points out there is a need for effective means of filtering which might need more attention.

63 Like the Distance Selling Directive, E-Commerce Directive, or the Directive on Distance Marketing of Financial Services.

64 Art. 3 (5): 'In case of conflict between the provisions of this Directive and other Community rules governing specific aspects of unfair commercial practices, the latter will prevail and apply to the specific aspects of unfair commercial practices.'

65 Explanatory memorandum, no. 45: 'Where a sectoral directive regulates only aspects of commercial practices, for example the content of information requirements, the framework directive will come into play for other elements, for example, if the information required in the sectoral legislation were presented in a misleading way. The directive therefore complements both existing and future legislation, such as the proposed Regulation on sales promotion, or the consumer credit Directive and the e-commerce Directive.'

66 As Distance Selling Directive and E-Commerce Directive, only the Financial Services Directive follows the maximum or full harmonization approach.

benchmark consumer only follows the case law of the European Court of Justice but by introducing it to the statutory law increases clarity.

The proposed Directive on Unfair Commercial Practices regards some core information as material, including the main characteristics of the product, price (including taxes), delivery charges and the right of withdrawal. These are indeed core information and their omission (or any misleading presentation) should result in dissuasive sanctions. The proposed Directive on Unfair Commercial Practices however, leaves the sanctions to the Member States. In areas where special EU legislation exists as for injunctions,[67] these will have to be taken into account. Unlike in previous directives the requirements for effective sanctions are specified and described in a rather detailed way. Due to the maximum harmonization approach of the proposed Directive on Unfair Commercial Practices sanctions will have to follow the requirements of this Directive.[68]

By introducing core – material – information the proposed Directive seems to distinguish information requirements into different categories. The non-fulfilment of these material information obligations should result in stricter sanctions than the non-fulfilment of other (less important) information obligations. This idea would amend the current structure of information obligations in European law and their distinction to pre-contractual and contractual obligations and therefore result in conflicts between the framework directive and the existing sector specific directives, but it would reduce the amount of information for the consumer as well as businesses to a manageable amount. The proposed Directive on Unfair Commercial Practices, however, introduces through Annex 2 of the proposed Directive many of the other existing information obligations as material information as well and by this introduction the specification of some information obligations as core information obligations becomes more or less redundant.

References

Bradgate, R., Brownsword, R. and Twigg-Flesner, C. (July 2003), *The Impact of Adopting a Duty to Trade Fairly*, at http://www.dti.gov.uk/ccp/topics1/pdf1/unfairreport.pdf.

Byrne, D. (2003), *Rough times for rogue traders: Commission proposes EU-wide ban on unfair commercial practices*, press release of 18 June 2003, available at http://europa.eu.int/comm/dgs/health_consumer/library/press/press_consumer_en.html.

Janal, R.M. (2003), *Sanktionen und Rechtsbehelfe bei der Verletzung verbraucherschützender Informations- und Dokumentationspflichten im elektronischen Geschäftsverkehr* (Berlin: Tenea).

Law Commission (December 2001), *Electronic Commerce: Formal Requirements in Commercial Transactions – Advice from the Law Commission*, at http://www.lawcom.gov.uk/files/e-commerce.pdf.

---

67 Directive 1998/27/EC of 19 May 1998 on injunctions for the protection of consumer's interests, OJ L 166 of 11 June 1998.

68 For effective enforcement means the Commission proposed recently an EU-wide network of national watchdogs, at http://europa.eu.int/comm/consumers/prot_rules/admin_coop/index_en.htm.

Madden, E. (2002), 'A safe distance?', Gazette of the Law Society of Ireland , pp. 14 *et seq.*
Mankowski, P. (2001), 'Verbraucherschutzrechtliche Widerrufsbelehrung und Sprachrisiko', *Verbraucher und Recht*, pp. 359 *et seq.*
Reich, N. and Nordhausen, A. (2000), *Verbraucher und Recht im elektronischen Geschäftsverkehr (eG)* (Baden-Baden: Nomos).

Chapter 7

Contractual Disclosure and Remedies under the Unfair Contract Terms Directive

Edoardo Ferrante*

Introduction

The EC Directive on Unfair Terms in Consumer Contracts (93/13/EEC),[1] privately referred to as the '*Klauselrichtlinie*' in the German literature,[2] is not just another directive. Given the varying and uncertain panorama of European private law, it might have been expected to play a central role from the very beginning. However, contrary to these expectations, its centrality has been above all qualitative or virtual, because the introduction of the directive into the legal orders of the Member States has, to date, had little impact on judicial decisions.[3]

In Germany, the directive did not require significant changes. It was sufficient to modify § 12, and to add § 24a of the *AGB-Gesetz* (which has now become, with some minor changes, § 310 (3) *Bürgerliches Gesetzbuch* (*BGB*)). However, outside Germany, the directive does not seem (at the moment) to have been a great success, or at least to have lived up to expectations. It is difficult to identify the exact reasons for this. One of several possible factors is surely the radically innovative scope of the text, at least in comparison with pre-existing national laws. This would also explain its easy reception into the German cultural environment.

---

* I would like to thank Professor G. Howells and Dr. A. Johnston from the University of Sheffield for their help and advice regarding my contribution to this book.

1 Official Journal (OJ) 1993 L 95/29.

2 They read in it, nearly unaltered, the '*Gesetz zur Regelung des Rechts der Allgemeinen Geschäftsbedingungen* (or *AGB-Gesetz*)' of 1976. This statute is today part of the German civil code (new §§ 305-310 *BGB*): see Pfeiffer and Schinkels (2001); Ulmer (2001). But many German consumer statutes have recently become part of the *BGB*. See some comments in Pfeiffer (2001); Roth (2001).

3 For Italy see Bin (1996). In fact the consumer protection has become an explicit and independent goal of the EU since 1992, thanks to the Maastricht Treaty on European Union (7 February 1992, Art. 3s, Titles XI, XVIII). In this perspective the Directive 93/13/EEC can be considered a first important step on putting into effect that communitarian policy, at least regarding consumer contract law.

One cannot infer from its inconsistent application that the directive has limited conceptual significance, if it is true that the directive lays the foundations (or '*allgemeiner Teil*', as the Germans would put it) for a general European law of consumer contracts. The directive summarizes and sets out the fundamental principles of consumer protection. In a virtuous circle these principles, which are already included in various sectoral directives, are summed up and clarified by directive 93/13/EEC, and then feed back into these same norms individually.[4] This gives rise to a constant interaction between directive 93/13/EEC, a type of base directive dealing with consumer contracts, and the various sectoral contractual-consumerist directives which both preceded and followed it (not least the important directive 99/44/EC on Certain Aspects of the Sale of Consumer Goods and Associated Guarantees[5]).

There is another aspect worthy of note, at least as regards those Member States that, like Italy, implemented the directive using a '*kleine Lösung*', i.e. they passively introduced the unaltered community text directly into national law.[6] This method of implementation, which often leads to the creation of statutes that simply reproduce their source, requires nothing more of the legislator than to 'make space' in the relevant code for the insertion of new articles. It is not coincidental that those national codes, including the Italian one, which simply incorporate the community text and refuse to apply its contents beyond the specific area of consumer law, have to co-ordinate the old and new laws in a single normative space.[7] A new law emerges alongside the existing 'residual' or 'common' law of contracts. This law is specialized, but still forms part of the general law of consumer contracts.

The possibility of viewing this process as a two-way dialogue – with one side aiming for the cohesiveness of European Union consumer law, the other for the domestic coordination of internal contractual law – remains largely unexplored.

The text of the European directive is well known and it is not necessary to present it here. It seems that the directive's general machinery and the solutions it proposes must be traced back plastically to two poles of attraction: judicial control of the content of the contract, aimed at guaranteeing a normative equilibrium by eliminating oppressive clauses, and the principle of transparency, aimed at balancing the information asymmetry which is typical of the consumer contract. However, the source of inspiration is unitary and consists of a political will to use

4 This discussion might introduce to a 'super-directive' on consumer contractual law, resulting from the coordination and recasting of the existing *aquis* in the subject of consumer contracts. See in particular no. 50 and no. 77 COM (2003) 68 final (OJ 2003 C 63), the so-called 'EC-Action Plan'. Some news about COM (2003) 68 are available in Schulze (2003) and also Ferrante (2003). Also in that context the normative material transfused in the Directive 93/13/EEC is going to play a fundamental role, being – as said in the text – a real and true 'general part'. See Alpa and Patti (2003), p. 25. See also Rochfeld and Houtcieff (2003).

5 OJ 1999 L 171/12. In connection to this directive, but also to the main point of the present contribution, see Lehmann (2000).

6 See with critical remarks Bin (1996); recently again Bin (2000), p. 403; even more critical Schlechtriem (2001), p. 335; Möllers (2002).

7 See Alpa (1997); Mengoni (1998), p. 546; Roppo (2002), pp. 25-57.

legislation to combat the abuse of bargaining power, which can occur where one party is a professional and the other is not.

Although there are two poles of attraction, the attention of market actors was fairly quickly captured by the first one, leaving the second one mostly in the shadows, at least until today. Certainly, control over content appeared to be a disruptive and revolutionary practice, at least for those legal orders which had for so long been used to proclaiming the virtues of private autonomy and non-interference with agreements. So it is not surprising that attention mainly focused on these profoundly innovative aspects, at least outside Germany. Nevertheless, there is another equally important aspect, which has perhaps been overlooked because of its relative silence, namely the principle of transparency of contract.[8]

On reading Art. 5 of the directive, one immediately realizes that, in this context, transparency is not entirely neutral. The requirement of good faith (or '*Treu und Glauben*') does not have a broad and definite application. It is not a bilateral criterion, which might be expected to pervade the behaviour of contracting parties, whatever their status, all by itself. Instead, it is a right of the consumer and a duty of the professional.[9] This brings us to the first theme of this research. Transparency in contracting, at least in the system designed by this directive, means a right to information for the consumer and a duty to supply information for the professional.[10] Accordingly, it is an instrument of struggle, even of class struggle, even if here the class is not 'social', but 'occasional', in the sense that the status of consumer is occasional.

From the Rhetoric of Will to Rhetoric of Information

As has been said, the directive is aimed at information asymmetry, and in particular at giving back to the weaker party, the consumer, an awareness of their actions in contracting which ignorance precluded from the beginning.[11] Whether or not the average consumer really wants more pre-contractual information, and whether this would actually counteract their own weaknesses (which are not only cognitive), is another matter altogether. On the one hand, more information does no harm, and the general propensity on the part of the consumer to make individual consumption choices on the basis of information received presumably remains an

---

8 In many directives in the field of consumer protection a contractual disclosure requirement is included. See Directive 99/44/EC (OJ 1999 L 171/12), Directive 98/6/EC (OJ 1998 L 80/27), Directive 97/7/EC (OJ 1997 L 144/19), Directive 94/47/EC (OJ 1994 L 280/83), Directive 90/314/EEC (OJ 1990 L 158/59) and Directive 87/102/EEC (OJ 1987 L 42/48).

9 Something similar can be read in Art. 4:107, comma 3th (a), of the Principles of European Contract Law (so-called 'Lando-Principles' or 'PECL').

10 More generally it can be noticed that 'consumer protection measures in contract law function primarily by reducing the reflexive qualities of private law regulation'. See Collins, (1998), p. 978.

11 Di Majo (1995).

important rationale for media propaganda. On the other, the consumer contract increasingly appears to be a mechanical exchange, a mutual *do ut des* devoid of dialogue or reflection, where the demands of brevity and economy of thought win out by a long distance over the formation of conscious and informed choices.[12]

Of course, this discussion is simplistic and overlooks many of the finer details. However, it seems clear that the transparency of the contractual conditions 'offered' to (but in reality 'imposed' on) the consumer is not a factor in safeguarding their freedom of choice. They would have this effect in a perfectly competitive market, in which the consumer is able and willing to compare the terms offered by each professional actor. They would also have this effect in the hypothetical – but altogether improbable – situation where the consumer is put in a position to negotiate, and actually contributes to the formation of the contract. However, this would require greater equality of bargaining power, something altogether incompatible with contracts of adhesion.[13] In the period preceding the formation of a contract, the consumer, as a rule, can neither choose nor negotiate, and normally would not be interested in doing so.

So What is the Point of Transparency?

Transparency appears above all as an element of post-contractual protection.[14] Underpinning the directive is a belief that more information essentially creates an increased awareness on the part of the consumer about the instruments of protection that the legal system offers them. Information is, in a sense, an aspect of publicity for civil justice. The different status of the parties gives rise to an imbalance in contracting power, and the law accordingly obliges the stronger party to undertake this 'promotional' activity. Returning to the directive's two poles of attraction – the struggles against abusive terms and for contractual transparency – one can well understand that the second issue is of lesser importance than the first. This would appear to justify the far greater attention which has been paid to control over contractual content, compared to elaborating the principle of transparency.

In Search of a Sanction

To describe the principle of transparency in terms of pre-contractual protection of the consumer, or in terms of an informational medium aimed at ensuring better access to civil justice, is to condemn the principle to anonymity, or at best to a lowly, non-justiciable status. To get out of this bind, it is essential to identify a secondary norm, or sanction, which is capable of elevating the principle of transparency beyond the status of mere fashionable declaration.[15]

---

12 Irti (1998), pp. 347-364. *Contra* Oppo (1998). Again Irti (1999); Irti (2000).

13 Very interesting on this point the so-called 'doctrine of inequality of bargaining power', which was formulated by Lord Denning in the famous case *Lloyds Bank LTD* v. *Bundy* (1974), *3 All England Reports*, p. 757.

14 Wolf (2001).

15 See in general Wilhelmsson (2003); Schwintowski (2003).

The sanction – it helps to repeat it – cannot consist of the spontaneous competitiveness of the market, or even the rational choices of the consumer, which are capable of expelling the 'non-transparent' professional actor from the commercial arena. This just does not happen. Nor can the sanction be limited to a judicial declaration of invalidity on the grounds of oppressiveness, the sanction which most typifies control over content, at least if one wants to avoid reducing contractual transparency to little more than a kind of 'advertisement' promoting consumer rights. If that were the case, we would also have to conclude that the impact of the principle on private autonomy and contractual justice would be close to nil.

True and False Problems Concerning the Transparency Principle in the Directive

Let us therefore examine a little more closely Art. 5 (1) of the directive (which became Art. 1469-quater, 1st comma of the Italian civil code,[16] and did not appear as such in the AGB-Gesetz before incorporation in the code,[17] although now it is expressed by § 307, 1st comma, 2nd period, BGB[18]):

> In the case of contracts where all or certain terms offered to the consumer are in writing, these terms must always be drafted in plain, intelligible language.

It is not necessary to analyze this provision in order to clarify the literal meaning of the phrase, as has been done so often regarding '*plain, intelligible language*' (or clauses which are '*klar und verständlich*'). It is not particularly important to understand whether the two words denominate two distinct indicators of transparency or a unitary concept.[19]

Consciousness or Conscionability of the Content of the Contract?

The legal wording, however one reads it, does not only aim to ensure that information is accessible, but also addresses the deeper issue of information communication. In other words, a contract is not transparent where its fixed terms

---

16 See under Italian law Rizzo (1999).

17 See however, about § 8 of the 'old' *AGB-Gesetz* (today § 307, comma 3th, *BGB*), Stoffels (2001). The principle of disclosure in contractual standard terms was elaborated by German legal scholars especially from § 9 *AGB-Gesetz*, and this doctrine was early approved by the German Supreme Court '*Bundesgerichtshof*' (BGHZ 106, 42, 49; BGH, *Neue Juristische Wochenschrift*, 1997, p. 1068; BGH, *Neue Juristische Wochenschrift*, 1999, p. 276). Today § 307, comma 1st, clause 2nd, *BGB* must be taken into account.

18 Lorenz and Riehm (2002), p. 56; Huber and Faust (2002), pp. 463-464.

19 On this 'problem', under Italian law, Giammaria (2003), pp. 1021-1023; Rizzo (1999), pp. 804-805; Di Giovine (1998), pp. 563-565.

are readily understandable, but where its terms are effectively known. The professional must bring them to the consumer's attention, as opposed to simply ensuring that they are understandable.

By contrast, where the more fundamental problem of absolutely incomprehensible terms arises, it triggers the application of specific sanctions. These sanctions are so well tried and tested in national law that they do not need to be specifically addressed here.

One must assume that the absolutely incomprehensible clause will be excluded from the contract, simply because it does not reflect a congruence of wills, even according to the logic of a contract of adhesion.[20] If the incomprehensible clause goes to the 'root of the contract', what at one time was called 'the object of the contract', then the contract itself will probably be null and void because the object is neither determined nor determinable.[21] There are, nevertheless, good grounds for believing that the Community legislator, in enacting Art. 5 of the directive, did not intend to take over the role of the national legislator in dealing with such infrequent defects, which are so simple to resolve. To give some meaning or application to the Community rule, it is essential to abandon the idea of comprehensibility so that we may grasp the aim of effective understanding. Its rationale here is to inquire into sanctions.

Meanwhile, let us add a new piece to the dense mosaic of our research. Above, we ascertained that the principle of transparency of contract is not neutral, but in fact a duty of the professional. It can now be added that the professional discharges this duty only by effectively supplying information; passively ensuring that the contract is merely comprehensible would not suffice.

The Meaning of 'Offer'

A further issue arises concerning the obligation to ensure that 'all or certain terms offered to the consumer are in writing'. This passage appears to raise two distinct questions, but in reality does not raise any.

The first question concerns the concept of 'offer': what does 'terms offered' mean? Does the reference only cover 'fixed terms or clauses which regulate specific contractual relationships in a uniform manner' (as Art. 1342, 1st Comma of the Italian Civil Code puts it), or does it also cover bespoke texts prepared from time to time for a single contract?[22]

What indicates the protective purpose of the legislation is not so much the clause in question's ability to regulate a greater or lesser number of contractual relations, so as to become almost a normative source for contracts of adhesion, but the simple fact of being 'fixed'. It does not matter much whether this leads to the conclusion of many contracts, or, to the contrary, simply regulates the individual contract in question. It remains beyond the perception of the consumer, and their need for protection is not reduced just because the standard terms were written by

---

20 See on this point Art. 1341, comma 1st, Italian *Codice civile*.

21 See Art. 1418, comma 2nd, Italian *Codice Civile*.

22 Rizzo (1999), pp. 806-807.

their author specifically for that occasion. Granting importance to the internal organizational solutions adopted by the professional or to his psyche appears to contradict the rules under discussion.

The Requirement of 'Writing'

The second question is less redundant, but equally scholastic, and concerns the requirement of 'writing'.[23] This does not require an elegant summary of the journeys of neo-formalism and an evaluation of its revival; rather, we have to deal with a raw fact, that is, the inconceivability in practice of a transparency problem arising in the context of oral contracting.[24]

Any inquiry into defects of clarity and comprehensibility of contractual terms requires analysis, but presupposes a temporal and logical divide between the facts to be analyzed and the analytic inquiry. It is essential therefore that the content of the contract should have 'solidified' in some way before the formation of the agreement – this constitutes a unilateral arrangement – and before the transparency analysis takes place. 'Oral solidification', namely the production of an unwritten text, which may be adjudged to fall foul of the transparency requirement, cannot be excluded per se. However, it is not easy to understand how this might happen, and so it is not surprising that the directive's field of application is limited to written contracts.

So there is an extra element – for the most part implicit – in the scheme put in place by the directive. The professional's duty of transparency, which obliges him to offer contractual terms which are clear and comprehensible, arises independently of the regularity with which he uses the term, provided that the term is embodied in a written document, which is a necessary precondition of any scrutiny on the grounds of transparency.

The Reason that the *Contra Proferentem* Rule Seems to be a Weak Sanction against the Stronger Party

Let us now return to our discussion of the sanction. This can help our enquiry because the duty of transparency puts pressure on the professional's freedom of contract. Art. 5 (2) of the directive supplements this incontrovertible principle with a rule of interpretation, which might also be considered to have some of the characteristics of a sanction. In a sense it does:

> Where there is doubt about the meaning of a term, the interpretation most favourable to the consumer shall prevail.

---

23 See again Rizzo (1999), pp. 798-802.

24 Jarach (1998), pp. 616-620. *Contra* Di Giovine (1998), pp. 557-561; Patroni Griffi (1995), p. 368; Giammaria (2003), p. 1018.

This is, of course, the well-known contra proferentem rule, with was familiar to both the German[25] and Italian[26] legal systems long before the directive.[27]

Accordingly, traditional reflections about the punitive effect of the rule may be relevant here. Since the ambiguous term originates with the stronger contracting party, who drafted it as an instrument of preventive self-protection and contractual bullying, they are precluded from relying on any ambiguity to gain further advantage beyond that already gained from using a contract of adhesion.[28]

It seems that this sanction, which is significant and deep-rooted in social consciousness, provides narrow and incomplete protection for the transparency principle. The first subsection of Art. 5, which sets out the transparency principle, actually has a broader meaning and application than the second subsection, the *contra proferentem* rule.[29] The latter rule both affirms the first principle and represents an important manifestation of it, albeit subject to certain limits.

In any event, the rule only becomes applicable when there is a 'doubt about the meaning of a term', which does not simply refer to a lack of intelligibility, but rather to the ability of the terms of the contract to bear multiple attributions of meaning. In other words, it is necessary that the writing should be capable of bearing a plurality of meanings, in such a way that the rule can lead to the choice of interpretation which is most favourable to the consumer. Where that is the case, the principle of transparency appears more comprehensive. It is not limited to the use of expressions which have more than one meaning, a moment of what might be termed 'qualified' literal obscurity. Instead, it covers the wider, generic category of lack of 'clarity and comprehensibility', and its ultimate limit is invalidity where the clause is absolutely without meaning.

If this rule of interpretation is really the only, exhaustive sanction for breach of the principle of transparency, and this is the only explanation for the rule, one must ask why the community legislator chose also to introduce this principle. Would it not have been sufficient simply to introduce *contra proferentem* as a rule of interpretation?

Beyond the *Contra Proferentem* Interpretation: Are Obscure Terms Simply Abusive?

This solution seems once again to relegate the principle of transparency to the status of fashionable declaration. However, other authors, who are broadly in

---

25 Old § 5 *AGB-Gesetz*, new § 305c, comma 2nd, *BGB*. See about this so-called 'Unklarheitenregel' Medicus (2002), pp. 163-164.

26 Art. 1370 Italian *Codice civile*, and after the Directive 93/13/EEC also Art. 1469-*quater*, comma 2nd. See also Art. 4.6 of the Unidroit-Principles and Art. 5:103 of the PECL.

27 For some comments Bigliazzi Geri (1996), p. 327; also Pardolesi (1995), p. 540.

28 See under Italian law, but with general comments on the meaning of the rule, Oppo (1943), p. 102; Grassetti (1938), pp. 204-211.

29 Rizzo (1999), pp. 786-789; Di Giovine (1998), pp. 555-557.

agreement with the above discussion, have tried to escape from this impasse by recognizing in transparency a strong remedial system which constitutes a key feature of the body of the directive. It has been suggested that lack of clarity and comprehensibility might be sanctioned by means of a declaration of substantive abusiveness. Simply by virtue of being obscure, a term would be suspected of being abusive, as if the merely obscure term were contained in the list of well-known presumptions set out in Art. 1 of the Annex.[30]

Where it is practicable, the *contra proferentem* interpretation seems to suggest a preliminary evaluation, aimed at excluding abusiveness, by giving the clause a meaning which is favourable to the consumer wherever possible and expelling it from the contract. In light of this, it seems clear that judicial use of the *contra proferentem* rule could become ambiguous, because it would always be necessary first to establish which interpretation would really punish the author of the term.[31] Which is the more punitive interpretation: the one which favours the consumer, but renders the clause non-abusive, or the one which apparently favours the professional, but exposes him to the gravest sanction, namely the clause's removal from the contract (which is certainly satisfactory from the weaker party's perspective)?

We should not rule out the possibility that a term which violates the transparency principle of Art. 5 could be considered by a judge to be oppressive (and for that reason, ineffective) on the basis of Art. 3 (1). Nor do we want to reduce the protective capacity of the *contra proferentem* rule, at least while the debate over its possible uses continues.[32] It should be accepted that an obscure term may be considered oppressive within the meaning of Art. 3 simply by virtue of its obscurity. In fact, if it is considered abusive under a different provision, on the grounds that it constitutes a significant imbalance contrary to good faith, it is beyond discussion that the appropriate sanction will be invalidity, and the clause's literal obscurity will simply reinforce a judgment reached for other reasons.[33] Relying on this sanction simply to safeguard the transparency principle will give rise to a declaration of invalidity on the grounds of abusiveness where the clause is simply obscure. This rules out any judicial control over the contents of the contract. The outcome of this thesis seems to be a classification of lack of transparency as a form of abusiveness, which unifies the two poles of attraction and makes content control the only instrument of consumer protection.[34] One can certainly doubt whether this is within the spirit of the directive. The problem is not

30 This conclusion seems to be 'approved' by the new rule of § 307, comma 1st, clause 2nd, *BGB*: 'Eine unangemessene Benachteiligung kann sich auch daraus ergeben, dass die Bestimmung nicht klar und verständlich ist'. See in the legal literature Huber and Faust (2002), p. 464; in Italy Giammaria (2003), pp. 1023-1025.

31 See Roppo (1997), p. 99; Di Giovanni (1997), p. 196; Sciarrone Alibrandi (1993), p. 727, note 50.

32 Di Giovine (1998), pp. 589-594.

33 Under French law Paissant (1995), p. 107.

34 Under Italian law Di Giovanni (1997), p. 183.

that the solution debases the principle of transparency; indeed, it provides a powerful sanction. Rather, it is the type of sanction that is not convincing.

On closer examination, an incompatibility between the rule and the sanction emerges. It is suggested that the two poles of the directive, judicial control over content on one side, and protection of transparency, on the other, should be kept separate. If the clause in question is difficult to understand but does not in itself violate the rule in Art. 3 (1), the sanction of invalidity for oppressiveness does not make sense.[35] That sanction is in fact applied where the contract is imbalanced, something that, at least hypothetically, does not apply in this situation. It is 'only' a problem of intelligibility.

A further argument in support of keeping these perspectives separate might be mentioned. As has been noted, between the negative criteria of oppressiveness set out in Arts. 3 (1) and (2), we find 'individual negotiation'. This rids the terms of oppressiveness, even if it is not easy to reconstruct definitively the minimum requirements from which one can conclude that the parties have effectively negotiated. Nevertheless, if the sanctions for lack of transparency and oppressive content were to be equated, one could draw comfort from the fact that, in both cases, the existence of a negotiation process will lead to the exclusion of the sanction. It is impossible to deny that an individually negotiated clause is by definition transparent.[36]

This conclusion seems somewhat superficial, because discussion about the wording of the clause, even when it rises to the level of authentic negotiation, does not necessarily guarantee the transparency of the written text. At most, it excludes unilateral arrangements. Accordingly, where one or more terms have been individually negotiated, the requirements of Art. 5 are not satisfied, and it has no application. Something similar happens as regards abusiveness, where willing participation on the part of the consumer tends to rule out any abuse of power, subject to the importance of the consumer's voluntary contribution. The individually negotiated parts of the contract may be too limited in scope to support a single sanction.

In Search of a Remedy outside the Directive

Let us look beyond the directive for a remedy. This tentative step should not cause a sensation and finds theoretical justification in another more general premise. Once implemented into the national legal systems, the directive can no longer be differentiated from national law, being united with it in constant dialogue. If this is the case, the likelihood of an external sanction appears quite plausible.

As anticipated, total incomprehensibility of a term, a phenomenon which violates the transparency principle, demands a response from the general law of contract. Since there must be a lack of consensus around a clause that is absolutely

35 Di Giovine (1998), p. 569.

36 Contra Jarach (1998), p. 607.

unintelligible, the only possible outcomes are non-incorporation in the contract or nullity, total or partial, of the contract, depending on whether or not the clause was determined by consensus. This is most obvious when a term that goes to the 'heart of the contract' is completely incomprehensible, making its object indeterminate and indeterminable. This not the proper scope of the transparency principle which, according to Art. 5, applies the requirements of clarity and comprehensibility to clauses which are still intelligible.[37] This is also different from significant imbalance contrary to good faith, where the obstacles pertain purely and typically to content.

Lack of Transparency as a Synonym for Contractual Fraud

How, then, can a sanction drawn from the general law of contract be imposed on a professional who imposes non-transparent clauses on consumers? Here one's thoughts can easily become national, but Europe's legal orders have many common traits.

The lack of transparency of contractual terms, understood as the result of the conduct of the stronger party, who drew up the obscure provision in question, can break down at various points. Some simplification is called for. It seems plausible that, although the facts may have been effectively divulged, they have been expressed in such a way as to prevent understanding by the addressee. Here we can identify a positive course of action which violates the duty to provide information. The professional is acting, but acting badly, and fails to comply with his legal obligation to inform. On the other hand, it is more or less inevitable, if one is dealing with obscurity, that some important information will not have been communicated. Such a failure of communication will impede the understanding not only of the facts which remain hidden, but also of those which have been effectively supplied, which probably would have been more transparent if they had been presented alongside the missing facts. This is an omission rather than a positive course of action, but it also contravenes the duty of transparency.

In summary, where writing that the professional should ensure is crystal clear is in fact scarcely intelligible, this constitutes objectively harmful conduct by the stronger party, resulting from a varying combination of legally relevant actions and omissions. If this course of action was deliberately pursued by the professional, violating his duty to inform in order to bring about an imperfect representation of his standard form contract, and thereby deceiving the consumer, this would certainly appear to open the doors to a claim of contractual fraud (dol). In fact, by preventing quick and correct access to the effective content of the general conditions drawn up by him, conditions which may be wrapped in nebulous or sibylline expressions, or perhaps in very small print, he induces an error in the other party, and extorts a vitiated consent.

---

37 See under Italian law Masucci (1996); Jarach (1998), pp. 603-613.

A Response Drawn from Italian Contract Law

It seems that all the conditions of applicability contained in Arts. 1439 and 1440 of the Civil Code are satisfied.[38] So in the most serious cases, where the fraud of the professional is shown to have induced the consumer to enter the contract, it will be voidable for lack of transparency, in addition to the obligation to provide compensation for any damage caused (Art. 1439). In less serious cases, where fraud is only incidental – i.e. where the consumer would still have entered the contract, but on different terms – the intransparent contract will still be valid, but the professional will be obliged to compensate any harm caused to the other party (Art. 1440).[39] This second hypothesis will be statistically more likely. The limited attention of the consumer and his inability to free himself from the grip of the market makes it difficult to believe that he would have avoided contracting entirely, even if a block of non-negotiable clauses were drafted in a more transparent manner.

This proposed solution seems balanced. The contract will survive under either hypothesis, since voidability on the grounds of fraud can only be invoked by the deceived consumer, while in the hypothesis of incidental fraud it is ruled out. In both cases the consumer has a claim to damages.

This can be made more explicit by inversion. If the professional does not comply with his obligation to inform, he will always have to provide compensation for any damage caused to the consumer, who would in any event have bargained for different terms. In the most serious cases, when the consumer would not have entered the contract at all, the contract is voidable. If the clause or clauses are actually incomprehensible, they will either not form part of the contract, or the contract will be partially or totally void, depending on whether this incomprehensibility affects the object of the contract. Control of content – rather than form – for oppressiveness is unaffected at all levels, and can also result in a judicial declaration of invalidity.[40]

Malice on the Part of the Stronger Party

Undoubtedly, this conclusion about sanctions for lack of transparency in contracting presupposes an apparently limiting requirement. The professional must have acted in subjective 'bad faith', as Art. 1440 of the Civil Code puts it. Simple culpable violation of informational obligations would not give rise to a sanction, so

---

38 Only statutory rules from the Italian *Codice civile* on the topic of contractual fraud are mentioned here, but it would be easy to transfer these observations also in the context of the German *BGB* (§ 123) or the French *Code civil* (Art. 1116). See also Art. 3.8 of the Unidroit-Principles and Art. 4:107 of the PECL. In the legal literature see Grigoleit (2003); Storme (2003).

39 In similar direction Majello (1995), p. 308.

40 Different solutions – but always coming from the national contractual law and not from the directive 93/13/EEC – are supported by Sacco and De Nova (1993), pp. 373-376; Pietrobon (1990), p. 251; see also Lener (1996), V, column 154.

often the professional would be able to take refuge behind an open claim of 'good faith'.

It is difficult to understand how a professional, who has drafted and, to a substantial degree, imposed contractual terms, would be able to claim that he was unaware of its lack of transparency. It is even more difficult to accept a claim that he did not realize that it would have negative consequences for the consumer. The very logic of a contract of adhesion leads one to doubt, from the start, the validity of such objections. The requirement of intention seems to be satisfied by the very fact of the arrangement.

Judicial Self-Restraint and the Need for an Unlikely Cultural Revolution

We now turn our attention to evaluating how this system of sanctions, constructed by the directive but in need of external integration, impacts on the autonomy and, in particular, the contractual freedom of the professional. In fact, the legal rules expose the professional to a notable degree of pressure. It is difficult to say whether this pressure will help to stabilize an effective equilibrium for this type of relationship, balancing the asymmetries typical of the contract of adhesion and especially the consumer contract, or whether it is in fact little more than a dead letter. The scarcity and lack of significance of decisions delivered to date – at least in Italy – seems to demonstrate some failings in the implementation of community law.

In any event, the main problem is not so much one of the text or the technical solutions connected with it, but rather one of the cultural revolution that it must bring about. The idea that courts can strike down a clause because it is oppressive or annul a contract because its meaning is obscure is a far from commonly-held judicial sentiment, at least in most European legal orders. The discussion should be more clearly articulated in Germany or the Scandinavian countries of the EU, where one can observe a greater propensity for judicial intervention in the modification or avoidance of contracts.[41] Elsewhere, judicial practice demonstrates a degree of reluctance to criticize agreements, which are the product of private autonomy, on the basis of externally imposed rules which are not imperative norms of the domestic legal system. This cultural resistance, which is capable of preventing or hindering the efficient operation of the new rules in the domestic order, bears witness to the diffuse conceptions of contractual autonomy as an intangible tenet of the private law system.[42] Such a deeply held belief creates a real paradox.

Before applying a norm which demands a very different approach from the one usually demanded by his cultural context, the judge necessarily hesitates. This

41 See on this point the important nos. 37-38 COM (2003) 68 final (OJ 2003 C 63). Vice versa in Italy a mental habit very scared on accepting such intrusions exists.

42 Legal scholars usually speak about 'sanctity of contract'. On the topic of contractual freedom the studies of Ludwig Raiser remain fundamental. See his articles published in Raiser (1977). In the common law area see Atiyah (1995); Atiyah (1979).

hesitation arises from traditional judicial self-restraint in the face of private agreements, and, since it is lawful, drives judges towards readings which limit the effects of norms as far as possible. The likely result of this is an easing of the pressure which the directive intended to impose on the professional. Whether this is a good or a bad thing is difficult to say, but it is a fact.

Lack of Transparency as a Key to Judicial Control on the Basis of Economic Justice

This concerns the balance of rights and obligations contained in the contract, and the requirements of transparency, which I have referred to as the 'poles' of the directive. However, there is a more fundamental area where the absentionism of the Courts will probably remain definitive, despite the directive. Art. 4 (2) of the directive allows the limits of control over content to be extended to include the 'definition of the main subject matter of the contract' and the 'adequacy' of consideration, when the clauses under consideration lack transparency.[43] Accordingly, obscurity could be considered as the key to accessing control over the economic balance of the contract, and would allow the judge to intervene where the consideration promised by the parties is not proportionate.[44]

A Judicial Decision on whether the Agreement is Economically Just Cannot be the Appropriate Remedy for Contractual Obscurity

If this were the case – and the letter of the law seems to confirm this – we would nevertheless have to admit to a double distortion of the system of sanctions. In fact, lack of transparency would not only give rise to a declaration of abusiveness and the consequent invalidity of the clause. In fact, this defect would actually legitimate judicial supervision of the economic justice of the relationship. Now, if the first scenario gives rise to a degree of uncertainty, the second opens a deep hole into which no judge would want to fall.

Conducting an inquiry into the balance between the rights and duties of the parties, which might lead to a finding of abusiveness, but for reasons that only relate to transparency, already seems anomalous.[45] Lack of balance would become a serious matter, especially if the 'formal' reasons opened the door for judges to criticize the bargain in question and to impose sanctions, for example, where the price is excessive. Once again, there is no agreement between rule and sanction or between primary and secondary norms. The confusion grows as one reflects on the consequences of the application of the rule, if understood as its terms appear to suggest.

---

43 See Collins (1998), pp. 988-990.

44 On this point Mengoni (1998), p. 546; Monticelli (1998); Di Giovine (1998).

45 In fact 'altro è perseguire la trasparenza, altro è perseguire l'equilibrio delle prestazioni', as it was written by De Nova (1993), p. 712.

Let us try to imagine the logical route. The judge, on a cursory reading of the contract, notices that the clause which stipulates the prices is barely comprehensible. The terms of the contract must be understandable and must not render the object of the contract indeterminable, since this would demand a decision of that contract is a nullity. This is in fact a simple example of lack of transparency, but which falls on the 'main subject matter of the contract', which is the payment due from the consumer in return for a particular service. At this point the judge consider both the balance of the contract – although this seems to be an inappropriate course of action – and inquire into the monetary equivalence of the consideration. Being obliged to identify any economic abuse, the judge will make use of economic criteria, although he will not find these in the law, even less in judicial precedent. On the basis of these criteria, will the judge decide the question of economic abusiveness, all the while hiding behind the language of defects of transparency?

There is more. If we recognize that the clause which deals with the object must fall for economic oppressiveness, what will be the fate of the contract? The object has to be an essential requirement of the contract, but if the clause becomes ineffective for economic oppressiveness, how can the contract survive in the light of Art. 6 (1) of the directive? Either the judge will insert his own clause, thereby guaranteeing that the contract survives, or the contract will have to collapse completely. There is no legal mechanism that can get around this defect in the object.[46] The first solution denies private autonomy and legitimates authoritative determinations on the economic justice of the agreement, for which there is a total absence of any cultural and legal background. The second frees the consumer from the presumptively disadvantageous contract, without adequately protecting them in the event that their primary interest is in the continuation of the relationship, albeit rectified.

It is improbable that a judge – even less a 'latin' judge – would choose to follow this route to the end.

How to Overcome the Traditional Self-Restraint of Judges without Waiting for a Cultural Revolution

The law could be read differently, without giving in to the vague language of the directive or to constructions which are difficult to reconcile with the demands of judicial practice.

As I have explained, according to Art. 4 (2), any inquiry into abusiveness cannot go as far as an inquiry into economic equilibrium – and so stops short of a judgment about the proportionality of the rights and duties of the parties – 'in so far as these terms are in plain, intelligible language'. This proposition could even be interpreted not as an implicit legitimation of 'economic justice' in the event of verbal obscurity, but as a specific reaffirmation of a more general principle, imposed by Art. 5. In other words, the parenthesis inserted in the principal phrase ('in so far as…') could refer to control of content which does not, as a rule, involve

46 See Sirena (2003), p. 856.

economic inquiry. Where the terms relating to the object are tainted by obscurity, these remain subject to Art. 5 and its sanctions, the centrality of which have already been referred to. If this is the case, the obscurity of terms which go to the 'heart of the matter' would lead not to a verdict of economic oppressiveness, for which credible instruments are lacking, but to the very sanctions which protect, in general terms, the transparency of the standard contract. This would once more trigger the applicablility of national rules about contractual fraud, or, more specifically, an obligation in every case to compensate the consumer for harm inflicted, and further, in the case of fraud which induces the consumer to enter the contract, voidability.

This reading of Art. 4 (2) seems to be compatible with the terms of the directive, and also recreates harmony between rule and sanction or, in even wider terms, between informational obligations and contractual freedom, safeguarding the inviolability of private autonomy within the limits of the law.

A Realistic Approach

Directive 93/13/EEC introduces two parallel and competing subsystems of consumer protection, which both make inroads into private autonomy, and more specifically the contractual freedom of the professional. In fact, both control over content, which leads to oppressive clauses being held to be ineffective, and the principle of contractual transparency, which gives rise to remedies like compensation or voidability for fraud, constitute instruments of legal pressure on the stronger party.

In any event, in order to prevent the pressure from becoming unbearable and leading to paradoxical outcomes, such as judicial disregard for Arts. 5 and 4 (2), it is essential that each violation should be matched with an appropriate remedy. Accordingly, the sanction for lack of transparency should be disengaged from judgments about oppressive content, in such a way as to grant to Arts. 3 (1) and 5 of the directive distinct and competing spheres of application.

Furthermore, if one wants an interpretation which facilitates the furtherance of community goals and interferes with judicial application of the rules, one must exclude *a priori* judicial interference with agreements on purely economic grounds. If this leads to defects of transparency, the only effective – and judicially 'possible' – sanction consists of applying those remedies designed by domestic law for contractual fraud.

Otherwise, one would be demanding from the judge an intrusion into the field of economic justice. This would lead, on the one hand, to excessive restrictions of contractual liberty, and on the other, to strong reluctance on the part of courts to abandon their long-standing practice of self-restraint. Such extreme statements would lead to substantial inertia, while more balanced interpretations could, by contrast, give rise to more productive applications, which are more respectful of private autonomy and in fact, more protective of the consumer.

References

Alpa, G. (1997), 'L'incidenza della nuova disciplina delle clausole vessatorie nei contratti dei consumatori sul diritto comune', *Rivista Trimestrale di Diritto e Procedura Civile*, pp. 237 *et seq.*

Alpa, G. and Patti, S. (2003), 'Introduzione', in Alpa, G. and Patti, S. (eds.), *Clausole vessatorie nei contratti del consumatore* (Milan: Giuffrè), pp. 1 *et seq.*

Atiyah, P.S. (1979), *The Rise and Fall of Freedom of Contract* (Oxford: Clarendon Press).

Atiyah, P.S. (1995), *An Introduction to the Law of Contract*, 5th edn. (Oxford: Clarendon Press).

Bigliazzi Geri, L. (1996), 'A proposito della proposta di attuazione della direttiva comunitaria sulle clausole abusive nei contratti stipulati con i consumatori', in Bianca, C.M. and Alpa, G. (eds.), *Le clausole abusive nei contratti stipulati con i consumatori. L'attuazione della direttiva comunitaria del 5 aprile 1993* (Padua: Cedam), pp. 327 *et seq.*

Bin, M. (1996), 'Clausole vessatorie: una svolta storica (ma si attuano così le direttive comunitarie?)', *Contratto e Impresa/Europa*, pp. 431 *et seq.*

Bin, M. (2000), 'Per un dialogo con il futuro legislatore dell'attuazione: ripensare l'intera disciplina della non conformità dei beni nella vendita alla luce della direttiva comunitaria', *Contratto e Impresa/Europa*, pp. 403 *et seq.*

Collins, H. (1998), 'Transnational private law regulation of markets', *Europa e Diritto Privato*, pp. 967 *et seq.*

De Nova, G. (1993), 'Informazione e contratto: il regolamento contrattuale', *Rivista Trimestrale di Diritto e Procedura Civile*, pp. 705 *et seq.*

Di Giovanni, F. (1997), 'Difetto di trasparenza e valutazione di vessatorietà delle clausole predisposte nei contratti del consumatore', in Ruffolo, U. (ed.), *Clausole 'vessatorie' e 'abusive'* (Milan: Giuffrè), pp. 196 *et seq.*

Di Giovine, G. (1998), 'Art. 1469-quater', in Cesàro, E. (ed.), *Clausole vessatorie e contratto del consumatore* (Padua: Cedam), pp. 546 *et seq.*

Di Majo, A. (1995), 'Libertà contrattuale e dintorni', *Rivista Critica di Diritto Privato*, pp. 17 *et seq.*

Ferrante, E. (2003), 'Brevi note a margine del "Piano d'azione" sul diritto contrattuale europeo', *Contratto e Impresa/Europa*, pp. 677 *et seq.*

Giammaria, P. (2003), 'Art. 1469-quater – Forma e interpretazione', in Alpa, G. and Patti, S. (eds.), *Clausole vessatorie nei contratti del consumatore* (Milan: Giuffrè), pp. 1011 *et seq.*

Grassetti, C. (1938), *L'interpretazione del negozio giuridico con particolare riguardo ai contratti* (Padua: Cedam).

Grigoleit, H.C. (2003), 'Irrtum, Täuschung und Informationspflichten in den European Principles und in den Unidroit-Principles', in Schulze, R., Ebers, M. and Grigoleit, H.C. (eds.), *Informationspflichten und Vertragsschluss im Acquis communautaire*, (Tübingen: Mohr Siebeck), pp. 201 *et seq.*

Huber, P. and Faust, F. (2002), *Schuldrechtsmodernisierung* (Munich: Beck).

Irti, N. (1998), 'Scambi senza accordo', *Rivista Trimestrale di Diritto e Procedura Civile*, pp. 347 *et seq.*

Irti, N. (1999), '"E' vero, ma ..." (replica a Giorgio Oppo)', *Rivista di Diritto Civile*, I, pp. 273 *et seq.*

Irti, N. (2000), 'Lo scambio dei foulards (replica semiseria al prof. Bianca)', *Rivista Trimestrale di Diritto e Procedura Civile*, pp. 601 *et seq.*

Jarach, A. (1998), 'Art. 1469-quater', in Cesàro, E. (ed.), *Clausole vessatorie e contratto del consumatore* (Padua: Cedam), pp. 599 *et seq.*

Lehmann, M. (2000), 'Informationsverantwortung und Gewährleistung für Werbeangaben beim Verbrauchsgüterkauf', *Juristenzeitung*, pp. 280 *et seq.*

Lener, G. (1996), 'La nuova disciplina delle clausole vessatorie nei contratti dei consumatori', *Foro italiano*, V, colums 145 *et seq.*

Lorenz, S. and Riehm, T. (2002), *Lehrbuch zum neuen Schuldrecht* (Munich: Beck).

Majello, U. (1995), 'Problematiche in tema di trasparenza delle condizioni contrattuali', in Rispoli Farina, M. (ed.), *La nuova legge bancaria. Prime riflessioni sul Testo Unico in materia bancaria e creditizia* (Naples: Jovene), pp. 308 *et seq.*

Masucci, S.T. (1996), 'Art. 1469-quater', in Barenghi, A. (ed.), *La nuova disciplina delle clausole vessatorie nel codice civile* (Naples: Jovene), pp. 135 *et seq.*

Medicus, D. (2002), *Allgemeiner Teil des BGB* (Heidelberg: C.F. Müller).

Mengoni, L. (1998), 'Problemi di integrazione della disciplina dei "contratti del consumatore" nel sistema del codice civile', *Studi in Onore di Pietro Rescigno, III, Diritto Privato, 2. Obbligazioni e contratti* (Milan: Giuffrè), pp. 546 *et seq.*

Möllers, M. (2002), 'Europäische Richtlinien zum Bürgerlichen Recht', *Juristenzeitung*, pp. 121 *et seq.*

Monticelli, S. (1998), 'Art. 1469-ter', in Cesàro, E. (ed.), *Clausole vessatorie e contratto del consumatore* (Padua: Cedam), pp. 503 *et seq.*

Oppo, G. (1943), *Profili dell'interpretazione oggettiva del negozio giuridico* (Padua: Cedam).

Oppo, G. (1998), 'Disumanizzazione del contratto', *Rivista di Diritto Civile*, I, pp. 525 *et seq.*

Paissant, G. (1995), 'Les clauses abusives et la présentation des contrats dans la loi n. 95-96 du 1er février 1995', *Dalloz 1995 Chron.*, pp. 107 *et seq.*

Pardolesi, R. (1995), 'Clausole abusive, pardon vessatorie: verso l'attuazione di una direttiva abusata, *Rivista Critica di Diritto Privato*, pp. 540 *et seq.*

Patroni Griffi, L. (1995), 'Le clausole abusive nei contratti conclusi con i consumatori (Direttiva 93/13/C.E.E.)', *Rassegna di Diritto Civile*, pp. 347 *et seq.*

Pfeiffer, T. (2001), 'Die Integration von "Nebengesetzen" in das BGB', in Ernst, W. and Zimmermann, R. (eds.), *Zivilrechtswissenschaft und Schuldrechtsreform*, pp. 481 *et seq.*

Pfeiffer, T. and Schinkels, B. (2001), 'Schuldrechtsmodernisierung und AGB-Gesetz', in Micklitz, H.W., Pfeiffer, T., Tonner, K. and Willingmann, A. (eds.), *Schuldrechtsreform und Verbraucherschutz* (Baden-Baden: Nomos), pp. 133 *et seq.*

Pietrobon, V. (1990), *Errore, volontà ed affidamento nel negozio giuridico* (Padua: Cedam).

Raiser, L. (1977), *Die Aufgabe des Privatrechts. Aufsätze zum Privat- und Wirtschaftsrecht aus drei Jahrzehnten* (Kronberg: Athenäum).

Rizzo, V. (1999), 'Art. 1469-quater. – Forma e interpretazione', in Bianca, C.M. and Busnelli, F.D. (eds.), *Commentario al capo XIV bis del codice civile: dei contratti del consumatore (art. 1469-bis – 1469-sexies)* (Padua: Cedam), pp. 783 *et seq.*

Rochfeld, J. and Houtcieff, D. (2003), 'Perspectives de développement du droit communautaire en matière de la consommation', in Schulze, R., Ebers, M. and Grigoleit, H.C. (eds.), *Informationspflichten und Vertragsschluss im Acquis communautaire* (Tübingen: Mohr Siebeck), pp. 49 *et seq.*

Roppo, V. (1997), 'La recezione della disciplina europea delle clausole abusive ("vessatorie") nei contratti fra professionisti e consumatori: artt. 1469 bis e seg. c.c.', *Diritto Privato 1996*, pp. 99 *et seq.*

Roppo, V. (2002), *Il contratto del duemila* (Turin: Giappichelli).

Roth, W.H. (2001), 'Europäischer Verbraucherschutz und BGB', *Juristenzeitung*, pp. 475 *et seq*.

Sacco, R. and De Nova, G. (1993), *Il contratto*, vol. I (Turin: Utet).

Schlechtriem, P. (2001), 'Die Anpassung des deutschen Rechts an die Klausel-Richtlinie und den Richtlinienvorschlag zum Verbraucherkaufrecht', *Zeitschrift für Schweizerisches Recht*, pp. 335 *et seq*.

Schulze, R. (2003), 'Der Acquis communautaire und die Entwicklung des europäischen Vertragsrechts', in Schulze, R., Ebers, M. and Grigoleit, H.C. (eds.), *Informationspflichten und Vertragsschluss im Acquis communautaire* (Tübingen: Mohr Siebeck), pp. 3 *et seq*.

Schwintowski, H.P. (2003), 'Informationspflichten und effet utile – Auf der Suche nach einem effektiven und effizienten europäischen Sanktionensystem', in Schulze, R., Ebers, M. and Grigoleit, H.C. (eds.), *Informationspflichten und Vertragsschluss im Acquis communautaire* (Tübingen: Mohr Siebeck), pp. 267 *et seq*.

Sciarrone Alibrandi, A. (1993), 'Prime riflessioni sulla direttiva comunitaria n. 93/13 (clausole abusive nei contratti stipulati con i consumatori)', *Banca, Borsa e Titoli di Credito*, I, pp. 713 *et seq*.

Sirena, P. (2003), 'Art. 1469-ter – Accertamento della vessatorietà delle clausole – 2° comma', in Alpa, G. and Patti, S. (eds.), *Clausole vessatorie nei contratti del consumatore* (Milan: Giuffrè), pp. 855 *et seq*.

Stoffels, M. (2001), 'Schranken der Inhaltskontrolle', *Juristenzeitung*, pp. 843 *et seq*.

Storme, M.E. (2003), 'Information Requirements and Remedies in the Principles of European Contract Law', in Schulze, R., Ebers, M. and Grigoleit, H.C. (eds.), *Informationspflichten und Vertragsschluss im Acquis communautaire* (Tübingen: Mohr Siebeck), pp. 231 *et seq*.

Ulmer, P. (2001), 'Integration des AGB-Gesetzes in das BGB?', in Schulze, R. and Schulte-Nölke, H. (eds.), *Die Schuldrechtsreform vor dem Hintergrund des Gemeinschaftsrechts*, (Tübingen: Mohr Siebeck), pp. 215 *et seq*.

Wilhelmsson, T. (2003), 'Private Law Remedies against the Breach of Information Requirements of EC Law', in Schulze, R., Ebers, M. and Grigoleit, H.C. (eds.), *Informationspflichten und Vertragsschluss im Acquis communautaire* (Tübingen: Mohr Siebeck), pp. 245 *et seq*.

Wolf, M. (2001), 'Party Autonomy and Information in the Unfair Contract Terms Directive', in Grundmann, S., Kerber, W. and Weatherill, S. (eds.), *Party Autonomy and the Role of Information in the Internal Market* (Berlin: de Gruyter), pp. 313 *et seq*.

Chapter 8

Information Disclosure about the Quality of Goods – Duty or Encouragement?

Christian Twigg-Flesner

Introduction

A well-known problem for consumers is the difficulty of evaluating the quality of goods before making a purchase and using the goods. This problem has many facets: consumers may not be able to establish the overall level of quality to be expected from a particular brand, or product sector; furthermore, consumers will usually find it difficult to establish the quality of the particular item they wish to purchase. Most legal systems recognize this problem and provide some protection to consumers, offering at least a basic set of rights for consumers who have bought faulty goods. In the Member States of the European Union, this area of law is now governed by Directive 99/44/EC on the Sale of Consumer Goods and Associated Guarantees (1999), OJ L 171/12 ('the Consumer Sales Directive'), which established a common set of rules in this sphere. Although the Directive does not make it obligatory for a seller (or, indeed, a manufacturer) to provide information to a consumer about the quality of goods, it is nevertheless possible to characterize many of the core provisions as information-based. This chapter will examine to what extent the Directive does address the information problems regarding the quality of goods. It will first review the general problem of inadequate information about quality. It will then consider the relevant provisions of the Consumer Sales Directive and consider the extent to which this encourages sellers to disclose quality defects to consumers. There will also be a brief analysis of whether above-average quality could be communicated to consumers through additional guarantees and to what extent this is supported by the Directive.

Informational Imbalance about the Quality of Goods

It will not be surprising to hear that consumers frequently encounter problems with the quality of goods they have bought. In 1999, the UK's Office of Fair Trading suggested that there were around 43 million consumer complaints and concerns about defective goods or substandard service in the United Kingdom per year.[1] This includes almost nine million instances of complaints about major household appliances, consumer electronics, cars and other household goods. Overall, just over half of those consumers who had reason to complain did so because goods they had bought were in some way defective. Such problems may be due to a variety of reasons. For example, there may be inherent weaknesses in the design of the goods, causing them to malfunction unexpectedly at some point after purchase. Alternatively, a particular item may fail to work as intended because of a manufacturing defect. Other instances may be caused by the way the goods were handled before they were delivered to the consumer, or by the way the consumer used the goods.

It is rarely possible for a consumer to identify any problems before purchase. Consumers therefore buy goods without knowing how reliable and durable the particular item will be. Indeed, defects will often not manifest themselves until after the consumer has used the goods for some time. It is therefore generally not possible to ascertain the level of quality of goods before purchase, because most consumer goods are 'experience' goods rather than 'search' goods. Whereas the attributes of 'search' goods can be discovered before purchase, those of 'experience' goods will only become apparent when the goods are in use.[2] Experience goods are technically complex, and consumers are usually not able to discover any defects simply by inspecting the goods. This makes it difficult, if not impossible, to discover quality defects in such goods.

This leads to a more general problem which Akerlof raised in his seminal paper.[3] He argued that the inability of consumers to identify whether particular goods are low-quality or high-quality, as well as the inability of sellers and manufacturers reliably to communicate the level of quality of their goods, may eventually cause a decline in the overall level of quality. This is because the inability to ascertain the quality of goods before purchase takes away the incentive for a seller to offer high-quality goods. Similarly, there is little encouragement for manufacturers to improve the design and manufacturing process for their goods. Eventually, low-quality goods ('lemons') could push high-quality goods off the market. According to Akerlof, the overall level of quality in a market will decline if consumers cannot discover the quality of goods before purchase. However, in order to be able to establish whether goods are of high or low quality, consumers need to be aware of the general level of quality to be expected in a particular product market in order to compare particular goods to the overall standard of quality. This, too, may decline because consumers cannot make this comparison. Consequently, the informational imbalance in the quality of consumer goods can be problematic both with regard to the quality of particular goods and the overall level of quality in the relevant product sector.

It has been suggested that the primary difficulty is the imbalance in the distribution of information about quality as between consumer and seller:

---

1 OFT (2000), p. 9.

2 Hadfield, Howse and Trebilcock (1998), no. 17.

3 Akerlof (1970).

> Consumers may often lack adequate information on the reliability, durability and running costs of products, and sellers will generally have superior information on these matters.[4]

Such information is regarded as central to the consumer's autonomy, because the availability of relevant information is regarded as fundamental in giving consumers the opportunity to make a rational and wealth-maximizing decision.[5]

It follows from this that persuading sellers to make available reliable information regarding the quality of goods would enable consumers to exercise a better-informed choice when making purchases. An obvious, and significant, problem with this view is that a seller will rarely have specific information about the quality of the particular items he sells. In the case of most consumer transactions, the seller's role will be little more than that of intermediary between manufacturer and consumer, with goods packaged and sealed by the manufacturer and not unpacked until delivered to the consumer. A seller may therefore not, in fact, know a great deal more about the quality of goods than the consumer. Admittedly, a seller will probably have taken some care in selecting the goods he sells and will have made sure that these meet a particular standard of quality, but even then it would be difficult to claim that a seller will always have superior information about the quality of goods.

There are, of course, a number of alternative sources which make available information about the quality of particular goods. A common practice is for consumer associations to carry out comparative testing of a number of different brands in a specific goods sector to give some general guidance about the prevailing level of quality in that sector, as well as which brands generally offer higher quality goods. In the United Kingdom, the primary source is the Consumers' Association's monthly magazine *Which?*; in Germany, the *Stiftung Warentest* carries out similar tests. Consumers can access this information to identify high quality goods. However, such information only reaches a limited number of consumers. Moreover, the information provided is only of a general nature and does not give the consumer concrete information about a particular item he may wish to buy.

Information Deficit: the Legal Response

The perceived imbalance in quality information is one reason for the adoption of rules to protect consumers in the sale of goods. It is now widely accepted that consumers have certain basic expectations about the minimum level of quality that goods should meet. At the very least, goods should work and be fit for their general purpose (functionality), but consumer expectations often go further. There are various factors which have a bearing on the precise expectations of consumers, such as price, brand image and statements made in advertising. Legislation on

---

4 Ramsay (1989), p. 415.

5 This is discussed extensively in Grundmann, Kerber and Weatherill (2001).

consumer sales seeks to enforce such expectations by specifying that goods must meet a certain level of quality, often expressed through a flexible test, such as the 'satisfactory quality' standard in English law or the 'conformity with the contract' test in the Consumer Sales Directive. In the absence of clear information about the actual quality of goods, the law requires that goods must reach a standard which, broadly speaking, a reasonable person / average consumer[6] would reasonably expect. Such expectations are shaped by a variety of factors, and the test therefore is flexible to allow for the relevant factors to be taken into consideration. One such relevant factor is whether a consumer is made aware of any defects in the goods before purchase.[7] If a particular problem is drawn to the consumer's attention before sale, then he could no longer reasonably expect the goods to work in the same way as they would without the defect. It has therefore been argued that the Consumer Sales Directive, far from requiring improvements to the quality of goods to ensure that consumers get what they could reasonably expect, is little more than a measure that requires disclosure of information about the quality of goods. Failure to make available such information would mean that the goods do not satisfy the requirement that they must be in conformity with the contract and would therefore make available the Directive's remedial scheme. This interpretation will be considered in more detail in the following section. However, it is argued in this chapter that it would be misguided to place too much emphasis on the disclosure character of the Consumer Sales Directive, because the information that may be disclosed by a seller in order to minimize his risk of liability under the Directive may not only be of limited assistance to the average consumer, but also potentially confuse and mislead consumers about the real quality of the goods they are purchasing.

Disclosure 'Rules' in the Consumer Sales Directive

In this section, the argument that the Consumer Sales Directive is, in effect, a form of disclosure regulation will be analyzed. This will be done in two stages: first, there will be a brief overview of the relevant provisions of the Directive; this will then be followed by an analysis of the disclosure characteristics of these provisions. The key provision for present purposes is Art. 2 of the Directive. This provides as follows:

---

6 The UK's 'reasonable person' for the purposes of the Section 14 (2A) of the Sale of Goods Act 1979 is very probably different from the 'average consumer' of EC law, although *quaere* whether the UK's test should now be the equivalent of the EC's average consumer (note Rott (2003)).

7 Art. 2 (3) of the Directive; Section 14 (2C) of the UK's Sale of Goods Act 1979.

Conformity with the contract

1. The seller must deliver goods to the consumer which are in conformity with the contract of sale.

2. Consumer goods are presumed to be in conformity with the contract if they:

(a) comply with the description given by the seller and possess the qualities of the goods which the seller has held out to the consumer as a sample or model;
(b) are fit for any particular purpose for which the consumer requires them and which he made known to the seller at the time of conclusion of the contract and which the seller has accepted;
(c) are fit for the purposes for which goods of the same type are normally used;
(d) show the quality and performance which are normal in goods of the same type and which the consumer can reasonably expect, given the nature of the goods and taking into account any public statements on the specific characteristics of the goods made about them by the seller, the producer or his representative, particularly in advertising or on labelling.

3. There shall be deemed not to be a lack of conformity for the purposes of this Article if, at the time the contract was concluded, the consumer was aware, or could not reasonably be unaware of, the lack of conformity, or if the lack of conformity has its origin in materials supplied by the consumer.

4. The seller shall not be bound by public statements, as referred to in paragraph 2 (d) if he:

- shows that he was not, and could not reasonably have been, aware of the statement in question,
- shows that by the time of conclusion of the contract the statement had been corrected, or
- shows that the decision to buy the consumer goods could not have been influenced by the statement.

5. Any lack of conformity resulting from incorrect installation of the consumer goods shall be deemed to be equivalent to lack of conformity of the goods if installation forms part of the contract of sale of the goods and the goods were installed by the seller or under his responsibility. This shall apply equally if the product, intended to be installed by the consumer, is installed by the consumer and the incorrect installation is due to a shortcoming in the installation instructions.

Although Art. 2 is not phrased in terms of reasonable, or legitimate, expectations (unlike the proposals originally made in the Commission's *Green Paper* (1993)), it is nevertheless clear that the general principle underlying the Art. 2 conformity requirement is that the goods should conform to the consumer's reasonable expectations. Thus, Art. 2 (1) essentially requires that the goods delivered to the consumer must conform to the consumer's reasonable expectations, which, in turn, are derived from the contract.[8] Art. 2 (2) provides a list of factors which are taken into account in creating a rebuttable presumption that goods are in conformity with the contract. Interestingly, the language of Art. 2 (2)(d) confirms that the reasonable expectations of consumers are significant, requiring that the goods 'show the quality and performance which are

8 Bradgate and Twigg-Flesner (2003), pp. 40-41.

normal in goods of the same type and which the consumer can *reasonably expect*'.[9] Such expectations may, in particular, be based on public statements such as advertising. This is qualified by Art. 2 (4), allowing the seller in certain circumstances to escape responsibility for public statements which are referred to in Art. 2 (2)(d). Finally, Art. 2 (5) extends the conformity requirement by treating a lack of conformity resulting from incorrect installation of the goods as a lack of conformity in the goods themselves.

For present purposes, Art. 2 (3) is of most significance. The restriction in Art. 2 (3) could be expressed in terms of reasonable expectations: if the consumer is aware of a defect in the goods he cannot claim that he *reasonably expected* the goods to be free of that defect. It is this provision, in particular, which may give the Directive its disclosure character, and it will be examined more closely in the following section.

Analysing Art. 2 in Terms of Information Disclosure

It would, of course, be wrong to state that the Consumer Sales Directive contains an express obligation to disclose information about the quality of goods.[10] However, it is easy to analyze the effect of Art. 2 as providing information to a consumer about the quality of the goods he wishes to purchase. Indeed, Riesenhuber has argued that it is possible to analyze the whole of Art. 2 in terms of information.[11] His suggestion can be summarized thus: Art. 2 (1) requires that goods be in conformity with the contract. Art. 2 (2) then lays down a number of criteria, compliance with which gives rise to the *presumption* that the goods satisfy the requirement of conformity. Art. 2 (2) creates a baseline for the quality which a consumer may reasonably expect of goods which are in conformity with the contract. These criteria come into play when the contract is silent as to the specific quality of the goods, and are therefore merely default principles, reflecting a basic minimum level of quality. If, however, there is a more specific express agreement regarding the quality of the goods, then compliance with the criteria in Art. 2 (2) may not be enough to establish that the goods are in conformity with the contract. Factors other than those in Art. 2 (2) may therefore be relevant in order to establish whether goods are in conformity with the contract,[12] both in addition to, as well as instead of, those in Art. 2 (2). However, as acknowledged by Riesenhuber, Art. 7 (1), which seeks to render ineffective any attempt to exclude the rights given by the Directive, means that it should not be possible to find that goods fail to meet the presumptive criteria in Art. 2 (2), but nevertheless are in conformity because they satisfy any express terms regarding the goods' quality.[13] The overall effect of Art. 2, he argues, is to provide a consumer with information about the quality of

9 Emphasis added.
10 Riesenhuber (2001), p. 352; Wilhelmsson (2003), p. 255.
11 Riesenhuber (2001).
12 Bradgate and Twigg-Flesner (2003), pp. 41-44.
13 Riesenhuber (2001), p. 352.

the goods in that, absent any contrary (express) indication, the consumer is told that the goods meet the basic standard of quality reflected in Art. 2 (2). If the seller is aware that the goods do not meet this standard, there is an incentive to disclose this.

Hedley has made a similar point in relation to English law, although he goes further in that he seeks to fashion an independent duty to provide information:

> If a court complains that goods are defective, but tendering identical goods along with information about them would have cured the 'defect', then surely an independent duty is at work.[14]

Many leading English cases could be analyzed in such terms, and, in Hedley's view, cases where information is entirely irrelevant would be rare.[15] However, although information about goods is clearly central, even he concedes that what also matters are the expectations of buyer and seller.[16] The difficulty with seeking to couch this entirely in terms of a *duty* to provide information is that it presupposes that such information is, in fact, available. This point will be returned to subsequently.

As noted above, in the case of most consumer goods, consumers lack adequate information about their quality. Although Art. 2 provides some compensation for this in that it reflects the notion that consumers have reasonable expectations as to quality, it does not mandate a particular standard of quality to be attained by all goods. Essentially, it offers consumers some protection against defects of which they were not aware at the time of purchase.[17] A consumer cannot claim that goods are not in conformity with the contract if the shortcomings complained of were drawn to his attention before purchase. If a seller is aware that there is a problem with the goods a consumer is about to buy, and he makes the consumer aware of this problem, then, by virtue of Art. 2 (3), the goods will still be deemed to be in conformity with the contract. A consumer would still be entitled to complain in respect of non-conformities not specifically drawn to his attention, unless the consumer 'could not reasonably [have been] unaware of' the lack of conformity. Wilhelmsson therefore concludes that

> [i]t seems quite natural to refer to an indirect information requirement considering the provisions of conformity in the Consumer Sales Directive.[18]

This requires further analysis. To begin with, one may quibble over the terminology. The language of the Directive never refers to a requirement to make a consumer aware of any shortcomings. At best, the provision in Art. 2 (3) encourages a seller to make the consumer aware of these, and to the extent that he

---

14 Hedley (2001), p. 116.
15 Hedley (2001), p. 119.
16 Hedley (2001), p. 123.
17 Cf. Hedley (2001), p. 123.
18 Wilhelmsson (2003), p. 256.

does so, he will not have to make good the lack of conformity under Art. 3. It might therefore be more appropriate to describe this as an 'encouragement to provide information', rather than a 'requirement'.

To what extent is a seller 'encouraged to provide information' under this provision? Art. 2 (3) merely refers to a lack of conformity of which the consumer was 'aware, or could not reasonably have been unaware'. It is therefore not even phrased in terms of disclosure of relevant information by the seller. This may be contrasted with the corresponding provision in Section 14 (2C)(a) of the UK's Sale of Goods Act 1979, which disapplies the requirement that goods must be of satisfactory quality with regard to

> any matter making the quality of goods unsatisfactory [...] which is specifically drawn to the buyer's attention before the contract is made [...].

Although this still falls short of a requirement to disclose, it is a very strong encouragement directed at the seller to draw any problems with the goods to the consumer's attention. It is also much more precise in setting out what is required to remove a particular problem from the ambit of Section 14 (2) – the matter rendering the goods unsatisfactory must be *specifically* drawn to the consumer's attention. This, it seems, would exclude matters which might be covered by a general description of the goods as 'ex display' or 'shop soiled' (note that Section 14 (2A), which provides that goods are satisfactory if a reasonable person would regard them as such, taking account of any description of the goods, the price and the other relevant circumstances. Thus, goods described as 'ex display' may still be regarded as satisfactory because in light of that description a consumer could reasonably expect, say, scratches on a DVD player or a small stain on a garment, and Section 14 (2C) may not come into play at all anyway).

Art. 2 (3) is much less precise. A consumer may be 'aware' of a lack of conformity for various reasons. One of these will obviously be where the seller expressly points out the problem. Another instance may be where the consumer has inspected the goods and has discovered a problem. For example, the consumer may discover a stain on a blouse and mention this to a shop assistant. At that point, the consumer is clearly aware of the problem and would, therefore, not be able to complain about this lack of conformity subsequently. So the scope of Art. 2 (3) appears to be wider than the corresponding provision of UK law.

In fact, it seems that Art. 2 (3) may apply even where the consumer does *not* pass on this information (which the consumer has about the non-conformity) to the seller. It may be asked why the independent knowledge of the consumer should result in the disapplication of Art. 2 (2).[19] Indeed, it has been doubted whether the fact that the consumer is aware of a defect of which the seller is ignorant should invariably bar the consumer from relying on this non-conformity. Although there is obviously a strong incentive on the consumer to inform the seller in order to obtain the best deal (e.g., a reduction in price), it does not seem to constitute unacceptable behaviour (*venire contra factum proprium*) if the consumer chooses not to do so

---

19 Schwartze (2000); Schermaier (2003).

and to rely on the non-conformity subsequently.[20] This wide scope of Art. 2 (3) therefore seems surprising, in particular because its inclusion in this form seems to lack a clear basis – an exclusion of Art. 2 (2) would seem more appropriate only where *both* parties are fully aware of the lack of conformity.[21]

Irrespective of these difficulties, it seems clear that one aspect of Art. 2 (3) is to encourage a seller to draw a lack of conformity to the consumer's attention (to make him 'aware'). It then needs to be asked *how* this should be done by the seller. Would it be enough for the seller to mention, in general terms, that there may be a problem, or would he have to be more precise? As noted above, the description of the goods may imply to the consumer that there may be certain problems. For example, if goods are described as 'second-hand' or 'ex display', the consumer is at least put on notice that there may be some problems. Small scratches on a TV set should therefore not come as a surprise. However, it is submitted that it would be wrong to allow broad descriptions to have the effect of deeming a consumer to be aware of specific functional defects. Take the example of a second-hand PC with a faulty disk drive. Although the description as second-hand may mean that the consumer should not be able to complain about, say, a worn-out but fully functional keyboard, this should not extend to the faulty disk drive. Surely this should be drawn to the consumer's attention in specific terms in order to benefit from the exemption in Art. 2 (3). Similarly, it should not be enough for a seller to say that 'sometimes, the disk drive on second-hand PCs may be faulty' to bring Art. 2 (3) into play. A consumer will only be aware of a lack of conformity if this is specifically pointed out to him. Overall, therefore, Art. 2 (3) encourages a seller to disclose specific problems, and only where the seller identifies such shortcomings should that particular problem be excluded from the conformity requirement.

Two additional observations need to be made on the scope of Art. 2 (3). It goes further in that it also covers non-conformities of which the consumer could not 'reasonably have been unaware'. The immediate question is when a consumer could not reasonably have been unaware. Presumably, this must be so with very obvious defects. It may also extend to matters which the consumer should have noticed following his examination of the goods. However, it is submitted that a consumer should not 'reasonably have been unaware' of a specific problem if the seller has simply made a very general statement. Moreover, nothing in the Directive requires a consumer to examine the goods, and it would be inappropriate to interpret Art. 2 (3) in such a way as effectively to require such an examination. However, if the consumer does examine the goods before sale, any shortcomings which should have been discovered by the consumer during that particular examination will be covered by Art. 2 (3).

Finally, Art. 2 (3) also deems there to be no lack of conformity if this has its origin in materials supplied by the consumer. Thus, if the consumer asks a tailor to make a suit from fabric supplied by the consumer, and there is a problem with the fabric which renders it unsuitable for that purpose, the tailor will not be liable for a

20 Schwartze (2000), p. 125.
21 Schermaier (2003), p. 11.

resulting lack of conformity. It should be noted that this applies even where the consumer has no information about this shortcoming, and, more significantly, where the seller is aware that the materials may have a defect. The question of whether a seller would be under a duty to inform the consumer about this falls outside the scope of the Directive.

Art. 2 (3) therefore provides the main route by which a seller can evade the application of the conformity requirement. In passing, it should be noted that Art. 2 (4) provides a further escape route for a seller in the case of public statements, which may be taken into account in assessing the conformity of the goods by virtue of Art. 2 (2)(d). Because of its narrow scope, it is not examined in more detail in this chapter.

To summarize: Art. 2 (2) creates a base-line standard for establishing the conformity of the goods with the contract. If the seller does not draw a particular shortcoming to the consumer's attention, the consumer is entitled to assume that the goods meet this basic level of quality. If it transpires that the goods do not conform, then the remedial regime provided for in Art. 3 of the Directive (repair or replacement; or price reduction/rescission) is triggered and the seller has to make good the lack of conformity.

On this analysis, it does not seem possible for a seller to escape the application of Art. 2 (2) by disclaiming all knowledge about the actual quality of the goods. However, just this argument was put forward by Riesenhuber:[22]

> There may, however, be cases where the seller does not know whether the quality of the goods is below the standard imposed by Art. 2 (2). In such a case, it is enough for the seller to point out that he cannot say whether the goods are of normal quality or not. If the consumer buys the goods none the less, that is an agreement to a more specific standard of conformity and the consumer may not later rely on the standard of Art. 2 (2).

It is not clear on what basis this suggestion could be sustained. Unfortunately, Riesenhuber does not explain fully the legal basis for his argument that a general disclaimer by the seller may be enough to displace the general standard of quality set by the presumptive criteria in Art. 2 (2). Within the overall scheme of Art. 2, it seems that it is only possible to displace the basic standard set by Art. 2 (2) in accordance with Art. 2 (3). Thus, there has to be a *specific* problem which would mean that the goods would not be in conformity with the contract, either because they do not meet the presumption in Art. 2 (2) or because the goods fail to comply with an additional express term in the contract. There is nothing in Art. 2 to suggest that a general disclaimer of knowledge such as the one suggested by Riesenhuber would fall within the scope of Art. 2 (3). Indeed, to allow a seller to escape the application of the criteria in Art. 2 (2) by stating that he has not examined the goods would, effectively, allow the seller to exclude the application of this article and would reduce the standard of quality legally required by the Directive below that which a consumer could reasonably expect. This is an

22 Riesenhuber (2001), p. 353.

exclusion of the rights granted by the Directive by another name and cannot have been intended by the legislator. It was noted above that sellers are generally acting as conduits between manufacturers and consumers, and will generally not have examined the goods. If Riesenhuber were correct, it would be enough for the seller to state that the goods had come straight from the manufacturer and that therefore the seller does not know what the state of the goods is to evade the application of the Directive. It is submitted that this is an incorrect interpretation of the Directive and should be rejected. It is clearly the underlying policy of the Consumer Sales Directive to protect the reasonable expectations of consumers, but such expectations are not affected by a seller disclaiming specific knowledge about the quality of the goods. At best, such a statement may enable a seller to argue that he has not 'accepted' the particular purpose for which the consumer requires the goods (as per Art. 2 (2)(b)), and it is this particular aspect of Art. 2 (2) which may then have no application. As a general principle, however, a deviation from the basic standard set by Art. 2 (2) requires that specific shortcomings are identified and clearly drawn to the consumer's attention. This is also the position taken in English law, as evidenced by Stuart-Smith L.J.'s observations in *Harlingdon & Leinster Enterprises Ltd.* v. *Christopher Hull Fine Art Ltd.* that it would be a 'serious defect in the law' if a seller could escape liability simply by claiming that he was not an expert in what was being sold.[23] The same must be true where the seller merely disclaims knowledge of whether the goods are of satisfactory quality, or in conformity with the contract.

Problem: The Extent of Information Failure

The preceding section has considered the extent to which Art. 2 may assist with the information problems regarding the quality of goods. In particular, Art. 2 (3) encourages sellers to make the consumer aware of any particular problems. It is important to note that this presupposes that the seller is, in fact, aware of such problems. If the seller is unaware of any defects, then it is obviously impossible for him to draw these to the consumer's attention. On the one hand, this may encourage sellers to be more careful about the goods they sell, and examine these before they sell them to consumers. On the other hand, it would be both impractical and unrealistic to expect a seller to test every individual item he sells. However, this cannot be a sufficient reason to allow a seller to evade Art. 2 (contrary to Riesenhuber's suggestion, discussed above). It may be an argument for imposing greater liability on a manufacturer, either through a guaranteed right of recourse, or through direct manufacturer liability. Neither is currently provided for in the Directive, although Art. 4 offers at least some protection for sellers.[24]

Even if the seller is aware of a problem and discloses this to the consumer, it may be asked whether this should, in itself, be enough for Art. 2 (3) to apply. It has

---

23 *Harlingdon & Leinster Enterprises Ltd.* v. *Christopher Hull Fine Art Ltd.* [1990] 1 All. E.R. 737, p. 748; cited in Hedley (2001), p. 119.

24 Bradgate and Twigg-Flesner (2002).

often been remarked that information disclosure in itself does very little to improve consumer protection unless consumers are able to make sense of the information and utilize it appropriately.[25] Many consumer goods are technically complex, and a consumer who is told that a particular component is faulty may not be aware of the overall implications of this on the usability of the goods. Moreover, he may not appreciate at the time he is told of the fault what may be required to put it right, and what the costs both in terms of money and inconvenience would be if he decided to go ahead with the purchase. This, too, could be classed as an information failure. Trebilcock and Elliott describe it thus:

> Information failure occurs where a transactor either lacks information about a proposed arrangement *or lacks the ability to process it.* [...] By processing information we refer both to the comprehension of complex legal and business facts and to the sorting and sifting of alternatives that people perform in an effort to decide which arrangement will best satisfy their utility functions. *The lack of an ability to process information is in a sense a form of incapacity* as some people lack the intellectual or experiential resources needed to synthesise and make sense of [information].[26]

This is a serious matter, and one that seems to have been largely ignored in the debate about the central role that information plays both in the sale of goods and in the protection of consumers more generally.[27] A consumer who goes to buy goods expects that these goods will do certain things for him. In other words, the consumer has a particular preference, which, at a basic level, is that the goods will be suitable for his needs and, even more fundamentally, work reliably. Assume that the consumer is told about a defect. The overwhelming view is that, by virtue of Art. 2 (3), the consumer is now aware of the defect and therefore cannot, on this basis, claim that the goods are not in conformity with the contract. In terms of information, the informational imbalance between seller and consumer has been corrected by the disclosure. Or has it? Following the definition of 'information failure' set out above, it is not the availability of the information about the existence of the defect alone that is the problem, but also the extent to which the consumer is able to process that information. Consequently, simply disclosing a defect may not correct an information failure at all; in fact, it may exacerbate the problem. Only if the consumer is able to process the information fully and correctly can the informational imbalance be redressed.

On this basis, it is submitted that Art. 2 (3) should be applied with some care, allowing a seller to benefit from it only where the consumer's 'awareness' of the lack of conformity encompasses both knowledge of the specific defect *and* the full implications of buying goods with such a non-conformity. As this is a European Directive, this could be subject to a presumption that if an average consumer (reasonably well informed and reasonably observant and circumspect) would be 'aware' on this basis, then the particular consumer will be so aware unless he provides evidence that this was not so. It is submitted that this would be the most

25 Seminally, Whitford (1973).
26 Trebilcock and Elliott (2001), p. 62; emphasis added.
27 Although it has been noted by Ulen (2001).

appropriate application of this provision and one that ensures that any information which is made available can be utilized by the consumer. Thus, all 'information failures' should be remedied before the consumer is deprived of the protection of the Consumer Sales Directive.

Providing Information about Above-Average Quality

So far, this chapter has focused on those provisions within the Consumer Sales Directive which have the effect of informing the consumer that goods meet the standard of quality which they can reasonably expect (such expectations being established on the basis of the criteria in Art. 2 (2)), as well as informing the consumer about specific shortcomings of the goods. However, does the Directive also create a framework for providing information that goods are of a standard of quality above the base line set by Art. 2? There are two possible ways in which this may be achieved. First, there is the possibility to include an express term in the contract of sale. As Art. 2 (2) only creates a presumption of conformity, there is nothing to prevent an express term in the contract mandating a higher standard of conformity. A breach of such a term would rebut the presumption created by Art. 2 (2) and render the goods non-conforming.[28]

Secondly, the Consumer Sales Directive contains rules on voluntary guarantees, and it has been suggested these may have the capacity to provide information to consumers about the quality of the goods to which the guarantee relates.

Guarantees and Information about Product Quality

It has often been suggested that manufacturers could provide a better indication of the quality of their goods through the use of guarantees:

> [Guarantees] seem like an incredibly useful device for getting around asymmetric information about product quality. There are many products sold with [guarantees], but I find it surprising that they are not used even more often.[29]

Guarantees could therefore be used to reduce the informational imbalance. This role of guarantees is commonly known as signalling theory.[30] According to this theory, guarantees can signal to consumers that goods meet a certain level of quality. In particular, a guarantee which is more generous than the average guarantee in a particular product sector suggests that the goods in question are of a

---

28 A question which is not addressed here is whether Art. 2 (3) could be invoked to disapply such an express term where the consumer is told that the goods do not, in fact, reach the higher standard. Intuitively, it seems that this should not be so, but further consideration elsewhere is required.

29 Grossman (1981), p. 479.

30 Twigg-Flesner (2003), Chapter 3.

higher level of quality. Guarantees could therefore provide information about the quality of goods, which might not be communicated through other means, such as a statement in advertising that the product is of 'superior quality'.[31] This, however, only works if the person sending the signal would incur a cost if the signal were incorrect. If a guarantee is a signal, then the cost to the manufacturer of providing the guarantee is systematically related to product reliability.[32] A guarantor will incur the cost of having to provide a remedy under a guarantee if goods do not match the level of quality 'communicated' in the guarantee (the signal has failed). The guarantor will want to keep such costs to a minimum, which is best achieved by using the guarantee to 'signal' a quality standard which is not higher than the actual level of quality of the relevant goods.

Despite the superficial logic of this argument, there is now a considerable body of research evidence which reveals that guarantees will rarely achieve their purpose as a quality indicator. For present purposes, a thorough discussion of this research is not required and an overview will suffice.[33]

Research on the Link between Guarantees and Quality

Agrawal *et al.* suggest that there is no clear relationship between guarantees and quality.[34] Guarantees were more likely to be accurate signals of quality when they were given on established goods with a high degree of market penetration. This contrasts with research evidence that consumers are more likely to rely on guarantees, if at all, when these are least likely to be an accurate reflection of quality, i.e., when goods are new on the market.[35]

The reputation of the guarantor is clearly of some significance.[36] If the guarantor has a bad reputation, it seems that a signal such as a guarantee will do little to suggest that the products covered by the guarantee are of a certain standard of quality. Consumers will only rely on guarantees where the reputation of the guarantor is positive.[37] Similarly, Purohit and Srivastava found that the signalling value of a guarantee benefited from the good reputation of the guarantor:

> [...] perceptions of quality were not influenced by [a guarantee] when the reputation of the manufacturer was poor [...].[38]

In addition, Srivastava and Mitra draw a distinction by dividing consumers into two broad categories, 'novices' and 'experts'.[39] Novices are consumers who have not previously bought particular goods, whereas experts have purchased such

---

31 Wiener (1985).
32 Spence (1977).
33 A detailed discussion can be found in Twigg-Flesner (2003), Chapter 3.
34 Agrawal, Richardson and Grimm (1996).
35 See also Shimp and Bearden (1982).
36 Bearden and Shimp (1982).
37 Boulding and Kirmani (1993).
38 Purohit and Srivastava (2001), p. 133.
39 Srivastava and Mitra (1998).

goods at least once previously. Experts largely ignore the reputation of the guarantor, possibly because of the experts' general awareness of the particular product market. Novices would only use guarantees as a signal of quality if the perceived reputation of the guarantor is high.

The existence of non-excludable statutory rights and the extent to which consumers are aware of this protection may also have an effect on the signalling value of guarantees.[40] If consumers are familiar with their legal rights, and the relationship between their legal rights and the rights they may have under the guarantee, the guarantee may not be as strong a signal of quality. This is because consumers know that they will in any event be able to obtain a remedy if they have acquired a product which is of lower quality than required by statute.

Trebilcock pointed out that consumers may find it difficult to understand the terms of a guarantee.[41] More significantly, he noted that guarantees were rarely, if ever, considered during the process of making a purchasing decision. Often, this is because guarantees are enclosed in the packaging with the goods, and consumers are therefore unable to inspect guarantees before purchase. Moreover, there is evidence that consumers are unlikely to be interested in the detailed terms of the guarantee, but merely in the fact whether a guarantee is offered at all.[42] This may be because the mere existence of a guarantee may be an indicator of the manufacturer's confidence in his product.[43] This is generally supported by empirical evidence. Thus, Adler reported that only ten per cent of consumers examined a guarantee before purchase.[44] In the United Kingdom, recent research suggests that 41 per cent of all consumers looked for information about product quality before purchase, but only 18 per cent of all consumers were interested in the existence of a guarantee.[45] However, this figure was higher for purchasers of domestic appliances (one quarter of all those who buy such appliances) and for cars (28 per cent of car purchasers). These findings suggest that consumers in the United Kingdom generally rely on other sources to obtain information about product quality. Of course, guarantors may not intend their guarantees to be a true quality indicator. Long guarantee periods increase the likelihood of factors outside the guarantor's control causing a defect.[46] Second, consumers use goods in different ways, and some consumers are more likely to cause goods to fail than others.[47] In addition, it cannot be predicted in advance how much care a consumer will take of his goods.[48] The conclusion that can be drawn from this brief exegesis is that guarantees do not always and certainly not consistently[49] provide information about the quality of goods. It is therefore clear that 'information

40 Cf. Price and Dawar (2002), p. 186.
41 Trebilcock (1972).
42 Gerner and Bryant (1981); Kelley (1988).
43 Willett (1992).
44 Adler (1994).
45 DTI (2001), p. 7.
46 Eddy (1977), p. 844.
47 Emons (1989).
48 Lutz (1989).
49 Agrawal, Richardson and Grimm (1996), p. 441.

failure'[50] exists not only in respect of the disclosure of quality shortcomings, but also of indicating higher quality.

The Consumer Sales Directive and Guarantees

Although the research evidence now strongly demonstrates that signalling theory is 'not useful for policy purposes',[51] the basic premise of signalling theory has taken root with policy makers both at national and the European level. Indeed, the European Commission's perception of the function of 'consumer guarantees' betrays the influence signalling theory must have had. In the *Green Paper* it was noted that:

> Guarantees are steadily becoming a preferred method of competition between firms and one of the most widespread arguments used in advertising (*consumers look on guarantees as a quality label*).[52]

To say that 'consumers look on guarantees as a quality label' is to suggest that consumers regard the existence of a guarantee as evidence of better quality – it is thus assumed that consumers perceive guarantees as signals of quality.

This is also reflected in the Consumer Sales Directive. Recital 21 states that:

> Whereas, for certain categories of goods, it is current practice for sellers and producers to offer guarantees on goods against any defect which becomes apparent within a certain period; whereas *this practice can stimulate competition*; whereas, while such guarantees are legitimate marketing tools, they should not mislead the consumer; whereas, to ensure that consumers are not misled, guarantees should contain certain information, including a statement that the guarantee does not affect the consumer's legal rights.[53]

This, too, is an indication that the signalling function of guarantees was a dominating factor in the approach taken by the EC. This is, perhaps, further re-inforced by the requirement in Art. 6 (3) of the Directive, according to which a guarantee has to be made 'available in writing or feature in another durable medium available and accessible to [the consumer]'. Although this provision has not been restricted to the pre-purchase context, it may be of relevance at that point. It may be noted that Riesenhuber disagrees with this view and asserts that it has no application in the pre-purchase context at all.

---

50 As per Trebilcock and Elliott (2001).

51 Schwartz and Wilde (1983), p. 1398.

52 Commission of the European Communities (1993), emphasis added.

53 Emphasis added.

> Article 6 (3) does not impose a pre-contractual obligation to provide information [...] rather than a pre-contractual duty to inform, Article 6 contains a contractual duty to inform the obligee about the contents of the agreement (once it has been formed) [...].[54]

This cannot be correct. Rather, it is the case that Art. 6 (3) may be relevant both before and after the consumer has made a purchase. As noted, Recital 21 regards guarantees as a matter on which sellers and producers may compete. However, such competition can only be obtained, if at all, by enabling consumers to compare guarantees on different goods before deciding which one to buy.

In practical terms, however, few consumers will do so, and it seems unlikely that guarantees will ever be a true indicator of the quality of goods.

Conclusions

Whenever consumers buy goods, they take a gamble as to whether the goods will be of the quality they can reasonably expect. In view of the difficulty in conveying information about the quality of goods, it is vital that the basic standard set by Art. 2 of the Consumer Sales Directive is maintained as much as possible. It should only be possible to depart from this standard and go below it where the particular problem is clearly pointed out to the consumer, and the consumer is fully aware of (i) the implications for the usability of the goods and (ii) the costs involved in rectifying the problem. To the extent that they are aware, sellers should be encouraged to disclose defects, but they should do so in a manner that consumers understand the consequences. Only such a reading of Art. 2 (3) would approach anything like a solution to the information failure this provision is aimed at. Whether this can be achieved in practice remains to be seen.

Similarly, it is difficult to provide assurances to consumers that goods are of higher-than-average quality. Although voluntary guarantees may provide some assistance, their accuracy is very limited and therefore, guarantees may only be a very basic indicator. In an ideal world, there would be more information available about the quality of goods, but in every-day transactions, this is not possible. That is why strong, non-excludable quality standards are vital.

So is the strong information-based analysis of the Consumer Sales Directive, and sales law generally, misguided? Not necessarily, because there clearly are information-based elements to it. However, it does not seem right to express this in terms of an overall 'duty' or 'obligation' to disclose information. At best, there is an *encouragement* to disclose. The fallacy of the information analysis, i.e., in reducing consumer sales law to a lowest common denominator of information, is that the seller may not have all the relevant information, and/or the consumer will not be able to process information accurately. Far from enabling a consumer to make the most rational, wealth-maximizing and autonomous decision, accepting information as the panacea increases the risk of consumers making a wrong

---

54 Riesenhuber (2001), p. 354.

decision, unless it can be said with certainty that all information failures have been corrected.

References

Adler, R.S. (1994), 'The Last Best Argument For Eliminating Reliance From Express Warranties: "Real-World" Consumers Don't Read Warranties', 45, *South Carolina Law Review*, p. 429.

Agrawal, J., Richardson, P.S. and Grimm, P.E. (1996), 'The Relationship Between Warranty And Product Reliability', 30, *Journal of Consumer Affairs*, pp. 421-443.

Akerlof, G. (1970), 'The Market for "Lemons": Quality Uncertainty and the Market Mechanism', 84, *Journal of Law and Economics*, pp. 488-500.

Bearden, W.O. and Shimp, T.A. (1982), 'The use of extrinsic cues to facilitate product adoption', 19, *Journal of Marketing Research*, pp. 229-239.

Boulding, W. and Kirmani, A. (1993), 'A consumer-side experimentation of signalling theory: do consumers perceive warranties as signals of quality?', 20, *Journal of Consumer Research*, pp. 111-123.

Bradgate, R. and Twigg-Flesner, C. (2002), 'Expanding the Boundaries of Liability For Quality Defects', 25, *Journal of Consumer Policy*, pp. 345-377.

Bradgate, R. and Twigg-Flesner, C. (2003), *Blackstone's Guide to Consumer Sales and Associated Guarantees* (Oxford: Oxford University Press).

Commission of the European Communities (1993), *Green Paper on Guarantees for Consumer Goods and After-Sales Services*, COM (93) 509 final.

Department of Trade and Industry (DTI) (2001), *Consumer Knowledge Survey* (London: DTI).

Eddy, J.A. (1977), 'Effects Of The Magnuson-Moss Act Upon Consumer Product Warranties', 55, *North Carolina Law Review*, pp. 835-877.

Emons, W. (1989), 'On the Limitation of Warranty Duration', 37, *Journal of Industrial Economics,* pp. 287-301.

Gerner, J.L. and Bryant, W.K. (1981), 'Appliance Warranties as Market Signals', 15, *Journal of Consumer Affairs*, pp. 75-86.

Grossman, S. (1981), 'The Informational Role of Warranties and Private Disclosure about Product Quality', 24, *Journal of Law and Economics*, pp. 461-483.

Grundmann, S., Kerber, W. and Weatherill, S. (eds.) (2001), *Party Autonomy and the Role of Information in the Internal Market* (Berlin: de Gruyter).

Hadfield, G.K., Howse, R. and Trebilcock, M.J. (1998), 'Information-Based Principles For Rethinking Consumer Protection Policy', 21, *Journal of Consumer Policy*, pp. 131-169.

Hedley, S. (2001), 'Quality of Goods, Information, and the Death of Contract', *Journal of Business Law*, pp. 114-125.

Kelley, C.A. (1988), 'An Investigation of Consumer Product Warranties as Market Signals of Product Reliability', 16, *Journal of the Academy of Marketing Science*, pp. 72-78.

Lutz, N.A. (1989), 'Warranties as Signals under Consumer Moral Hazard', 20, *RAND Journal of Economics*, pp. 239-255.

Office of Fair Trading (OFT) (2000), *Consumer Detriment* (London: OFT).

Price, L.J. and Dawar, N. (2002), 'The Joint Effects of Brands and Warranties in Signalling New Product Quality', 23, *Journal of Economic Psychology*, pp. 165-190.

Purohit, D. and Srivastava, J. (2001), 'Effect of Manufacturer Reputation, Retailer Reputation and Product Warranty on Consumer Judgments of Product Quality: A Cue Diagnostic Framework', 10, *Journal of Consumer Psychology*, pp. 123-134.

Ramsay, I. (1989), *Consumer Protection Law – Cases and Materials* (London: Butterworths).

Riesenhuber, K. (2001), 'Party Autonomy and Information in the Sales Directive' in Grundmann, S., Kerber, W. and Weatherill, S. (eds.), *Party Autonomy and the Role of Information in the Internal Market* (Berlin: de Gruyter), pp. 348-370.

Rott, P. (2003), 'Minimum Harmonisation for the Completion of the Internal Market? The Example of Consumer Sales Law', 40, *Common Market Law Review*, pp. 1107-1135.

Schermaier, M.J. (2003), 'Rechtsangleichung und Rechtswissenschaft im kaufrechtlichen Sachmängelrecht' in Schermaier, M.J. (ed.), *Verbraucherkauf in Europa – Altes Gewährleistungsrecht und die Umsetzung der Richtlinie 1999/44/EG* (Munich: Sellier ELP).

Schwartz, A. and Wilde, L.L. (1983), 'Imperfect Information in Markets For Contract Terms: The Examples of Warranties and Security Interests', 69, *Virginia Law Review*, pp. 1387-1485.

Schwartze, A. (2000), *Europäische Sachmängelgewährleistung beim Warenkauf* (Tübingen: Mohr Siebeck), pp. 127-145.

Schwartze, A. (2003), 'Sachprobleme für die Umsetzung aus Genese, Inhalt und Dogmatik der Richtlinie über Verbraucherkäufe' in Schermaier, M.J. (ed.), *Verbraucherkauf in Europa – Altes Gewährleistungsrecht und die Umsetzung der Richtlinie 1999/44/EG* (Munich: Sellier ELP).

Shimp, T.A. and Bearden, W.O. (1982), 'Warranty and other extrinsic cue effects on Consumers' Risk Perceptions', 9, *Journal of Consumer Research*, pp. 38-46.

Spence, M. (1977), 'Consumer Misperceptions, Product Failure and Producer Liability', 44, *Review of Economic Studies*, pp. 561-572.

Srivastava, J. and Mitra, A. (1998), 'Warranty as a Signal of Quality: The Moderating Effect Of Consumer Knowledge On Quality Evaluations', 9, *Marketing Letters*, pp. 327-336.

Trebilcock, M.J. (1972), 'Manufacturers' Guarantees', 18, *McGill Law Journal*, pp. 1-44.

Trebilcock, M.J. and Elliott, S. (2001), 'The Scope and Limits of Legal Paternalism' in Benson, P. (ed.), *The Theory of Contract Law* (Cambridge: Cambridge University Press), pp. 45-85.

Twigg-Flesner, C. (2003), *Consumer Product Guarantees* (Aldershot: Ashgate).

Ulen, T.S. (2001), 'Information in the Market Economy – Cognitive Errors and Legal Correctives' in Grundmann, S., Kerber, W. and Weatherill, S. (eds.), *Party Autonomy and the Role of Information in the Internal Market* (Berlin: de Gruyter), pp. 98-129.

Wein, T. (2001), 'Consumer Information Problems – Causes and Consequences' in Grundmann, S., Kerber, W. and Weatherill, S. (eds.), *Party Autonomy and the Role of Information in the Internal Market* (Berlin: de Gruyter), pp. 80-97.

Willett, C. (1992), 'Consumer Guarantees, Citizen's Charters and Access to Justice', 11, *Civil Justice Quarterly*, pp. 99-105.

Whitford, W.C. (1973), 'The Function Of Disclosure Regulation In Consumer Transactions', 68, *Wisconsin Law Review*, pp. 400-470.

Wiener, J.L. (1985), 'Are warranties accurate signals of product reliability?', 12, *Journal of Consumer Research*, pp. 245-250.

Wilhelmsson, T. (2003), 'Private Law Remedies against Breach of Information Requirements of EC Law' in Schulze, R., Ebers, M. and Grigoleit, H.C. (eds.), *Informationspflichten und Vertragsschluss im Acquis communautaire* (Tübingen: Mohr Siebeck), pp. 245-265.

Chapter 9

Information and Product Liability – A Game of Russian Roulette?

Geraint Howells

Introduction

Information as an aspect of consumer rights has been developed mainly in the context of consumer contracting. Ensuring that the consumer is provided with sufficient information to determine whether he wants to enter into a contract is obviously a way of promoting his autonomy whilst not unduly interfering with the autonomy of the trader.[1] Although the trader's freedom is inhibited through procedural and information requirements these should not unduly inhibit innovation and in fact should promote competition (and hence innovation) through market forces. For many consumer contracts, where the risks associated with making a bad decision are economic in nature and often limited in impact, information rights are a sensible way of encouraging self-reliance by the consumer and transparency from traders. Of course, there are limits to such a laissez-faire attitude, especially where the contracts concerned are for high value, of long duration or involve consumers who may not be able to look after their own interests. These issues are explored by many of the other contributors.

This chapter is concerned with the role consumer information plays in relation to consumer safety and in particular its impact on liability. In relation to consumer safety it might be expected that information would play a lesser role. The principles of freedom and autonomy might suggest that consumers should be free to enter into a risky financial services contract so long as they are informed of the risks; but surely, consumers should not be allowed to expose themselves to dangerous products? Of course, safety is always a matter of degree. Some products are so unsafe that no degree of warning will justify their marketing to consumers, but for others product information can help to make them as safe as possible. Thus where it is accepted that products should be legitimately marketed despite posing some risks, information can be viewed as a sensible response. However, it will be suggested that whilst information has a role to play in making products safer in the public law of consumer safety, its role as a potential excluder of liability for products that have caused harm is more debateable. It will be suggested that where

1 Grundmann, Kerber and Weatherill (2001).

the consumer is asked to play a game of Russian roulette – in the sense that although he knows of the risks he cannot predict whether they will affect him personally or be present in any particular product – then information should not be an excluder of liability.

This book is primarily concerned with contractual fairness. This chapter could be seen as outside that framework as consumer safety is public law and product liability is traditionally viewed as tort liability. However, many of the issues discussed will be familiar to those who have read the contractual chapters. The responsibilities the parties have to inform one another and how that impacts on liability are not too dissimilar in the product liability context. This should not be entirely unexpected given that product liability can be viewed as having its origins in the contract law just as much as tort law. Contract law models of product liability tend to assess defectiveness by whether products fail to meet consumer expectations; tortious models are more centred around risk:utilty analysis. The European product liability directive[2] is concerned with whether a product 'does not provide the safety which a person is entitled to expect'.[3] Therefore it could be viewed as influenced by the contractual product liability model, which helps explain why the following discussions fit easily alongside contractual discussions.

Forms of Information

First, a few notes on the different forms of safety information provided with products may be in order. One key distinction is between information providing instructions on how to use a product and information warning consumers about the risks of products. Instructions for use provide ways in which products can be used safely. Lack of instructions or inadequate instructions may render the product unsafe. Some instructions relate to obvious risks and nothing else needs to be said as the instruction makes the risk obvious. Thus instructing that an eye guard should be worn when using an angle grinder, obviously relates to the risk of stone splintering off and damaging the eye. On the other hand, when the risk to which the instructions relate is not obvious, a warning as well as an instruction may have to be given. In a famous article Dillard and Hart cite the case of a new toothpaste that permanently discolours teeth if used more than twice a day.[4] The instruction 'For Best Results Use Twice Daily' or even 'Do not Use More Than Twice Daily' would be insufficient without an accompanying warning of the dangers of not complying with the instructions. The warning is needed to bring home the need to follow the instructions.

This last point can serve to underline an important general point about information and liability. Information should only affect liability when it makes a risk so obvious that it can be equated with a risk that does not need to be warned against. Even then it will be argued that the risk must be one which society accepts

2 Directive 85/374/EEC, OJ 1985 L 210/29.

3 Art. 6 (1).

4 Dillard and Hart (1955), pp. 145 *et seq.*

does not warrant compensation should harm materialize. In particular it will be argued that compensation will continue to be expected unless the consumer is both alerted to the risk and able by virtue of the information to avoid the risk.

Information and Safety

Public law controls on unsafe products place emphasis on the provision of information to make the product as safe as possible. Thus the latest General Product Safety Directive[5] includes in its definition of a safe product considerations of 'the presentation of the product, the labelling, any warnings and instructions for its use and disposal and any other indication or information regarding the producer'.[6] Producers must 'provide consumers with the relevant information to enable them to assess the risks inherent in a product throughout the normal or reasonably foreseeable period of its use where such risks are not immediately obvious without adequate warnings, and to take precautions against those risks'.[7] Member States must also have powers to require warnings to be given with respect to products that pose risks in certain conditions[8] or for certain persons.[9]

This chapter does not seek to discuss in detail the issues relating to the use of warnings in consumer safety law. It accepts that it may on occasions be legitimate to allow products to be marketed notwithstanding they carry risks and that warning of those risks is a responsible policy response. What is questioned is whether, just because public policy finds it socially acceptable to market the product, this should mean the warning immunizes the product from strict product liability.

Three criteria are studied: (i) the obviousness of the danger following the warning; (ii) the social acceptability of the risk; and (iii) the ability to avoid the harm following the warning. Criteria (i) and (iii) give rise to similar questions in both product liability and public consumer safety law concerning whether information has been effective in rendering a product safe. By contrast, criterion (ii) regarding the social acceptability asks fundamentally different questions. In consumer safety law the issue is whether it is acceptable to market the product in that condition with that warning; in product liability law the issue is whether it is socially acceptable that no compensation for harm is paid because of the presence of the warning. To be blunt, a producer might be allowed to market a product so long as he is prepared to pay for any harm caused.

---

5 Directive 201/95/EC, OJ 2002 L 11/4.
6 Art. 2 (b).
7 Art. 5 (1).
8 Art. 8 (b).
9 Art. 8 (c).

Strict Product Liability and the Rationale for Imposing Liability despite Warnings

The policy behind strict liability is notoriously difficult to discern. Indeed suggesting how the law is intended to apply is dangerous as the jurisprudence is still in its infancy in Europe and the Product Liability Directive gives no clear lead as to what the underlying rationale is. The drafter of the directive Professor Taschner clearly views it as a strict standard, whereas other commentators like Stapleton would place it closer to negligence.[10] In truth most commentators' viewpoints can find some support in the rather opaque wording of the Directive. Indeed as the motivations for the Directive were mixed it is hard to discern a clear underlying policy favouring one approach over another.

Hanson and Logue, admittedly in the perhaps unique context of tobacco liability, have argued for a strict regime that imposed liability on tobacco producers for all harm caused by smoking.[11] They argue that tobacco companies presently have incentives to minimize the impact of warnings and in fact are driven by market considerations to do so in order to remain competitive. Moreover given the insights of behavioural economics it is arguable that smokers are not always able to react rationally to such warnings. Therefore the only way forward is to impose the full costs of harm caused by the product on producers so that they will have incentives to reduce the harmful affects of their product so far as possible. The product price will also then reflect its true cost with a corresponding impact on demand.

Although the addictive qualities of tobacco raise special issues, it could be argued that the broad insights of behavioural economics concerning the ability of consumers to process information might suggest that this model of strict causation based liability should be extended to all products. This is, however, surely not the regime introduced by the Directive and probably not a realistic policy option.

Making the Risk Obvious

It seems safe to state that the intention was at least to exclude liability for inherent known risks, where it is nevertheless considered justifiable to market the product.[12] Some of these risks are so obvious that they do not need even to be warned of: everyday examples include the risk that a knife can cut you or that cars can be involved in accidents. Without additional factors being involved one would not make knife or car manufacturers liable just because their products were involved in accidents. Other risks are less obvious and a product will only be non-defective and avoid liability if the public is made sufficiently aware of the risk. That such warnings should be relevant seems implicit from the definition of defect that includes as a relevant circumstance the presentation of the product.[13]

---

10 See Taschner and Frietsch (1990); cf. Stapleton (1994).

11 Hanson and Logue (1998).

12 Dahl (1975) labels this 'system damage'.

13 Art. 6 (1)(a).

An interesting sub-set of questions relates to how information can best be communicated to the consuming public. When should the information be supplied – with the product (labelling, package inserts etc.) or through public information (the internet, consumer information campaigns, advertising). This chapter will look at two English cases which both raise different aspects of this interrelationship between private and public communication. The first case concerns toxic shock syndrome allegedly caused by a tampon, where it will be argued that one dimension of whether the instructions and warnings should suffice to absolve the producer of liability relates to whether the risk of that infection was sufficiently obvious to users to make them aware that there would be information they should read.[14] The second case concerns the supply of blood infected by Hepatitis C. This raised the issue of whether supplying information to a learned intermediary, such as a doctor, is adequate given that often the patient will not be in a condition to receive the information, for instance, when they come into hospital in an unconscious state. Moreover, whether the blood authorities could have done more by raising public awareness and how that impacts on liability will also be considered.

What is interesting is that awareness of a risk has to be assessed not merely on the basis of what information is provided directly with the product, but also through other information and media sources. The debate is likely to turn on whether it is enough for the user to have been warned of the risks or whether the warning has to be so clearly brought home to the consumer that he will accept it as an inherent risk in the product. In a strict liability regime it is not a question of whether the producer has behaved reasonably. Rather liability turns on whether the product meets the consumer's expectations. Unless a consumer is made clearly aware of risks, products will fail to meet their expectations. Risks mentioned in small type or hidden away on web-sites should not be found to have a sufficient impact on expectations.

Social Acceptability

Not all warnings will render the risks warned of socially acceptable. It would not be acceptable for a producer of a product that posed a high risk and offered little utility, or for which there was a ready substitute, to seek to escape liability simply by warning of the risk. For instance, clothing impregnated with a carcinogen would not be acceptable even with a warning.[15] More controversially it might be argued that if tobacco was introduced today, simply warning of its dangers might not justify its marketing.

However, some products can carry high risks and still be justifiably marketed. Thus a drug to counter HIV may be acceptable despite having severe, even

---

14 *Worsley* v. *Tambrands Ltd.* [2000] PIQR P95.

15 Such as the US children's night-wear treated with the fire-retardent chemical TRIS (2,3-dibromopropylphosphate). When it was found to be carcinogenic many manufacturers tried to sell their stock to developing countries leading to reforms in the law: see Schulberg (1979), p. 331.

possibly potentially fatal side-effects, if the potential benefits were correspondingly greater. Equally, given current social attitudes, tobacco is accepted so long as the risk of harm is explained.

A possible distinction between warnings in consumer safety and product liability laws can be detected. Although some products might be justifiably marketed with appropriate warnings and thus satisfy consumer safety laws, this might not excuse their producers from product liability. Thus, under 'the producer as insurer of the product' rationale for strict product liability, people who suffer side-effects, especially where these affect people randomly, should be compensated even if they have been warned of the risks. Equally if a cost internalization model is used then making producers pay for all the harm caused by their product can also be justified. Making tobacco (and other) producers pay for the harm their product caused can be seen to internalize the costs of the product and ensure only an efficient amount of it is consumed.[16]

Sometimes warnings are not given for justifiable reasons. The likely harm (taken as numbers affected × extent of harm) may not justify the need for a warning. Those affected should be within the scope of a strict product liability regime as the product did not afford the safety they were entitled to expect. Compensating them is more efficient than giving a warning. Where a warning is given the position is more complicated. The Hanson-Logue line could be followed to its conclusion by arguing that if the warning was not successful in avoiding harm the producer should nevertheless be liable. Such an approach might be justified by the sceptical approach to cognitive evaluation of risk highlighted by behavioural economics. However, there are also issues of individual self-responsibility and it seems clear that the Directive would not have intended to impose liability in all such circumstances. Nevertheless reasonableness should not be the touchstone of liability. The mere fact that the producer has given the best warning possible should not protect him. It will be argued that where the warning does not allow the producer to identify the risk precisely enough to permit the user to determine whether he will be affected then the risk should fall on the producer. This is in line with the Directive's intention to seek a 'fair apportionment of risks inherent in modern technological production'[17] and informed by studies which show that consumers are unable to properly process such risk calculations and tend to be over-optimistic that risks will not affect them. In particular it will be argued that warnings should not be excluders of liability when they warn of risks, but cannot predict who will be affected or which units of products carry the risk.

Warnings Must Allow the Risk to be Avoided

Thus the third criterion that the warning must allow the risk to be avoided, interacts with the second criterion of social acceptability. A warning may make products socially acceptable for the purposes of consumer safety laws if it is as specific as possible, but for it to be an excluder of product liability it must allow the consumer

16 Hanson and Logue (1998).

17 Recital 2.

to assess whether the risk will in fact affect him. It will be argued that a consumer should only be deprived of compensation because of a warning if it is sufficiently precise for him to avoid the harm. This is in fact a principle found in other areas such as occupier's liability where warnings of dangers on land will only be effective if they permit the visitor to be reasonably safe.[18]

Many warnings will do exactly that and show the consumer how to use the product safely. For instance, a warning might state that it is dangerous to use the product above a certain speed; for more than a certain period of time; or without safety equipment. Such warnings are in effect a form of instruction for use and so long as it is clearly brought to the consumer's attention so that the risk of behaving inappropriately is obvious, then most people would agree this would form part of the 'system damage' that falls outside the product liability regime. Any harm is the fault of the user not the product.

A problem arises when the warning relates to non-specific risks that the consumer cannot assess accurately. General warnings about the risks of stock market fluctuations seem generally to be accepted. The same should not be true of a warning relating to health and safety. Statements which says something like:

> 'This drug, like all drugs, can have side-effects' or
>
> 'All blood might be contaminated'

should not be acceptable. They add nothing. They are just too general to be meaningful and the only way to avoid the harm would be to avoid the product and that would not be a rational response to such a broad statement.

Sometimes warnings may not allow you to avoid a risk as such, except by deciding not to use the product at all. For instance, a drug may cause hair loss. If the drug was only used to reduce dandruff then presumably the risk is unacceptable given the limited benefits and the product should not be marketed at all. If the drug was treating a life threatening illness most people would accept that risk, but there should be a warning so the user can make an informed choice. The less serious the illness, the less likely that the risk will be acceptable, but arguably so long as the illness being treated is more serious, or might be considered by some to be more serious than hair loss, there is an argument that the product should be marketed so long as it is accompanied by the warning. If someone encounters a risk knowingly then there is an argument which says the risk becomes an obvious one and no compensation should be payable. It can be criticized that such an approach is mistaken, because it places too much emphasis on the ability of consumers to assess the warnings and make rational informed decisions. Nevertheless, under existing European law it would be hard to argue for liability where such warnings are sufficiently obvious and on balance the product is considered one that should legitimately be marketed.

---

18 See *Roles* v. *Nathan* [1963] 1 WLR 1117 where Lord Denning gave the example of a warning that the only means of access over a rotting footbridge was dangerous. If this was the only way to enter then the warning did not make the visitor reasonably safe.

Warnings are particularly useful from a regulatory perspective where the side-effects only affect a portion of the population. It would be an unjustified restriction on the general population to ban a product, just because some people suffer an adverse reaction to it. It has already been noted that in some instances the overall harm is so small that no warning need be given and yet a case can be made out for the producer having to pay compensation. Many of these will involve situations of mild and rare adverse reactions. In practice the courts will often find that a warning need not have been given. In other cases products will affect certain groups of consumers with such severity and/or in such numbers that on balance a warning would be expected. However, such warnings do not necessarily rule out compensation: this must depend on whether the warning made the risk obvious to the individual. That would turn on questions such as whether the user would be alert to that product posing such a risk and the nature and prominence of the warning given. This might depend therefore both on the quality of the information supplied with the product and general public education alerting at risk groups to seek out such warnings.

The scenarios considered so far concern risks that the consumer can decide whether he wants to encounter. The first situation covered risks inherent in the product for all consumers. Everyone knows the benefits of the product and the risks that come with the benefits. The second situation is the same save it is restricted to specific but identifiable at-risk groups, whose characteristics mean they face additional risks not shared by other users. It is assumed that the Directive did not intend for producers to be liable in such situations so long as the nature of the warning made it clear to users that they faced these risks. In contrast the next two scenarios involve warnings where the consumer knows there is a risk but is unable to predict whether he will be affected by it. One approach might be to suggest that if the consumer could calculate the percentage chance of his being affected, he should be free to decide on that basis whether he wants to use the product on the understanding that the producer will not be responsible should any harm materialize. However, this seems to be making it too easy for producers to evade their responsibilities. It fails to take sufficient account of the cognitive limitations of consumers and moreover does not differentiate between negligence and a strict liability regime. If strict liability is to mean anything more than negligence it should place the risk of calculating risks created by the product on the producer who seeks to benefit from its sale rather than the consumer who is less well positioned to assess such risks or take insurance against them occurring.

Sometimes the producer is able to say that a certain percentage of the population will suffer a particular side-effect, but cannot determine who will be affected. The side-effects are random. The consumer cannot be sure whether he will be affected, but he knows there is a risk that he will suffer a certain side-effect. In effect the consumer is being asked to play a game of Russian roulette. It is not irrational to consume the product or else the side-effects would have meant the product failed consumer safety law standards. Indeed, it is probably in most cases rational to take the risk. For example, some users of aspirin might suffer internal bleeding, but many people sensibly continue to use that drug. Even if that risk were warned about should the producers of aspirin be liable to compensate? It is a hard case as it is difficult to contemplate a court would actually find aspirin defective, but such random side-effects seem to be just the scenario that should be covered by risk spreading and cost internalization rationales for product liability. Aspirin is an emotive example as the idea of imposing strict liability for everyday products seems unreasonable, but strict liability is not about reasonableness. Aspirin, when it causes a user to bleed, does not provide the safety expected, because the user did not expect it to harm him. He knew there was a risk of harm, but could not react rationally to the information in order to avoid the risk. Using Aspirin as an example risks undermining my argument because so many people consider that it should fall outside a strict liability regime. Indeed most courts would probably not impose liability along the lines suggested. However, hopefully the reader can see the argument that if strict liability is to mean something different from negligence such cases are candidates for liability.

Would the position be different if the risk was specified? If you knew there was a one in two chance that you would be affected or a five in six chance say, is this different from a one in one million chance? These issues seem more related to whether the product should be marketed in the first place. If a product has a five in six chance of causing you harm then the harm must be very small in comparison to the benefit to justify the marketing of the product. Once the product is considered legitimate to market it essentially turns into an insurance question. The greater risk of harm the more insurance costs rise and hence the price of the product increases. As it becomes more expensive usually less of it is consumed or the product is priced out of the market. In the latter case if governments still consider it desirable for the product to be marketed they may have to offer subsidies, perhaps by stepping in as insurer of last resort.[19]

Another instance of the consumer being asked to play Russian roulette occurs when producers warn of a potential risk, but cannot tell the user whether any particular product is affected. A producer who can only say that there is a percentage chance that any particular product is contaminated, but that the affected products either cannot be detected or only at too great an expense may be justified in some circumstances, in marketing the product. We shall see that such an argument arises in relation to contaminated blood, where it was impossible to tell which samples were contaminated. Where expense is the only excuse this will not be a defence in a strict liability case. Equally an argument can be made out for compensation to be payable even where detection was impossible following the principle that the consumer should be given the means to avoid the risk. As on balance society must have assumed the product worth marketing, the rational consumer would expose himself to the risk and has no means on taking any steps to avoid harm, except for irrationally avoiding the product. Using the product should not imply the consumer agrees to give up his claim to compensation if the product harms him.

---

19 See US Swine Flu Act (1976) which made the Government rather than the producer the defendant in product liability claims.

Warnings and Exclusions

Warning of risks can come very close to being exclusions of risks. Indeed, general warnings should probably be treated as exclusion clauses and not be allowed. However, in a system based on defect rather than simple causation there must be a role for warnings fashioning expectations so that when a harm materializes it does not lead to liability. This should be where: (i) the warning made the risk so obvious that the consumer expected to encounter it, (ii) it was considered socially acceptable that the injured party is not compensated for the loss, (iii) and the consumer had the means to avoid a known and predictable risk either by not using the product or using it in an safe manner. In essence the harm must have been caused by the consumer freely accepting a risk.

***Worsley* v. *Tambrands Ltd.*[20]**

Mrs Worsley had suffered toxic shock syndrome after using a tampon. Her claim for compensation turned on whether the warnings had been adequate. The package contained a warning about the risk of toxic shock syndrome, but that notice directed the reader to a leaflet within the box and advised the reader to 'read and save the enclosed information'. The leaflet listed a series of symptoms including vomiting and diarrhoea and said: 'If you have any of these symptoms and are using a tampon, remove it and contact your doctor for immediate treatment, telling him you have been using a tampon'. The claimant had lost the leaflet and failed to consider toxic shock syndrome as she believed that since the symptoms had lasted for more than a few days it could not be that or else she would have been dead by then. Had she retained and read the leaflet she would have been warned that the syndrome can cause flu like symptoms rapidly to move to a serious illness that might be fatal. Originally she thought it had been food poisoning following a wedding. She mentioned that she was menstruating to her doctor, but not the fact she was using a tampon.

The judge held that it was appropriate to have a warning on the package referring to an insert and that the leaflet was 'legible, literate, and unambiguous and contained all the material necessary to convey both the warning signs and action required if any of them were present'. The injury was really due to the loss of the leaflet or the failure to replace it. In particular the judge held that it was reasonable to rely on a warning on the package and that the warning was satisfactory despite more prominent and detailed warnings being given in the US. The differences were explainable by the multi-lingual nature of the British leaflet. Of course all these conclusions sound reasonable, but strict liability does not necessarily turn on what is reasonable. It is not argued that the outcome was necessarily wrong in this particular case. Rather it is hoped to demonstrate simply

20 [2000] PIQR P95.

that the facts could be looked at in a different light when judged against the criteria of obviousness, social acceptability and avoidability.

Obviousness

It was interesting that Mrs Worsley's awareness of toxic shock syndrome increased after reading an article about it in a women's magazine in 1985 or 1986, which caused her to re-read the insert leaflet. In fact the leaflet at that time stressed the rareness of the syndrome, simply mentioned some symptoms and advised seeing a doctor. Only in the 1990s did the explanations expand and become more detailed.

Was the risk so well known that anyone using the product would treat it as an inherent risk? It is hard, perhaps, for a man to answer that question. Objectively the warning on the package would seem to suggest it is. But there must be an element of doubt as to whether people take much notice of such warnings on everyday products. This is not to critizise the use of warnings, but simply to suggest that sometimes liability might be justified despite the use of all reasonable warnings. Indeed Mrs Worsley seemed a well educated person, being a graduate and a primary school teacher at the time of the incident, but she had been using the product for five years before reading the magazine article that alerted her to the dangers. Especially with younger users of the product, whether the danger is so obvious as to be regarded as an inherent risk is perhaps debateable. Awareness probably depends as much on health education and media profile of the danger, as with the warnings accompanying the packaging. Although the risk is extremely serious the rareness of the danger may dilute it in the minds of consumers so they do not consider it as an inherent risk every time they use the product.

Social Acceptability

Tampons are a regular part of many women's monthly routine. The small risk of toxic shock syndrome may be considered justified given the practical utility of the product. In might be countered that there are practical alternatives in the form of sanitary pads, but the small additional risk associated with tampons might be justified as they give women the choice of method for controlling their menstruation. However, it may be a different analysis if one asks whether tampon manufacturers should be responsible for harm caused by their product. Given the rareness of the syndrome, the possible impact of that on women's awareness and the difficulties of avoiding the risk (mentioned below), the public might consider it acceptable that the cost be internalized to tampon producers in their role as 'insurer'.

Avoidability

The leaflet does advise consulting the doctor if certain symptoms occur. Those suffered by Mrs Worsley – vomiting and diarrhoea – although listed on the leaflet are, however, also unfortunately quite common. Many people would not immediately link them to the use of a tampon. Indeed Mrs Worsley first linked it to possible food poisoning suffered at a wedding. The judge impliedly criticized her for telling the doctor she was menstruating, but not mentioning that she was using a tampon. However, this seems harsh for faced with those symptoms one might in fact have expected the doctor (rather than the ill patient) to have asked about tampon use. Certainly this suggests that Mrs Worsley's mistake was understandable and that is was not necessarily an easy thing to avoid the risk by following the instructions, laudable and well intentioned though they might be.

Moreover, the instructions only tell you how to react once the symptoms emerge. Presumably by stopping using a tampon and visiting a doctor for treatment the disease can be treated, but it clearly would not prevent it from being contracted. Tampons involve a non-specific risk that consumers have to weigh up when deciding whether to use the product. Still, given that the risk cannot be avoided otherwise than by avoiding the product (which may not be a rational response), there may be grounds for justifying compensation even if the product has been legitimately and responsibly marketed.

A v. *National Blood Authority*[21]

At a time when there was no way of detecting Hepatitis C, the National Blood Authority supplied blood that carried the risk of infecting patients. The medical community was informed about the risks, but not the general public. In a judgement acclaimed by many as very pro-claimant Mr Justice Burton held the authority liable.[22] It was indeed, in many respects, a remarkably strong endorsement of strict liability. He was vigorous in ensuring the assessment of defectiveness did not slip back into the language of negligence and held that avoidability of harm was not a relevant circumstance in a strict liability regime. However, this chapter will concentrate on what the judgment tells us about the role of information in the product liability regime.

Obviousness

In typically forthright terms the judge made it clear that it was not inappropriate of the public to 'expect the unattainable',[23] unless it had been informed that it was unattainable or impossible. The public could not be expected to play a game of Russian roulette. The blood would only be non-defective if the risk was socially acceptable and for that there needed to be at least publicity and probably warnings.[24]

Here one sees support for the idea that the risk must be obvious. Whether the standard is quite as high as that suggested in this chapter is unclear as the judge did

21 [2001] 3 All ER 289.
22 Howells and Mildred (2002), p. 95.
23 *A* v. *National Blood Authority* [2001] 3 All ER 289, para. 57.
24 *A* v. *National Blood Authority* [2001] 3 All ER 289, para. 65.

not go into detail, but his reference to the probable need for express warnings suggests a fairly demanding standard. Moreover, there is some hesitation in the judgment about whether warnings can ever exempt liability given the prohibition on exclusions in Art. 12. Certainly this is a point the judge has been keen to debate in academic seminars subsequent to the case and perhaps serves to emphasize that the courts will most likely be rigorous in assessing the extent to which the risk has been drawn to the public's attention.

There are further problems in applying this obviousness standard, both in general and to blood in particular. For most products the warning would presumably be required to be on the product or its packaging. This would raise the same debates as in *Worsley* v. *Tambrands Ltd.* about the positioning, prominence and form of warning. For blood, however, this is often not an option. Many patients may indeed come into a hospital unconscious and there may be no opportunity for consultation before blood is given to them. Assuming the debate about safety should not be purely one carried out within medical circles,[25] how should the National Blood Authority have informed the public about the risks to give itself a chance of defending a strict liability claim? Simply posting something on its website should not be enough: few citizens could be expected to consult that site. Presumably it should attempt to place stories in the media so that knowledge of the risk becomes such that all (or by far the majority) know that all blood carries the risk of being contaminated with Hepatitis C. However, it will be a very difficult call for the judge to make as to whether sufficient efforts have been made so that the risk can be said to be obvious to the public.

Social Acceptability

Simply making a risk obvious to the public does not make it socially acceptable. Mr Justice Burton seems to suggest that knowledge of the risk was a pre-condition for a finding of non-defectiveness, not the basis for excluding liability in itself. Of course, since the risk had not been drawn to the public's attention there was no need for the judge to dwell on which risks would be socially acceptable. In fact he only really raises the issue of whether Art. 12 prevents warnings from serving as excluders of liability and does not touch on the more fundamental question of what inherent risks are socially acceptable. Here socially acceptable refers not merely to social acceptability in the sense of justifying their marketing, but also as a shield from liability to pay compensation.

In the *National Blood Authority* case various factors made the judge's task of imposing liability less difficult than it might have been. First, the defendant was a state quango and not a private company. Although a private law dispute, it might be thought to be easier to take on board public policy debates about the responsibility of the suppliers of products when the state is the ultimate defendant. Second, a method of detecting Hepatitis C has subsequently been developed and so the problem was limited in scale and not on-going for the future. Finally, it seems important that the judge was able to use hindsight analysis to separate out the

---

25 Cf. Hodges (2001), p. 528.

contaminated blood and to characterize it as non-standard. Indeed he describes as too philosophical the argument that the defect might lie in the risk, present in all the blood, that it might be contaminated.[26]

However, let us take as an example the possible case of British blood carrying a risk of CJD contamination. Such a risk may exist since most countries refuse to accept blood from people who have lived in Britain during the 'mad cow' crisis. Such a risk is probably not obvious to the British public, but, if it were, would it be socially acceptable? One argument against acceptability would be that blood should have been used from overseas sources. However, even if the British public is sanguine enough to accept that such steps could not be justified on economic grounds and was willing to accept exchanges of blood from within its citizenry, the answer might be very different when it came to compensation. They might be prepared to play Russian roulette so long as the consequences of losing were tempered for them and their families by compensation. Once again we see that social acceptability can have a different function in consumer safety than in product liability.

Avoidability

Clearly in the *National Blood Authority* case any warning would have had little impact. There was no alternative product that was safer and often there would be no choice as to whether or not to use the product. Mr Justice Burton characterized the defect as the contamination of the blood. In reality one suspects it was more the failure to warn of the risk of contamination, but if this line had been taken then it would have been a viable argument to suggest the defect had not caused the harm. One suspects few people needing a blood transfusion would have changed their mind and refused on being informed of a marginal risk that could not be avoided. Mr Justice Burton mentioned that patients would not expect to play a game a Russian roulette.[27] It is unclear as to the extent to which the judge would accept no liability for engaging in such a game where the risks were known of and socially acceptable in the consumer safety sense. Where the risks are undetectable and the consumer is forced into a game of Russian roulette one can make a convincing argument for why society might not criminalize such products under consumer safety law, but might still impose civil product liability. The product should bear its full social costs and the injured be compensated through the price paid by those who benefit from the product (rather than the society as a whole). In many ways this is the ideal situation for strict product liability to apply – in a context when no blame need be attached to the producer, but nevertheless he should be accountable for the harm caused by his products.

---

26 *A* v. *National Blood Authority* [2001] 3 All ER 289, para. 65.

27 *A* v. *National Blood Authority* [2001] 3 All ER 289, para. 65.

Russian Roulette?

Product liability does not compensate for all harms linked to the use of products. The problem is that beyond the incantation that liability does not depend upon the reasonableness of the producer's conduct, there is no certainty as to what is included within the definition of defect. Information, instructions for use and warnings all seem to provide mechanisms through which producers can limit their liability leaving consumers to play a game of Russian roulette with many products. It may seem desirable, sensible or necessary for them to use the product, but there is no way of knowing whether they will be the victim of acceptable risks. Information may justify the marketing of products with acceptable risks, but should it absolve the manufacturer of liability for harm caused when those rules materialize? Three criteria have been put forward as prisms through which to assess that question – obviousness, social acceptability and avoidability. Information should be an enhancer of consumer safety, not simply an easy way for producers to avoid liability for the harm caused by their products.

References

Dahl, B. (1975), 'Product Liability in Denmark', in European Association for Legal and Fiscal Studies (ed.), *Product Liability in Europe* (Deventer: Kluwer).

Dillard, H.C. and Hart, H. (1955), 'Product Liability: Directions for Use and Failure to Warn', 41, *Virginia Law Review*, pp. 145 *et seq.*

Grundmann, S., Kerber, W. and Weatherill, S. (eds.) (2001), *Party Autonomy and the Role of Information in the Internal Market* (Berlin: de Gruyter).

Hanson, J.D. and Logue, K.D. (1998), 'The Cost of Cigarettes: The Economic Case for Ex Post Incentive-Based Regulation', 107, *Yale Law Journal*, pp. 1163 *et seq.*

Hodges, C. (2001), 'Compensating Patients', 117, *Law Quaterly Review*, pp. 528 *et seq.*

Howells, G. and Mildred, M. (2002), 'Infected Blood: Defect and Discoverability: A First Exposition of the EC Product Liability Directive', 65, *Modern Law Review*, pp. 95 *et seq.*

Taschner, H.C. and Frietsch, E. (1990), *Produkthaftungsgesetz und EG-Produkthaftungsrichtlinie*, 2nd edn. (Munich: Beck).

Schulberg, F. (1979), 'United States Export of Products Banned for Domestic Use', 2, *Harvard International Law Journal*, pp. 331 *et seq.*

Stapleton, J. (1994), *Product Liability* (London: Butterworths).

Chapter 10

Duties to Inform versus Party Autonomy: Reversing the Paradigm (from Free Consent to Informed Consent)? – A Comparative Account of French and English Law

Ruth Sefton-Green

L'obligation pour l'homme de renseigner ses semblables dans certaines circonstances, dite obligation de renseignements, [...] constitue l'une des manifestations de cet esprit de solidarité qui caractérise notre époque, par réaction contre l'individualisme excessif du XIXème siècle.[1]

Introduction

Why are duties to inform opposed to party autonomy?[2] Do duties to inform play a role in reversing the paradigm of party autonomy in the law of contracts, and if so, what role? If party autonomy no longer prevails, does a new pattern of behaviour and expectations between contracting parties bring us closer to achieving contractual fairness?

In order to explain why party autonomy and duties to inform are in opposition with one another the motto of '*Liberté, Egalité, Fraternité*' will be used as a

---

1 De Juglart (1945), p. 1.

2 It is self-evident that party autonomy is an indeterminate notion. It may encompass a nineteenth century libertarian view of contract as well as a welfarist-fairness oriented view of contract – see for example Trebilcock (1993), pp. 241 *et seq*. Furthermore, the concept of autonomy needs to be clarified. Broadly speaking it encompasses the idea that a person has control or influence over his actions: this inevitably means making choices. For an explanation of autonomy as a 'self-rule', see Smith (1996), p. 177, who offers a 'positive liberty' conception of autonomy, suggesting that autonomy must be exercised in the pursuit of the valuable.

metaphor. Party autonomy can be assimilated to freedom of contract:[3] here is *liberté*. In the classical version of contract, freedom of contract and the autonomy of the parties are paramount.[4] The classical belief presumes that the parties are equal: here is *égalité*.[5] However, these two presumptions have long since been decried; an awareness of the parties' inequality highlights the deficiency of classical contract values. It is widely admitted that in an increasing number of contractual situations the parties are neither free nor equal. Next, it is contended that the classical paradigm needs to be reversed, *inter alia*, since the prevailing value of party autonomy is anachronistic.[6] Indeed very few contracts actually fit the classical model today: it represents myth rather than reality. Moreover, greater recognition of the need for contractual fairness means that the paradigm must be changed because party autonomy and freedom of contract often lead to contractual unfairness.[7]

It is submitted that contractual fairness may be achieved by putting a greater emphasis on contractual solidarity: here is *fraternité*. Freedom, equality and solidarity must all be present in order to achieve this ideal. This needs explaining.

Schematically, there are two conceptions of the contract: the first where the binding force of contract is based on party autonomy and free consent.[8] This model represents the contract as a compromise of conflicting adversarial interests from

3 Likewise, freedom of contract has many meanings: see for example, Brownsword (2000), pp. 36 *et seq.* who identifies freedom to contract (party freedom), freedom of contract (term freedom) and sanctity of contract. The second narrow meaning of term freedom, which means that the law respects party autonomy, is adopted here.

4 See Atiyah (1979).

5 Atiyah (1979), pp. 402 *et seq.* points out that the notion of dealing 'at arms length' is crucial to the model of the market upon which the classical law of contract is based. See also Collins (2003), pp. 22 *et seq.*, who suggests that the market order respects the ideal of equality in that everyone has the opportunity to make transactions and attain social improvement.

6 Party autonomy can be criticized on the grounds that it is old-fashioned as it represents nineteenth century classical values of contract which no longer correspond to the needs of 21st century contract making. See Atiyah (1979), Part III on 'The Decline and Fall of Freedom of contract', pp. 571 *et seq.* The criticisms are too numerous to cite here, they may be based on, *inter alia,* welfarist concerns for the protection of the consumer or awareness of economic dependence, see Collins (2003), Chapter 2 on 'The Transformation of the Law of Contract', pp. 20 *et seq.*

7 Indeed the classical theory of contract is not over-concerned with considerations of fairness, see Atiyah (1979), pp. 402 *et seq.* evoking a 'retreat from interest in substantive justice or fairness'.

8 In French law, the will theory (*le principe de l'autonomie de la volonté*) plays an important role in this viewpoint, see Gounot (1912). For a criticism of the autonomy of the will as founding a modern basis for the law of contract, see Ghestin (1993), pp. 27 *et seq.* On the influence of this theory on the English law of contract see Atiyah (1979), pp. 405 *et seq.*

which it is inferred that each party behaves individualistically.[9] The rule of *caveat emptor*, long prevailing in the English contract of sale, sums up this viewpoint: the parties do not have a duty to inform one another of facts unknown to the other and each person looks after his own interests. The second conception posits that solidarity[10] lies at the heart of the contract, on the basis that each party has a positive duty to help and cooperate with the other contracting party; that the parties must behave transparently towards one another. Duties to inform must be imposed to produce informed consent[11] and to enable the parties to work together.[12] It follows that the model focusing on duties to inform, as means of achieving contractual solidarity, is opposed to that of party autonomy. The antithesis can be summarized by antagonism versus co-operation.

This chapter endeavours to explain the relationship between duties to inform and contractual solidarity and examines whether imposing duties to inform does actually reverse the paradigm of party autonomy towards increasing contractual fairness. A preliminary methodological explanation is necessary: this chapter aims to give a comparative account of French and English law. Since French law has recognized and imposed duties to inform, by case law and legislation, to a greater extent than English law, French law will mainly be used as a starting point for comparison. However, this method has proved somewhat tricky since it will be seen that in attempting a comparison sometimes there is a gap, or at other times the comparison falls in an unexpected place. Moreover, certain concepts and methodological choices need to be explained.

Defining the Scope of Duties to Inform

The term duties to inform will be used rather than information rights and obligations since duties to inform correspond to the French concept of *l'obligation d'information*. A semantic distinction may be helpful: duties to inform are referred to as duties of disclosure in English law. In my view, there is a difference between disclosing and informing, disclosure presupposes that one has something to hide which must be disclosed or divulged whereas informing does not connote the same idea.[13] Information has a wider scope than disclosure since one party can inform

---

9 Brownsword (2000), pp. 15 *et seq.* refers to this underlying ethic of contract law as individualism where priority is given to one's self-interest. For a judicial recognition of this principle see *Walford* v. *Miles* [1992] 2 AC 128, per Lord Ackner, at p. 138.

10 See Demogue (1932), no. 3, p. 9: 'Les contractants forment une petite société où chacun doit travailler dans un but commun qui est la somme des buts individuels poursuivis par chacun'.

11 If duties to inform aim to improve the quality of the parties' consent it may be inferred that such duties have as their goal merely procedural (as opposed to substantive) requirements. This inference must be verified.

12 This may be described as co-operativism, where each party gives equal value to his own interests, rather than giving priority to one party's interests. See Brownsword (2000), pp. 15 *et seq.*

13 See Sefton-Green (forthcoming), General Introduction.

the other of information which is not necessarily secret or exclusive to the party who possesses it.[14] Another distinction must be highlighted: duties to inform must be differentiated from duties to advise. There can be an overlap between these two duties in the sense that sometimes it is not entirely clear where informing ends and advising begins.[15] Moreover, in English law, failure to inform or advise or giving negligent advice may be the subject matter of tort rather than of contract.[16] It can be inferred that duties to inform in some relationships are inevitably related to issues of professional liability, classified as contractual in some legal systems and tortious in others. This observation highlights the inevitably asymmetrical nature of comparative analysis.

What Constitutes a Breach of a Duty to Inform?

To start with, if a party is under a duty to inform, his failure to do so constitutes a breach. However, it is submitted that information rights also imply that the party receiving information has a right not only to receive certain information, but also that the information supplied is true and accurate. It follows therefore that a breach of a duty to inform can also be constituted by a party informing defectively. The English concept of misrepresentation fits this pattern since representations (statements or conduct) given negligently, fraudulently or innocently are inaccurate and untrue information.[17] However, English law only requires that the information given is true, which is not the same as requiring that the information must be given in the first place.[18] In this respect, the positive obligation incumbent on contracting parties differs in French and English law. There is no general duty to disclose facts

---

14 A related issue is how much information is necessary for a contracting party to exercise an autonomous choice: see Trebilcock (1993), Chapter 2 on 'Asymmetric Information Imperfections', p. 103, citing Scheppele (1988), p. 25, who suggests that information plays a dual role in rational choice theory.

15 For example, advice may cover providing information as to risk and the options for treatment in a contract between doctor and patient or advice may cover information given in relation to the fitness for purpose of goods in a contract of sale. See below for examples.

16 *Hedley Bryne & Co.* v. *Heller & Partners Ltd.* [1964] AC 465.

17 Cartwright (2002).

18 To illustrate this idea, it is worth recalling that an attempt to exclude liability for misrepresentation would have to satisfy the reasonableness provisions of Section 3 of the Misrepresentation Act 1967 or Section 2 (2) of the Unfair Contract Terms Act 1977, whereas a clause excluding liability for non-disclosure was recently held to be valid in the Court of Appeal for the simple reason that no such duty to disclose exists in English law, therefore such a duty can be excluded by the parties. See *National Westminster Bank* v. *Utrecht-America Finance Co.* [2001] EWCA Civ. 658.

known to one party and not to the other in English law[19], such duties only arise as an exception: the classic example being contracts of insurance (*uberrimae fidei*).

It is thus inferred that a breach of a duty to inform can either be an omission, a failure to inform, or that performance has been defective in the sense that the party who is under the duty has not informed, i.e. by not giving all the information or by giving inaccurate information etc. This is important since French law treats the different kinds of breach of a duty to inform under different heads (of defective consent and precontractual liability respectively). A failure to inform gives rise to liability under the head of *dol* or fraud, understood as *réticence dolosive* or fraudulent concealment[20] whereas defective performance may either be ordinary fraud (*dol*) or a *faute* under Arts. 1382 *et seq.* of the *Code civil.*[21] Under English law, by contrast, an innocent party can rely on the Misrepresentation Act 1967, which covers innocently and negligently supplied information, as well as the separate tort of deceit.[22] However, an aggrieved party cannot invoke a failure to inform (breach by omission) in English law, unless a specific duty to inform exists.

Methodological Choices

In order to examine whether duties to inform can be linked to contractual solidarity and to illustrate how, or whether, such duties can reverse the paradigm of party autonomy, concrete examples of recent case law will be used from which a number of inductive observations will be made. No attempt is made to be exhaustive; cases have been chosen as illustrations and the presentation proceeds on the basis of the type of contract under review. A deliberate choice has been adopted not to classify in terms of stereotypes such as the relationship between persons acting in the course of business and consumers and/or relationships involving two parties acting in the course of business.[23] It will become apparent that duties to inform are not just imposed in situations where parties are obviously unequal, although this is often the case. Moreover, if the parties are unequal, this does not mean that there is

---

19 *Bell* v. *Lever Bros.* [1932] AC 161, *Norwich Union Life Insurance Co. Ltd.* v. *Qureshi* [1999] 2 All ER (Comm) 707, *Clarion Ltd.* v. *National Provident Institution* [2000] 1 WLR 1888, at p. 1905.

20 Art. 1116 of the *Code civil*: 'Le dol est une cause de nullité de la convention lorsque les manœuvres pratiquées par l'une des parties sont telles, qu'il est évident que, sans ces manœuvres, l'autre partie n'aurait pas contracté. Il ne se présume pas, et doit être prouvé'. See Ghestin (1993), pp. 519 *et seq.*, especially 534 *et seq.*

21 Art. 1382 of the *Code civil*: 'Tout fait quelconque de l'homme, qui cause à autrui un dommage, oblige celui par la faute duquel il est arrivé, à le réparer'. See Ghestin (1993), pp. 565 *et seq.*

22 See Cartwright (2002).

23 For example, when considering the relationship between doctor and patient, is it apt to classify the doctor-patient relationship in the category of professionals and consumers? A series of questions follow: do patients have a choice? Do they act as rational agents on the market? Can the provision of public health-care be compared to the provision of goods and services on a private and competitive market?

a 'weak' and a 'strong' party. More precisely, it is necessary to assess constantly, which party is weak, which party is strong and why. Nor can it be assumed that the weaker party is automatically the person who is the recipient of the information.[24] Duties to inform are also imposed where the parties are supposed to be equal; it is necessary to investigate whether the difference is one of nature or of degree.

Doctor-Patient Relationship

First, the most startling evolution in French case law regarding the increasing imposition of the duty to inform has been in the doctor-patient relationship. Of course, it may be contended that this is not the best example because of the special nature of the relationship between doctor and patient. Be that as it may, it is a highly instructive example particularly as case law in other types of contracts has mirrored some of the evolutions in this particular field.[25] It should be recalled that claims made by a patient against a doctor must be contractual in French law,[26] since the refusal to admit concurrent liability in contract and tort (*le principe de non-cumul*) precludes a patient from bringing an action in tort,[27] unless the patient is not party to a contract with the doctor (e.g. a child making a claim against a doctor for a harm arising out of a situation which occurred during the mother's pregnancy etc.).

Two points[28] in relation to a doctor's duty to inform his patient are of interest:

Particular obligation to inform and burden of adducing evidence In 1997 the *Cour de cassation* held that:

> A doctor is under a particular obligation to inform his patient and it is incumbent on him to adduce the evidence that he has fulfilled this obligation.[29]

---

24 See, for an example, the insurance contract below.

25 The rule reversing the burden of proof has been applied to *notaires*, architects, and more recently *avocats*. In relation to the latter, see *Cour de cassation, 1re chambre civile* (*Cass. 1re civ.*), 29 April 1997, *Revue trimestrielle de droit civil* (*RTD civ.*) 1997, p. 925, where it was held that *avocats* must prove they have fulfilled their duty to inform (cf. Art. 1315 (2) *Code civil*). This is interpreted as amounting to a reinforcement of the existence of the duty to inform.

26 *Cass. 1re civ.*, 20 May 1936, *Mercier. Dalloz (D.)* 1939.I. 88 *concl.* Matter, *rapp.* Josserand.

27 Viney and Jourdain (1998), pp. 698 *et seq.*

28 The third trend exceeds the scope of this enquiry since it concerns a tortious claim for lack of information given by a doctor to a claimant's mother at the moment of the child's birth. *Cass. 1re civ.*, 9 October 2001, *D.* 2001, p. 3470, *rapp.* Sargos, *note* D. Thouvenin. The case is extremely important since it gives a constitutional flavour to a doctor's duty to inform stating that the medical obligation to inform is derived from respect for the constitutional principle of safeguarding a person's dignity ('dans l'exigence du respect du principe constitutionnel de sauvegarde de la dignité de la personne humaine').

As a preliminary observation, it should be noted that by stating that the doctor is under a 'particular duty to inform', the duty itself, derived by case law is both recognized and reinforced. Secondly, the *Cour de cassation*'s formula (based on Art. 1315 (2) of the *Code civil*) has reversed the ordinary rules about the burden of proof.[30] Until this decision the patient had to prove the existence of the obligation incumbent on the doctor and that the obligation had not been performed, i.e. that he had not been informed. This decision reverses the burden of proof[31] in that the onus now lies on the doctor to prove that he has fulfilled his duty to inform, not on the patient to prove he has *not* been informed.[32] If the doctor fails to prove he had informed the patient, the latter will obtain a remedy for the breach, evaluated as the loss of his opportunity to refuse treatment (*perte d'une chance*).[33] The consequence of this decision and its interpretation are not open to doubt since the duty to inform and the onus of proof on doctors have been incorporated in the *Code de la santé publique* by a law of 2002.[34] As already mentioned, the reversal of the burden of proof is a trend that has been applied to other types of contracts. At first sight, the emphasis on an evidential rule might lead us to infer that the end-goal is procedural fairness and not substantive fairness.[35] However, it will be observed that reversing

---

29 *Cass. 1re civ.*, 25 February 1997, *Bulletin civil* (*Bull. civ.*) I, no. 75; *Gazette du Palais* (*Gaz. Pal.*) 1997.I.274, *rapp.* Sargos, *note* Guigue; *Juris-Classeur periodique* (*Semaine juridique*) (*JCP*) 1997.I.40255, no. 7, *obs.* G. Viney; *RTD civ.* 1997, 434, *obs.* P. Jourdain; *RTD civ.* 1997, 925, *note* J. Mestre and B. Fages.

30 Art. 1315 of the *Code civil*: 'Celui qui réclame l'exécution d'une obligation doit la prouver. Réciproquement, celui qui se prétend libéré, doit justifier le payement ou le fait qui a produit l'extinction de son obligation'.

31 On one reading this amounts to a literal interpretation of the evidential rules contained in Art. 1315 of the *Code civil.*

32 Some commentators have suggested, *RTD civ.* 1997, p. 925, *note* J. Mestre and B. Fages, that it would be in the doctors' interest to clarify the risk to their patients and that it would be advisable to get patients to sign a paper (not to relieve the doctor of liability) but to constitute evidence that the patients have been informed. See also Noiville (1999).

33 See Viney and Jourdain (1998), pp. 71 *et seq.*, 194 *et seq.*, on the case law concerning the concept of the loss of a chance. It should be noted that the dividing line between creating a risk (by a failure to warn) and the loss of a chance (arising out of a lack of information) is extremely fine. Using the loss of a chance as a means to compensate partially the loss has been criticized either because compensation is inadequate as partial or because compensation is governed by arbitrary principles of evaluation. The courts, however, continue to use the concept as a palliative, in order to compensate the loss. Confirmed again, more recently *Cass. 1re civ.*, 13 November 2002, *Legros épouse Riallant* v. *Duval et autres, Bull. civ.* I, no. 265, where it was held that if there was no evidence that the absence of information caused a loss, i.e. the patient would have had to have the operation anyway (whether informed or not), then there is no claim for compensation.

34 Art. L. 1111-2 (7) of the *Code de santé publique* states: (*Loi* no. 2002-303 of 4 March 2002): in case of litigation it is up to the professional or institution to adduce evidence that the information had been delivered to the interested person in the conditions provided for by law.

35 Atiyah (1988), pp. 329 *et seq.*

the burden of proof can have an effect on the content and significance of the duty to inform. Moreover, it can also be induced that obliging doctors to inform their patients about the risks of proposed treatment, for example, changes the nature of the relationship between the parties. There is inevitably more transparency between the contracting parties: indeed in view of the special nature of confidence inherent in a doctor-patient relationship, it would seem irrelevant to talk in terms of party autonomy. The explanation can even be reversed: it is because of a need for confidence and trust between the contracting parties that it is necessary to impose a duty to inform since imposing this duty has the effect of reinforcing the parties' confidence in one another. It is in this respect that it is suggested that imposing a duty to inform may have the consequence of imposing norms of behaviour.[36] Imposing a duty to inform on the doctor also conditions the patient's freedom to contract. If the patient subsequently consents to the proposed medical treatment, his freedom to do so is understood in the light of his fully informed consent. Making an induction from this instance, it is thus contended that duties to inform come first, freedom of contract second.[37] In other words, consent is understood in the light of information given prior to the contract's conclusion. It might even be said that information pre-conditions consent.

'Honest, clear and appropriate' information In 1998[38] the *Cour de cassation* emphasized the quality and content of the information to be given in that it must be 'honest, clear and appropriate'.[39] This illustrates once again the expectation of transparent behaviour between the contracting parties. Moreover, it can be inferred that information that is honest and clear must also be exact. As mentioned above, the duty to inform implies the duty to give accurate information, or to put it another way, coincides with a moral duty to tell the truth.

Without getting side-tracked by the many issues involved in this type of relationship, it is important to focus on contractual fairness. It has been suggested that this new model, allowing patients access to full information replaces a former model of medical paternalism.[40] Furthermore, the consequences of the change need emphasizing. If the doctor-patient relationship moves away from a paternalistic

36 See Sefton-Green (forthcoming).

37 See the law of 2 March 2002. The statement is perhaps categorical and needs to be nuanced since the patient's consent prevails over and above the doctor's duty to treat patients and to save life and has also altered the nature of this relationship, thus contractualizing it to a certain extent.

38 *Cass. 1re civ.*, 7 October 1997, *Mme C.* v. *Clinique du Parc et autres, JCP* 1998, II. 10179; *concl.* Sainte-Rose, *note* P. Sargos.

39 In relation to exceptional risks, the case is important as the decision clarifies the ambit of doctors' duties to inform: any information relating to serious risks must be disclosed regardless of the exceptional nature of the risk. The law of 2002 modifies this.

40 For a commentary on the new law, see Bellivier and Rochfeld (2002), pp. 574 *et seq.*

model, what does it turn into? If doctors supply the necessary information, does this have the effect of shifting the risk onto the patient or onto society as a whole?[41]

What if a doctor fails to give information to a patient in English law? In English law, the doctor-patient relationship belongs to both contract and tort law. English law does not consider that there is a contract between the national health-service and the patient, though there may be a duty of care in tort. However, there is a contract between a private doctor and patient and in this instance there could be a claim under both heads. A patient could make a claim in tort, for negligent misstatement, for example. A patient would have a claim in tort against a doctor for failure to inform about the risks of medical treatment, the case of *Sidaway* v. *Bethlem Royal Hospital Governors*[42] being an example where a doctor is under a duty of care when giving advice about a proposed course of treatment or operation.[43] Likewise, the case of *Thake* v. *Maurice*,[44] concerns a claim in contract and tort relating to a doctor's failure to warn the patient about the after-effects of a vasectomy operation. A claim could also be made for misinformation; a recent land-mark case concerns a doctor erroneously informing his patient of the results of a sperm test after a vasectomy – *McFarlane* v. *Tayside H.B.*;[45] the consequences of the erroneous information led to the patient's wife's pregnancy and the birth of a fifth (unexpected) child. The wife made a claim against the doctor for the losses caused by the misinformation, namely the cost of the pregnancy and the costs of bringing up the child. Briefly, the claim for the inconvenience caused by the pregnancy was admitted but not the costs of bringing up the child. Is there a material distinction between a duty to advise patients of risks and a failure to warn patients of risks? Professor Treitel[46] suggests that a doctor's duty to disclose illustrates the relationship between a professional and the person who has engaged his services: what is important then is the relationship between the two parties, not the presence or absence of a contract.

---

41 Recall the individualistic or welfarist conceptions of contract already mentioned. No doubt, the doctor-patient relationship is envisaged along the lines of a welfarist model. Note that the law of 2002 refers to a '*démocratie de santé*'.

42 [1985] 1 All ER 643, HL.

43 The House of Lords considered and rejected the doctrine of 'informed consent' developed in the US case of *Canterbury* v. *Spence* [1974] 464 f. 2d 772, as being imprecise. The doctrine lays down an objective test of a doctor's duty to advise about the advantages and disadvantages and risks involved in proposed treatment. It could be inferred that English judges prefer the paternalistic model. The majority view give greater weight to doctors choosing when it is opportune to warn patients or not. Lord Scarman, however, puts forward the view that the law should decide when doctors should advise and inform, not the medical profession.

44 [1986] 1 All ER 497. In this case, the doctor failed to inform the patient's wife, after a vasectomy had been performed on her husband, that the effects of sterility might not be permanent. Consequently, she did not realize that she was pregnant until it was too late to have an abortion.

45 [1999] 4 All ER 961.

46 Treitel (2003), p. 400.

To summarize the contractual implications of these developments in French law it would seem as though the model has been transformed from medical paternalism to that of greater transparency between the parties. This is confirmed by the use of language: in the law of 2002 patients have a right to information and this rights language is not coincidental. The emphasis now focuses on the informed consent and hence self-determination of the patient. The paradigm has been reversed: two inferences can be drawn. First, in a contractual relationship where party autonomy was not paramount (due to the relationship of trust and confidence), it might be suggested that party autonomy has been introduced, but this time it is understood quite differently in terms of self-determination and free choice. Secondly, the doctor-patient relationship is just one example of contractual relationships where trust, confidence and dependence[47] exist between the parties (others include for example, lawyer-client, architect-client, accountant-client, trustee-beneficiary, bank-customer, perhaps even supplier-distributor), which shows that party autonomy, in the classical meaning, is not a paradigm for a large number of contracts.

Seller and Buyer Relationship

Two hypotheses in contracts of sale must be examined: (i) that of a professional seller and a consumer and (ii) that of a non-professional seller and a professional buyer.

A professional seller and a consumer A professional seller's duty to inform the buyer. about the price, characteristics of the goods etc. is contained in Arts. L. 111-1 *et seq.* of the *Code de la consommation*. As the duty is incorporated in legislation it is arguable that the duty is considerably reinforced, since the buyer, as recipient of the information, does not need to prove the existence of the obligation, but can simply plead the breach. The obligation is perceived as being precontractual and sometimes cumulated with claims for defective consent.[48] For example, in 2002,[49] in relation to a buyer's claim for annulment of a contract of sale for a second-hand car, on the grounds of fraudulent concealment (*réticence dolosive*), where the seller had concealed that the car had been in an accident, it was held that it is up to the seller who is under an obligation to inform, to adduce evidence that the obligation has been performed. Secondly, it should be pointed out that usually, in case of fraud, the claimant must prove fraud. Here the reversal of the burden of proof is

---

47 See Collins (2003), pp. 198 *et seq.*, who suggests that 'dependence' justifies an exception from the general rule of non-disclosure in English law.

48 For example, examining the consumer Code provisions reveals that there seems to be little case law brought for breach of the duty to inform under this head. It might be inferred that the legislation is sufficiently protective and efficient and no claims need to be made. Or, more plausibly, that small claims are simply not brought before the courts.

49 *Cass. 1re civ.*, 15 May 2002, *Bull. civ.* I, no. 132; *JCP* 2002.I. 184, no. 1, *obs.* F. Labarthe.

highly significant and confirms the emerging pattern outlined above. Here is yet another example of a reinforced duty to inform, implying greater transparency between the parties.

On another analysis the seller's obligation to inform can also be conceived of as contractual since the information relates to the parties' performance of the contract.[50] Likewise, it is arguable in English law, that despite the cry of *caveat emptor*, the rule has little content today. In a parallel sale between a professional and a consumer buyer,[51] implied terms (as to the description, satisfactory quality and fitness for the purpose of the goods[52]) may fill the gap. In other words, in order to circumvent a lack of duty to disclose, the buyer will have other remedies for breach of contract that may be just as efficient or adequate. Liability is strict and damages are awarded on a contractual basis.[53] Once again, it is easy to identify a relationship of dependence or even trust between the parties since the professional will have skill and expertise and the buyer will rely on it. The same relationship can be identified as between lawyer and client. A lawyer's duty to inform his client about the price of his services, for example, has been the object of a recent development in case law[54] where it was held that *avocats* have such an obligation to inform. As mentioned above, a seller acting in the course of business is required by law to inform a consumer about the price of the goods.[55] More importantly for our purposes, it is submitted that if an *avocat* is obliged to inform his client about the price of his services, then the *avocat*'s freedom of contract is limited. Here is a clear-cut example where imposing a duty to inform displaces or reverses the primacy of party autonomy and freedom of contract. Furthermore, this development reinforces the hypothesis that an awareness of one party's reliance or dependence on the skill and expertise of the other is reflected by an increasing recognition of duties to inform.

---

50 Fabre-Magnan (1992). Some contributors made a distinction between information given prior to the conclusion of the contract and information provided during performance of the contract, suggesting that the former was a procedural requirement and the latter substantive (See Wendlandt, Chapter 5 of this volume, pp. 72 *et seq.*). Personally, I am not convinced that the dividing line is so clear-cut.

51 The same is also true for sales as between professionals.

52 Moreover, actions for non-conformity of goods will now be caught under the Sale of Goods and Supply of Services Act 2002 as will sellers' and manufacturers' liability for misleading information; see Willett, Chapter 1 of this volume.

53 See Zimmermann and Whittaker (2000), pp. 194 *et seq.* for an example where failure to give information or warning of the use of goods could be caught under the implied terms of the Sale of Goods Act 1979.

54 *Cass. 1re civ.*, 18 July 2000, *Garnier* v. *Haran, RTD civ.* 2000, p. 828, *note* J. Mestre and B. Fages who suggest that the duty is general and its scope is wide-ranging. This inference is drawn from the fact that the decision does not use an article of the Consumer code as a legal ground whereas it could have done; *a contrario* the duty is not limited to professionals and consumers and could also apply to other sorts of contracts.

55 Art. L. 111-1 of the *Code de la consommation*.

A non-professional seller and a professional buyer The cases of a non-professional seller selling to a professional buyer have produced inconsistent solutions with respect to the duty to inform. An explanation for this apparent lack of coherence is that the cases show that duties to inform are developed casuistically. Moreover, it can be inferred that despite an increasing tendency to recognize and enhance duties to inform, as examined above, there are limits. Two recent cases come to mind; the first is *l'affaire Baldus*,[56] the facts of which contrast nicely with the *Poussin* case.[57] In 2000 the *Cour de cassation* held that the buyer of photos by Baldus, which the buyer, and not the seller, knew to be by Baldus and therefore much more valuable than the contract price, was not under an obligation to inform the seller of this fact. The seller could not plead her mistake even though the buyer was a professional and she was a consumer. On one interpretation, this case represents a swing in the attitude of the French courts to the seller's position of ignorance (lack of expertise), i.e. it is less protective than previous case law. On another interpretation the decision can be justified and explained by the following facts: the seller had made a first sale to the buyer at a public auction; the seller then sought out the buyer for a second (private sale) of more Baldus photos at the same price. It may, therefore, be wrong to induce from this decision a general lack of duty to inform on the buyer to the seller and more realistic to interpret the case in the light of its precise facts: i.e. there was no duty on this particular buyer to inform the seller of the value of the photos; the latter should bear the consequences of her behaviour. Although the argument is not spelled out, this amounts to saying that the courts will not intervene in a bad bargain.

To substantiate the argument that this is an isolated case and does not give rise to a general principle, reference can be made to another case. In 2002,[58] a professional buyer dissimulated his identity to a non-professional seller and was held liable for fraud. The buyer was aware of the value of the underground resources of the land sold whereas the seller was not. Not only did the buyer lie about his identity (the managing director of the company was held out as an individual buyer whereas in fact the company was buying the land) but also about the use for which he intended the purchase. Interpreting *a contrario* from fraud leads us to infer that the buyer was liable for failing to inform the seller of the truth (about the value of the land and his own identity). Clearly therefore, it is difficult to deduce that professional buyers are not liable to inform non-professional sellers, as each case is judged on its facts.

Despite differing legal analysis, speculation about English law's solutions in the above two cases may reveal a convergence of result. For example, in the

---

56 *Cass. 1re civ.*, 3 May 2000, *Bull. civ.* I, no. 131, *Clin* v. *Mme Natali*, *RTD civ.* 2000, p. 566, *JCP* 2001, J. 10510, C. Jamin, 757, B. Fromion-Hébrard, *Petites Affiches* no. 242, 5 December 2000, p. 14.

57 *Affaire célebre! Cass. 1re civ.*, 22 February 1978, *JCP* 1978.II.18925, cf. Ghestin, 1993, pp. 479 *et seq.*

58 *Cass. 3e civ.*, 15 November 2000, *Carrières de Brandefert* v. *Palaric-Le Coent*, *JCP* 2001, I.I.301, no. 1, *note* Y.-M. Serinet; *RTD civ.* 2001, p. 355; *D.* 2002, *somm.comm.* p. 928, *note* O. Tournafound.

Baldus case, an absence of a duty to disclose (from buyer to seller) would also mean that the result would be the same.[59] As for the second case, perhaps the buyer's fraudulent conduct before the sale might be characterized as fraudulent misrepresentation so the buyer might be liable. If so, the seller could annul the contract and claim damages under this head.

To summarize, in French law a professional seller's duty to inform a consumer buyer is reinforced by legislation. Whether this makes a great deal of difference has yet to be demonstrated. As far as contracts of sale between two parties acting in the course of business is concerned, under French law the seller owes a duty to inform the buyer whose own expertise constitutes a limit to this duty. For example,[60] in a contract of sale for a fishing boat with a propeller usually used for pleasure boats the buyer alleged that the seller had failed to inform him that the boat would not be suitable for professional purposes. The seller replied that the buyer had the requisite knowledge of fishing boats. Liability was apportioned on a 50:50 basis as it was held that the buyer had professional knowledge of the goods. It is sometimes said that a manufacturer is only liable to inform the buyer to the extent that the buyer's own skill and expertise do not enable him to understand the characteristics of the good delivered.[61] As far as a non-professional seller and a professional buyer is concerned, the cases are decided on their facts but it should be clear that no relationship of dependence exists, which might explain the absence of such a duty. Considerations of fraud stand apart as they are, of course, remedied on the grounds of defective consent. In addition, the gap between French and English law might not be as stark as it may first appear: this is because in practice a buyer may have remedies (other than for breach of a duty to inform) under the implied terms contained in statute in English law.[62] Once again, party autonomy in the contract of sale appears to be rather mythical; to a certain extent duties to inform and greater transparency between the parties have replaced this model. However, highlighting duties to inform does not allow us to replace one dogmatic model with another. Just as the paradigmatic model of party autonomy is untrue, so the need to impose duties to inform in all types of contractual situations is equally false.

---

59 *Smith* v. *Hughes* [1871] LR 6 QB 597; *Bell* v. *Lever Bros.* [1932] AC 161.

60 *Cass. 1re civ.*, 20 June 1995, *Bull civ.* I, nos. 277, 83.

61 *Cass. 1re civ.*, 3 June 1998, *RTD civ.* 1999, p. 89. Or more recently, the *Cour de cassation* held that a professional seller owes a duty to a professional buyer : 'in so far as the latter's expertise does not give him the means to appreciate the exact scope of the technical characteristics of the goods that are delivered to him', see *Cour de cassation, chamber commerciale* (*Cass. com.*), 19 February 2002, *RTD civ.* 2003, p. 82. Likewise the seller is not under an obligation to inform the buyer about all and sundry, i.e. labour law provisions, where the sale of a video surveillance cameras was contrary to protective rules: *Cass. 1re civ.*, 25 June 2002, *RTD civ.* 2003, p. 83.

62 Furthermore, it is arguable that a further convergence may be reached because of the implementation of the EU 1999/44 Directive on consumer guarantees but this has not happened yet since France has still not transposed the Directive.

Insurance Contracts

Contracts of insurance represent the exception to the rule in English law, as classified as *uberrimae fidei.*[63] Briefly, under English law the insured is under a duty to disclose all material information affecting the risk to the insurer. Theoretically, the insurer is also under a duty to disclose. In the event of non-disclosure, each party can avoid the contract. In practice, actions against the insurer are rare. Moreover, the courts have pointed out that the burden on the insurer is not too onerous, for example, it has been suggested that 'a professional should wear a halo but not a hair shirt'.[64] So far as insurance contracts are concerned, the question of who is the weak and who is the strong party must be addressed. In my view, the most interesting point about this relationship is that the insurer is informationally weak, but is plausibly the stronger party overall, especially in terms of bargaining power. It would seem that transparency is required, but the emphasis is on the interests of the commercially stronger party and the market as a whole. It is therefore submitted that duties to inform are clearly imposed for the benefit of the insurer and that the insurer is not the weak party in the generally accepted understanding of the term. It is worthwhile pointing out that French law is coming round to this point of view and information requirements on the insured are clearly more for the benefit of the insurer than the insured, although this was not always the case.[65] An extreme case of cumulative (seven) insurance policies taken out by the insured for personal injury accidents illustrates this idea. The insured lost a finger after an accident with a firearm. The insurers alleged deception (*escroquerie*) and refused to pay out under the policy. After the insured was criminally acquitted he sued the insurers to pay for the accident. The insurers refused to pay on the grounds that the insurance policy was void as the insured had made a false declaration about the existence of other insurance policies covering the same risk. It was held (contrary to previous case law) that the insured did indeed have an obligation to inform the insurer of the existence of other insurance policies. Here it could be argued that the reinforced transparency acts against the insured in favour of the insurer but follows the same pattern we have seen emerging since freedom of contract (the insured's freedom is clearly fettered) is subsumed by the need for transparency on the market. If this hypothesis is true, perhaps it is not so surprising to note that French and English law converge in the sense that they both impose duties to inform on the insured, this being a case of an exception to the rule in English law, as already mentioned. Realizing that increased transparency can be imposed for the benefit of the 'stronger' party is important. Up

---

63 *Carter* v. *Boehm* [1776] 3 Burr. 1905.

64 *Banque Financière de la Cité SA* v. *Westgate Insurance Co. Ltd.* [1991] 2 AC 249.

65 See *Cass. 1re civ.*, 13 May 1997, *RTD civ.* 1997, p. 923. A further decision reinforcing the insured's duty to inform follows the same trend. See *Cass. 1re civ.*, 9 December 1997, *Bull. civ.* I, no. 356, *RTD civ.* 1999, p. 83, where it was held that the burden of proof that the obligation to inform has been fulfilled lies on the insured who subscribes to group insurance to inform the other subscribers of the group. This constitutes a reversal of the burden of proof.

till now, we may have had the impression that duties to inform were mostly beneficial and do help achieve contractual fairness. This may be true, but the statement is subject to qualification. It may be necessary to qualify that greater transparency does not necessarily imply contractual fairness per se for both parties and that greater transparency also favours the informationally weak party (in the contract) who is not inevitably and systematically the weaker party overall. It does not necessarily follow therefore that the party who is in an informationally weak position is always worthy of protection in the eyes of everyone.[66]

Distribution Agreements

In French law, information requirements concerning franchise and distribution agreements are set out in Art. 1 of the *Loi Doubin* (31 December 1989), which regulates the provision of information to be given by a supplier to the distributor prior to the contract's conclusion.[67] To elucidate the reasons behind this legislative intervention it is worth mentioning that these contracts had long since been criticized as creating a situation of dependency and, inexorably, inequality.[68] The legislation looks protective; in fact its subsequent interpretation by the *Cour de cassation*[69] renders it less so in practice as it has held that a failure to respect the information requirements does not automatically lead to the contract being annulled, it is still also necessary to prove defective consent. If information requirements must be cumulated with defective consent remedies, it is arguable that the new duties to inform, imposed by law, are formalistic and empty of real protection. We go back to classical values where the emphasis lies on free and unvitiated consent. Thus the law can be interpreted as paternalistic: the law accepts that you are dependent as long as you have chosen freely to be so and therefore party autonomy prevails. The law can also be interpreted as a sham: it appears as if duties to inform prevail: a party must be properly informed to choose to enter into the contract and therefore party autonomy no longer prevails. This would suggest that reversing the paradigm is not easy (or once again that the paradigm does not exist). However, the courts' interpretation of Art. 1 of the *Loi Doubin* is not linear. In another recent case the *Cour de cassation* allowed the franchisee to rely on the franchisor's failure to comply with Art. 1 as a defence to the franchisor's claim for payments under a partly performed and then retrospectively terminated franchise agreement so that failure to comply was treated as precluding the franchisor from obtaining any benefit whatsoever under the contract.[70] On one analysis, this could

66 Of course whether a contracting party is worthy of protection is an open question and depends on whose point of view the fairness of contract is perceived.

67 For a more detailed enquiry into the information requirements in commercial agency, distribution and franchise agreements, see Janssen, Chapter 11 of this volume.

68 Virasamy (1986).

69 *Cass. com.*, 10 February 1998, *D.* 1999, Chronique, p. 431, Y. Marot. See Béhar Touchais and Virassamy (1999), nos. 30 *et seq.*

70 *Cass. com.*, 4 April 1991, *RTD civ.* 1999, p. 87. The franchisor had not respected Art. 1 of the *Loi Doubin*, the contract was partly performed, goods had been delivered by the franchisor but the franchisee had not paid for them. After termination, the franchisor

be considered either as a deterrent or a punishment for the franchisor's failure to comply with information requirements.[71]

This illustration is confronted by a comparative gap in English law. As a generalization, it seems that distribution and franchise agreements are more often the subject of litigation in French law, whether on grounds of breaking-off negotiations (*rupture abusive des pourparleurs)*, non renewal of a fixed term contract, abuse in fixing the price (*abus de droit*) than in English law.[72] Why this is so is largely a matter of speculation. Do contractual practices differ, i.e. does the market work differently or is French law more concerned than English law to redress the balance and encourage the parties to behave transparently and in co-operation with one another? If the suggested criterion of dependence could be used to create an exception to the rule of non-disclosure in English law then distribution agreements could be presented as fitting this category. This suggestion could be countered with at least three objections of a different nature: first, some might disagree that the parties are in a situation of dependency to one another and contend that they are both professionals, acting in the course of business at arm's length. A counter-argument would contend that distribution agreements are an example of long-term contract involving co-operation where the need for solidarity is particularly overwhelming in order for the contract to succeed.[73] Secondly, objections might be raised about creating another exception to the rule. Thirdly, a more critical objection points to the ineffectiveness of the information requirements as illustrated. In other words, this may not be the best solution. It is submitted that information requirements are not a perfect answer but they may at least have the merit of raising our awareness that the party autonomy paradigm fails to correspond to reality.

---

sued for payment of the goods. The claim was dismissed by the Court of Appeal and approved by the *Cour de cassation* since the franchisor had lied and given inexact information to the franchisee at outset. See also *Cass. com.*, 7 March 2000, *RTD civ.* 2000, p. 829 where it was held that the franchisor is under an obligation to inform the franchisee about his own legal situation.

71 See also M. Behar-Touchais, *Revue des Contrats* 2003, pp. 158 *et seq.*, *note* to *Cass. com.*, 14 January 2003, *Barahona* v. *Sté Hygiène Diffusion,* who suggests that the ineffectiveness of information requirements set out in the *Loi Doubin* should be remedied by independently depriving the supplier or franchisor of sums due under the contract in the event on non-compliance with Art. 1. This would amount to a self-help remedy and also a private punishment (*peine privée*), similar to the forfeiture of the insurance premium in contracts of insurance (*déchéance*). For an enquiry on the notion of *peine privée*, see Carval (1995).

72 See Collins (1999), p. 245.

73 The numerous works of I.R. MacNeil on relational contracting support this idea, see Campbell (2001) with further references.

Conclusion

What conclusions can we draw from these heteroclite examples? First, it should be observed that there is not one contractual paradigm but many. The classical mythical model of party autonomy is being eroded and abandoned. Of the two proposed models: that of the parties pursuing their individual and adversarial interests and that of the parties working towards a common goal, requiring transparency and co-operation, there should be added a third. Many contracts today where there is an imbalance do not follow either of these models. In relations of trust, confidence and dependency, the parties must work in co-operation but moreover one party may sometimes be required to act altruistically, in the interests of the other.[74] I am not in any way suggesting that contracting parties should be angelized. However, special relationships with a high level of trust, confidence and dependence may require a balancing counterpart to redress the inequality.[75] A minimal requirement, where one party has the upper hand, so to speak, is to require that party to inform the other: so that the weaker party can give informed consent. Requiring the parties to work in co-operation may be an ideal, it may also be redolent of a paternalistic model which may not necessarily be preferable to a libertarian one of presumed equality. If duties to inform can be exploited towards achieving greater contractual fairness, at the very least, let us hope that contracting parties know what they are doing when exercising their choices. This then may be a new freedom of contract.

References

Atiyah, P.S. (1979), *The Rise and Fall of Freedom of Contract* (Oxford: Oxford University Press).

Atiyah, P.S. (1988), *Essays on Contract* (Oxford: Clarendon).

Beatson, J. (ed.) (2002), *Ansom's Law of Contract*, 28th edn. (Oxford: Oxford University Press).

Béhar Touchais, M. and Virassamy, G. (1999), *Les contrats de la distribution* (Paris : Librairie Générale de Droit et de Jurisprudence (LGDJ)).

Bellivier, F. and Rochfeld, J. (2002), 'Chroniques – Législation française', *Revue Trimestrielle de Droit Civil*, pp. 569-591.

Boussard, S. (2004), 'Comment sanctionner la violation du droit à l'information de l'usager du système de santé', *Revue du droit public*, pp. 169-206.

Brownsword, R. (2000), *Contract Law: Themes for the Twenty-first Century* (London: Butterworths).

---

74 This is said to be the key feature of a fiduciary relationship, *Bristol & West BS* v. *Matthew* [1998] 1 Ch 1, at p. 18, see Beatson (2002), p. 267.

75 For an interesting illustration in English law, it is worth mentioning that the House of Lords 'implied' a duty, incumbent on the employer, to inform an employee of his rights to a pension scheme arrangement. The employment relationship is typically one where enhanced trust, confidence, dependence and co-operation are present: *Scally* v. *Southern Health and Social Services Board* [1992] AC 294, HL.

Campbell, I.D. (ed.) (2001), *The Relational Theory of Contract: Selected Works of Ian MacNeil* (London: Sweet & Maxwell).

Cartwright, J. (2002), *Misrepresentation* (London: Sweet & Maxwell).

Carval, S. (1995), *La responsabilité civile dans sa fonction de peine privée* (Paris: LGDJ).

Collins, H. (1999), *Regulating Contracts* (Oxford: Oxford University Press).

Collins, H. (2003), *The Law of Contract*, 4th edn. (London: Butterworths).

De Juglart, M. (1945), 'L'obligation de renseignements dans les contrats', *Revue trimestrielle de droit civil*, pp. 1 *et seq.*

Demogue, R. (1932), *Traité des obligations*, vol. 6 (Paris: Rousseau).

Fabre-Magnan, M. (1992), *De l'obligation d'information dans les contrats: Essai d'une théorie* (Paris: LGDJ).

Ghestin, J. (1993), *La Formation du contrat*, 3rd edn. (Paris: LGDJ).

Gounot, E. (1912), *Le principe de l'autonomie de la volonté en droit privé; Contribution à l'étude critique de l'individualisme*, Ph. D. thesis (Dijon).

Jamin, C. (2001), 'Plaidoyer pour le solidarisme contractual in Crise du contrat', in *Le Contrat au début du XXième siècle, Etudes offertes à J. Ghestin* (Paris: LGDJ), pp. 441 *et seq.*

Jamin, C. (2003), 'Introduction', in Jamin, C. and Mazeaud, D. (eds.), *La nouvelle crise du contrat, Thèmes et commentaires : Actes du colloque du 14 mai 2001* (Paris : Dalloz).

Noiville, C. (1999), 'L'obligation d'information du médécin', *Petites Affiches*, no. 89, 5 May 1999, pp. 4 *et seq.*

Scheppele, K.L. (1988), *Legal Secrets: Equality and Efficiency in the Common Law* (Chicago: The University of Chicago Press).

Sefton-Green, R. (ed.) (forthcoming), *Mistake, Fraud and Duties to Inform in European Contract Law* (Cambridge: Cambridge University Press (CUP)).

Smith, S.A (1996), 'Future Freedom and Freedom of Contract', 59, *Modern Law Review*, pp. 167 *et seq.*

Trebilcock, M. J. (1993), *The Limits of Freedom of Contract* (Cambridge, Massachusetts: Harvard University Press).

Treitel, G.H. (2003), *Law of Contract*, 11th edn. (London: Sweet & Maxwell).

Viney, G. and Jourdain, P. (1998), *Les conditions de la Responsabilité*, 2nd edn. (Paris: LGDJ).

Virasamy, G. (1986), *Les contrats de dépendence* (Paris : LGDJ).

Zimmermann, R. and Whittaker, S. (2000), *Good Faith in European Contract Law* (Cambridge: CUP).

Chapter 11

The Information Requirements in the Principles of European Private Law 'Long-Term Commercial Contracts: Commercial Agency, Distribution, Franchise' – A Model for a European Civil Code?*

André Janssen**

Introduction

The Europeanization of private law is progressing at an ever-increasing pace. The creation of a European Civil Code, which only a few years ago was nothing more than a Utopian ideal and whose discussions were confined to a small group of legal scientists, is increasingly becoming a reality. The discussion has received unexpected impetus particularly from the European Commission's Action Plan on a more coherent European Contract Law of February 2003, which *inter alia* puts forward the possibility of the creation of a European Civil Code.[1]

The exact content of this Civil Code (leaving aside the many other difficulties) is currently unclear. What is certain is that a codification of general and special contract law will not take place on a '*tabula rasa*'. The regulatory codes on private law created by numerous European jurists will provide an important source of

* This publication has been written within the Research Network 'Uniform Terminology for European Private Law'. The member universities are Turin (Coordinator), Barcelona, Lyon, Münster, Nijmegen, Oxford and Warsaw. The research network is part of the Improving Human Potential (IHP) Programme financed by the European Commission (Contract no. HPRN-CT-2002-00229).

** The author would like to thank Christopher Dallimore LLB, LL.M. for the translation of this chapter.

1 Action Plan on a More Coherent European Contract Law, COM (2003) 68 final. Concerning the Action Plan see also Grundmann and Stuyck (2001); Najork and Schmidt-Kessel (2003); Staudenmayer (2003).

inspiration in addition to domestic laws and the Acquis Communautaire.[2] The most important examples in this respect are the *Principles of European Contract Law* (in the following PECL),[3] the *Unidroit-Principles of International Commercial Contracts*[4] and the *Code Européen des Contracts* under the auspices of Professor Giuseppe Gandolfi.[5]

However, all these regulatory codes display a 'common defect'. They do not contain any rules regulating special types of contract and for that reason their applicability in such areas is very limited. A European Civil Code – in whatever form – will sooner or later have to adopt rules for special types of contract as well.

The *Study Group on a European Civil Code*[6] led by Professor Christian von Bar has recognized this 'defect' in relation to the PECL and formed several working groups dealing with certain types of contract.[7] This Study Group was founded in 1997 following a conference entitled '*Towards a European Civil Code*' in Scheveningen. It now has almost 80 members from more than 20 countries. The Study Group represents the successor to the *Commission on European Contract Law*, (the '*Lando-Group*'). This network also set up various working groups in order to deal with different subjects. Accordingly, the Study Group is working on model laws on sales,[8] services, long-term commercial contracts, unjust enrichment, compensation,[9] management without mandate and the transfer of title.

The aim of the *Amsterdam Group*[10] under the auspices of Professor Martijn Hesselink is to formulate Principles of European Private Law for 'Long-term Commercial Contracts: Commercial Agency, Distribution, Franchise' (in the following 'PECL-LTCC'). After years of work, the PECL-LTCC will be published in 2004. This contribution mainly concerns these Principles.[11]

Approach and Aim of the Investigation

The following investigation concentrates on the information model upon which the PECL-LTCC are based and how they relate to party autonomy. Accordingly, the first step will be to investigate the influence that the information rules contained in the PECL-LTCC have on party autonomy. The second, smaller step will then answer the question as to whether the PECL-LTCC – in terms of information

2 For details on the Acquis Communautaire see Schulze (2003).

3 Lando and Beale (eds.) (2002). See also Blase (2001).

4 Unidroit (1994).

5 Gandolfi (2002).

6 Information at http://www.sgecc.net.

7 Von Bar (2000).

8 Cf. Heutger (2003).

9 Cf. also von Bar (2001).

10 This group consists of Martijn Hesselink, Jacobien Rutgers, Odavia Buenodiaz, Manolo Scotton and Muriel Veldman.

11 In the version of the 8th draft as approved by the Co-ordinating Committee of the Study Group on a European Civil Code. See the annex of this volume.

duties and their influence on party autonomy – constitute a functional model for a potential European Civil Code in relation to long-term commercial contracts or whether they simply amount to a regulatory code and nothing more.

In this respect, the contribution will only deal with the information duties required by all three types of contract under consideration (commercial agency, distribution, franchise). It will not consider information duties which are only intended for parties to a certain type of contract.

The Relationship to the PECL and the Structure of the PECL-LTCC

The Relationship of the PECL-LTCC to the PECL

Like the other Principles which have arisen under the aegis of the Study Group, the PECL-LTCC represents an invaluable supplement to the general law contained in the PECL relating to long-term commercial contracts in a later European Civil Code. Together they will therefore constitute a uniform system within a European Civil Code, in which the PECL will deal with general law and the Principles of the Study Group with special contracts.

The Structure of the PECL-LTCC and Background Information

The PECL-LTCC concentrate on commercial agency, distribution and franchise contracts and consist of four chapters: the Chapter One: 'General Provisions' applies to all commercial agency, distribution and franchise contracts. The other three chapters (Chapter Two: 'Commercial Agency', Chapter Three: 'Distribution', Chapter Four: 'Franchise') contain rules specific to these different types of contracts. The definitions of commercial agency, franchise and distribution are each found at the beginning of the respective chapter (cf. Art. 2:101 PECL-LTCC, Art. 3:101 PECL-LTCC, Art. 4:101 PECL-LTCC). There are no significant differences to the terminology used in existing law and so the terms will presumably be familiar.

The choice of structure has been determined by the fact that commercial agency, distribution and franchise contracts display many common characteristics. First, they perform the same economic function of bringing goods and services to the market. Thus, they are all vertical agreements. Second, they usually share a relational character: they are intended to last for many years and their success largely depends on loyal and intense co-operation. Such similarities justify a comparable or even uniform regulation of Chapter One.

However, there are also major differences. Although a commercial agent is an independent entrepreneur, he generally acts in the name of his principal, contrary to a distributor and a franchisee who act in their own name. In other words, whereas the commercial agent sells the principal's products to the public, the distributor and the franchisor sell their own products (which they have bought from the supplier or franchisor, or a third party). This implies different – and usually more extensive – risks. Another important difference is that in the case of franchise contracts the grant of intellectual property rights is a central issue whereas most commercial agency contracts and many distribution contracts do not involve any intellectual property rights at all. These are merely a few examples; there are further differences which fall out with the scope of this presentation. For this reason, rules relating to specific types of contract were also incorporated into the PECL-LTCC.

Status Quo at European Level

The European Community has long recognized the need for specific rules in this area. Indeed, the first Directive it enacted in the field of contract law was the Council Directive of 18 December 1986 on the Co-ordination of the Laws of the Member States relating to Self-employed Commercial Agents (86/653/EEC) (in the following 'CAD').[12] This Directive aimed at full harmonization in relation to the law on commercial agents and imposed numerous information requirements on both parties. However, in comparison to the PECL-LTCC (dealt with in greater detail below) it contains considerable restrictions to its scope of application. First and foremost, the CAD only applies to commercial agency and not to distribution contracts or franchise contracts. In addition, the CAD only affects the contractual and not the pre-contractual relationship which means that it does not regulate the pre-contractual information requirements (unlike the PECL-LTCC).

Transposing the CAD in the individual Member States largely harmonized the contractual relationship of commercial agency and thereby the contractual information duties incumbent on both parties. However, the contractual relationship concerning franchise und distribution contracts was left to national law. As already stated, the latter two display great similarities to commercial agency with the result that many courts in Member States apply a great number of CAD rules with the approval of legal commentators.[13] Regarding the pre-contractual phase and pre-contractual information requirements, recourse is usually had to general national law concerning all three types of contract.[14] Only a few countries (e.g. France and Spain) have special rules concerning franchise contracts.[15]

---

12 See Radley-Gardner, Beale, Zimmermann, Schulze (2003), pp. 139 *et seq.*

13 See, e.g., von Hoyningen-Huene (1996), before § 84 *Handelsgesetzbuch* nos. 16, 19-20; Kroll (2001); Küstner and Thume (1998), nos. 1186 *et seq.*, 1692; Westphal (1994). In England the majority opinion rejects an analogous application (see Hagemeister (2004), pp. 105 *et seq.*).

14 See, e.g., Bortolotti (2001), p. 118; Janssen (2001), p. 100; Küstner and Thume (1998), nos. 1638-1648.

15 See Ferrier (2001), pp. 103 *et seq.*; Pellisé De Urguiza (2001), pp. 138 *et seq.*

Some Brief Comments on the Information Models of the PECL

The PECL do not regulate the private law phenomenon of information requirements by means of an autonomous regulatory scheme (unlike, for example, the European Contract Code under the auspices of Professor Giuseppe Gandolfi).[16] A number of rules which concern information requirements are found in the chapter on the validity of the contract, especially in the rules governing incorrect information and fraud (cf. Art. 4:103 PECL; Art. 4:107 PECL).[17]

However, this should not disguise the fact that, as a rule, the PECL do not provide either general pre-contractual obligations to inform or general obligations to inform during the performance.[18] Nevertheless, the facts of the individual case can lead to the creation of obligations to inform due to the obligation of good faith (Art. 1:201 PECL), which also governs contractual negotiations (Art. 2:301 PECL) and especially due to the general obligation to co-operate (Art. 1:202 PECL).[19]

The Information Model in the PECL-LTCC

Upon closer examination it soon becomes clear that the PECL-LTCC contain numerous provisions relating to information duties. They indicate the particularly close relationships of co-operation and trust characteristic of long-term contractual relationships (cf. Art. 1:202 PECL-LTCC). These duties require a systematic arrangement. This contribution will attempt to do so on the basis of the sub-division made by the PECL-LTCC. Accordingly, information duties will be divided into the following categories:

- Pre-contractual obligation to inform.
- Obligation to inform during the performance.
- Obligation to warn.
- Entitlement to receive a signed written document.

Pre-contractual Obligation to Inform

The general rule of Art. 1:201 PECL-LTCC Art. 1:201 PECL-LTCC is found in Chapter One under the heading 'General Provisions'. It imposes on both parties a mandatory (cf. Art. 1:201 (4) PECL-LTCC) pre-contractual obligation to inform with regard to long-term commercial contracts. Accordingly, contractual parties

---

16 Gandolfi (2002), Art. 7, p. 5.

17 Cf. in detail Grigoleit (2003), p. 202.

18 Cf. Grigoleit (2003), pp. 202 *et seq.*

19 In commercial agency, franchise and distribution contracts and in other long-term commercial contracts the obligation to co-operate (Art. 1:202 PECL) is fundamental and especially intense. In particular, it requires the parties to collaborate actively and loyally and to co-ordinate their respective efforts in order to achieve the objectives of the contract (see Art. 1:203 (1) PECL). See also Grigoleit (2003), p. 202.

must furnish each other with adequate information within a reasonable time before the contract is concluded. Art. 1:201 (2) PECL-LTCC defines the term 'adequate information' as being information sufficient to enable the other party to decide on a reasonably informed basis whether or not to enter into a contract of the type and on the terms under consideration. The information which must be communicated to the opposite party therefore depends on the individual case.

Specification of the pre-contractual obligations to inform on the franchisor in accordance with Art. 3:102 PECL-LTCC Although there are no other rules governing pre-contractual information for commercial agency and distribution contracts, Art. 3:102 (1) PECL further specifies the franchisor's pre-contractual information duties. This provision therefore reflects the special importance that pre-contractual information occupies in the field of franchising which very often represents a bone of contention in court proceedings.

In accordance with Art. 3:102 (1) PECL-LTCC, the franchisor must disclose the following information to the franchisee before the contract is concluded:

(a) the franchisor's company and experience,
(b) the relevant intellectual property rights,
(c) the characteristics of the relevant know-how,
(d) the commercial sector and the market conditions,
(e) the particular franchise method and its operation,
(f) the structure and extent of the franchise network,
(g) the fees, royalties or any other periodical payments,
(h) the terms of the contract.

In this connection, Art. 3:102 (3) PECL-LTCC makes clear that the rule is mandatory.

Analysis of function and influence on party autonomy In order to understand the influence which the mandatory pre-contractual information duties have over party autonomy (which can be derived from Art. 1:102 PECL), one must draw a distinction between (mandatory) information rules on the one hand and (mandatory) substantive rules on the other.[20] The latter reduce variety to one option or to a smaller range of options.[21] This is typical in the law on unfair contract terms, for example. The information rules may be mandatory by construction (the duty to disclose is not subject to party autonomy), but they aim to allow the parties to take an autonomous decision in substance.[22]

If one applies this distinction to the provisions under investigation then it becomes clear that purely mandatory information rules are at issue. Certainly, both contractual parties must comply with (mandatory) pre-contractual obligations to

20 Grundmann (2000), p. 1137; Grundmann, Kerber and Weatherill (2001), pp. 3 *et seq.*

21 Mandatory substantive rules reduce the diversity of legal relationships and are therefore less able to satisfy different preferences of demand. Therefore, they are only suitable if an information rule cannot dispel market failure.

22 Grundmann (2000), p. 1137; Grundmann, Kerber and Weatherill (2001), pp. 3 *et seq.*

inform, but how they ultimately affect the contract remains a matter for the parties and is subject to their party autonomy. In other words: once e.g. the franchisor has informed the franchisee of all relevant facts in accordance with Art. 3:102 (1) PECL-LTCC the parties are free to control the substance of the contract. Therefore, the pre-contractual information duties of the PECL-LTCC merely create the situation that both parties have access to all information in order to make an informed decision tailored to the facts of the individual case. They enable a private individual to make decision by offering a number of possible arrangements and ensuring that individual needs are respected.[23] Therefore, they are intended to foster party autonomy and facilitate market transparency.[24]

However, one may object that there is no need to impose such an (mandatory) obligation in any given case because both the parties are professionals. Either party should be capable of giving free and informed consent to the contract after having looked for and obtained all the necessary information.[25] However, a party may only be a 'future professional'. In addition, owing to the relationship of trust and collaboration between the parties either one may expect the other to provide information which is important for the contract. Moreover, parties are not always in a position to obtain all the relevant information themselves. Some salient information (such as projects for the creation of certain products or the renewal of a series or any information regarding the financial situation and industrial/commercial policies of the parties) may be the subject of a trade secret. Accordingly, there is asymmetry of information (familiar from consumer protection law), i.e. one contractual party has a clear advantage in terms of information over the other.[26] Such an advantage is not negative *per se*: the possibility that information is distributed asymmetrically provides an incentive to produce information and is therefore necessary for the mechanics of selection which is based on market activity and essential for it.[27]

However, problems occur if one side cannot remove the information asymmetry or this is only possible at a prohibitively high cost (as is the case with the contracts under consideration).[28] In such cases one contractual party necessarily acts on information which does not provide an adequate basis for decision-making. In this case, the market will fail in structural terms if provision is not made for balancing the information duties. A departure must be made from the 'normal' information model (in which each party is responsible for obtaining the

23 Grundmann (2000), pp. 1137 *et seq.*

24 Riesenhuber (2003a), pp. 293 *et seq.*; Riesenhuber (2003b), pp. 128 *et seq.*

25 *Ibid.*

26 Grundmann, Kerber and Weatherill (2001), p. 21; Kerton and Bodell (1995).

27 Grundmann (2000), p. 1137; Riesenhuber (2003a), pp. 293 *et seq.*; Riesenhuber (2003b), pp. 128 *et seq.*

28 This is particularly apparent in the case of the Consumer Credit Directive and the Credit Transfer Directive since both were expressly motivated by the lack of transparency in the market (see Riesenhuber (2003b), p. 129).

information he is required to provide) in order to counteract this undesired information asymmetry and owing to the high transaction costs.[29]

Some comparative comments According to leading opinion, the CAD does not regulate the pre-contractual phase of the commercial agency agreement.[30] The regulation of the pre-contractual phase of long-term commercial contracts therefore remains the preserve of the national legislator.

Almost all European legal systems contain a specific obligation of pre-contractual disclosure for long-term commercial contracts but most Member States do not regulate this matter by statute. General rules relating to pre-contractual information apply. For example, in Germany the contractual parties to long-term commercial contracts have comprehensive pre-contractual information duties owing to good faith (*Treu und Glauben*) in accordance with § 242 *Bürgerliches Gesetzbuch* depending on the party, facts and type of contract. German courts have repeatedly imposed comprehensive pre-contractual information duties particularly on the franchisor due to the especially close relationship of co-operation and the franchisee's special dependency on the information provided by the franchisor.[31] Such information duties comply with those of Art. 3:102 (1) PECL-LTCC, even if no express catalogue has been provided. That pre-contractual information duties for long-term commercial contracts represent a difficult subject in need of regulation (especially with regard to franchising) is shown by the French *Loi*

---

29 Grundmann (2000), p. 1137; Riesenhuber (2003a), p. 293; Riesenhuber (2003b), pp. 128 *et seq.*

30 See Riesenhuber (2003a), pp. 307 *et seq.*; Riesenhuber (2003b), pp. 135 *et seq.*

31 Legal writers (Küstner and Thume (1998), nos. 1637-1649; Martinek and Semler (1996), § 19 nos. 1-4) and the courts (*Bundesarbeitsgericht, Der Betrieb* 1980, p. 2040; *Oberlandesgericht* Munich, *Betriebsberater* 1988, p. 865; *Oberlandesgericht* Munich, *Neue Juristische Wochenschrift* 1994, p. 667) believe that there is a pre-contractual obligation of disclosure in franchise contracts based on good faith under § 242 *Bürgerliches Gesetzbuch.* The information given to the franchisee must be correct (see, e.g., no. 3.2. of the Code of Ethical Conduct of the German Franchise Association). Due to the fact that there are no judgments of the *Bundesgerichtshof* regarding the duty of disclosure in franchise contracts, the two quoted decisions of the *Oberlandesgericht* Munich are considered to be 'leading cases'. In 1987, this court (*Oberlandesgericht* Munich, *Betriebsberater* 1988, p. 865) held that the franchiser had violated his duty of disclosure because he did not correctly inform the franchisee about his company (i.e. he did not inform the franchisee that 52 franchisees had stopped running the franchise business). In 1994, the *Oberlandesgericht* Munich also held that the franchisor is obliged to inform the franchisee completely and correctly about the profitability of the system (*Neue Juristische Wochenschrift* 1994, p. 667). In both cases, the franchisor was liable under the regime of *culpa in contrahendo* (now: §§ 241 (2), 311 (2), 280 (1) *Bürgerliches Gesetzbuch.* The courts have not yet decided when the duty of disclosure commences. According to legal writers, the duty commences as soon as the parties come into contact with each other (Flohr (1998), p. 16). There are no formal requirements *per se.* In principle, the franchisor can communicate information orally. However, written disclosure is common in practice (Martinek and Semler (1996), § 19 nos. 15-17; see also 3.3. of the German Code of Ethical Conduct).

Doubin,[32] Spanish law,[33] the Model Franchise Disclosure Law of Unidroit[34] and the European Code of Ethics for Franchising.[35] All these regulatory codes impose pre-contractual information duties – particularly on the franchisor – which are, on the whole, more comprehensive than those contained in the PECL-LTCC.

Viewed as a whole, it can be stated that by means of its pre-contractual information duty for all long-term commercial contracts and its specification or intensification in relation to the franchisor, the PECL-LTCC convey the laws and practice of EU Member States well even if the CAD could not serve as a model in this regard. The creation of Art. 1:201 PECL-LTCC and the specification of the pre-contractual information duties of the franchisor in Art. 3:102 PECL-LTCC mean that they are more advanced than most of the European legal systems in terms of legal certainty and clarity. This is also an element which can promote party autonomy – especially that of the 'weaker party'.

Obligation to Information during the Performance

The general rule of Art. 1:203 PECL-LTCC Both parties not only have an interest in being informed before the conclusion of the contract, but also in being informed of facts and developments relevant to their performance. It can make their performance easier and more successful. In accordance with Art. 1:203 PECL-LTCC, which is contained in Chapter One and applies to all long-term commercial contracts, each party must provide the other in due time during the contract with all the information which the first party has and the second party needs in order to achieve the objectives of the contract. This mutual obligation to inform is a specific instance of the general obligation of good faith in accordance with Art. 1:201 PECL and the especially important obligation to co-operate in the field of long-term commercial contracts (Art. 1:202 PECL; Art. 1:202 PECL-LTCC). As with the pre-contractual obligation to inform, the obligation to inform during the performance is mandatory (Art. 1:203 (2) PECL-LTCC).

Specification for the individual types of contract The general obligation to inform during the performance is specified by further provisions applicable to both contractual parties in relation to commercial agency (Art. 2:203; Art. 2:307 PECL-LTCC), franchising (Art. 3:205; Art. 3:302 PECL-LTCC) and distribution (Art. 4:202; Art. 4:302 PECL-LTCC). It would be beyond the scope of this contribution to describe these in detail. However, there are clear similarities in all the

32 Law No. 89-1008 of 31 December 1989 regarding the development of commercial and trade enterprises and the improvement of their economic, legal and social environment. See also Ferrier (2001).

33 Administrative order 2485/1998 of 13 November 1998, implementing Art. 62 of Act 7/1996 of 15 January 1996 on the Retail Trade Code concerning the regulation of the franchise trade and creating a register of franchisors. See also Pellisé De Urguiza (2001), pp. 138 *et seq.*

34 Unidroit (2002). See also Feuerriegel (2002); Peters (2001).

35 See Jeanmart (2001); Wormald (2001).

specifications mentioned: on the one hand, the notion of all specifications is that they are simply basic requirements (e.g. information concerning the characteristics of the product or the prices and terms for the sale of the products), not too burdensome and ultimately in the interests of both parties. On the other hand, the information duties of the 'stronger party' (i.e. principal, franchisor, supplier) are usually far more obvious than those of the weaker party (commercial agent, franchisee, distributor).

It is debatable whether all specifications of the obligation to inform during the performance are mandatory or optional. There is no express stipulation in the text of the provisions, which could suggest that the special rules are optional and can be modified. However, this would not accord with the mandatory general obligation to inform during the performance in accordance with Art. 1:203 (2) PECL-LTCC. It would be almost impossible to depart from the requirements of a specification (e.g. from the requirement to provide information about the characteristics of the product or the price), without infringing the expressly mandatory general rule to inform during the performance in accordance with Art. 1:203 (1) PECL-LTCC. Accordingly, the specifications for the individual types of contract must be regarded as mandatory as well. However, it would have been helpful and conducive to legal certainty had the regulatory framework clarified this point.

Analysis of function and the influence on party autonomy Both obligations to inform investigated so far serve different purposes: whilst the pre-contractual obligation to inform aims to create market transparency, the obligation to inform during the performance facilitates the successful performance of the contract.

If one now takes the distinction between (mandatory) information rules and (mandatory) substantive rules as a basis in this case as well, then one cannot avoid categorising the mandatory general obligation to inform during the performance (Art. 1:203 PECL-LTCC) and its specifications as a mandatory substantive rule unlike the pre-contractual obligation to inform (Art. 1:201 PECL-LTCC). This is because it reduces the possibilities of forming a contract; i.e. it no longer completely leaves the substance of the contract to the parties. Accordingly, the franchisor is bereft of the opportunity to exclude the obligation to inform the franchisee of e.g. market conditions (cf. Art. 3:205 PECL-LTCC). Party autonomy is therefore limited.

However, the question now arises as to whether restricting party autonomy by the obligation to inform during the performance is significant. This is not the case here: the mandatory character of the obligation to inform during the performance ultimately only prevents the contractual parties from requiring obligations which emanate from the contract itself owing to the increased obligation to co-operate and act in good faith. The fact that a franchisor (Art. 3:205 PECL-LTCC) or a supplier (Art. 4:202 PECL-LTCC) is obliged to provide information concerning the characteristics of the products will hardly be regarded as a serious incursion into party autonomy. If they want their distribution system to be successful, then they must also provide their contractual partners with the necessary information. In effect, this has a minor effect on party autonomy – even if it is a mandatory substantive rule.

Some comparative comments When formulating the general obligation of both parties to inform during the performance in accordance with Art. 1:203 PECL-LTCC, the Study Group was clearly guided by the CAD (i.e. Art. 3 (2)(b) and Art. 4 (2)(b) CAD). This is because the CAD provides the similarly mandatory obligation in relation to both the agent and the principal (Art. 5 CAD), i.e. to furnish the opposite party with the 'necessary information' during the performance. One can speak of a European 'common ground' because the CAD has been transposed in all the Member States.

However, the PECL-LTCC supplements the CAD in two important respects: first, the Study Group also extends the obligation to inform during the performance (which is not so extensive in the CAD) to other long-term commercial contracts such as franchise or distribution contracts. It therefore regards the notions contained in Art. 3 and 4 CAD as applicable to other long-term commercial contracts. In this respect, the Study Group is supported by a number of Member States which also accept this. The legal basis in many countries is provided by drawing an analogy to the CAD provisions which have been transposed and/or good faith.[36]

Second, in contrast to the CAD and most national laws, the PECL-LTCC further specify the obligation to inform during the performance. Without examining this in detail, such specifications merely concern 'fundamental pieces of information' which must be provided and are recognized by most national courts and legal commentators.

Warnings

Contents of Art. 2:309, Art. 3:206, Art. 4:203 PECL-LTCC The PECL-LTCC also impose an obligation to 'warn' on the supposedly 'stronger party', i.e. of the principal, the franchisor and the supplier (Art. 2:309, Art. 3:206, Art. 4:203 PECL-LTCC).[37] Generally speaking (and disregarding the peculiarities of the individual provisions) the obligation requires the 'stronger party' to warn the 'weaker party' within a reasonable time if the former foresees or ought to foresee that the volume of the contracts that he will be able to conclude or perform (principal) or his supply capacity (franchisor, supplier) will be significantly less than the latter had reasons to expect. This 'obligation to warn' is mandatory for the principal, franchisor and for the distributor who has concluded an exclusive purchasing contract. Ultimately, the obligations amount to a mandatory specification of the very intense obligation to co-operate (Art. 1:202 PECL, Art. 1:202 PECL-LTCC) and the obligation of good faith (Art. 1:201 PECL). The use of the word 'warning' serves to highlight this intensity of the obligation to inform during the performance owing to the particularly close co-operation.

---

36 See Kroll (2001); Küstner and Thume (1998), pp. 314 *et seq.*; Janssen (2001), pp. 93 *et seq.*

37 In exclusive and selective distribution contracts the distributor also has an obligation to warn the supplier (Art. 4:303 PECL-LTCC). However, a detailed examination is beyond the scope of this chapter.

Analysis of function and influence on party autonomy The provisions concerning the warning (excluding non-exclusive purchasing contracts) constitute mandatory substantive rules. Generally speaking, reference can be made here to previous comments concerning the 'obligation to inform during the performance'. This is because it is no longer possible for the parties to give their contract a different substance than that contained in the provisions on the warning. Party autonomy is therefore restricted. However, drawing on the justification stated earlier, this restriction to party autonomy cannot be regarded as significant either. Ultimately, the only obligation which is mandatory is that which emanates from the co-operative character of the contract itself. If the principal, franchisor or distributor is interested in successfully continuing the system of distribution with the contractual partner he will warn him as quickly as possible.

The difference between the obligations to inform during the contract therefore does not lie in the restriction to party autonomy, since both cases concern mandatory substantive rules. Rather, the difference lies in the somewhat modified function: the obligations to warn do not affect the performance of the contract *per se* (unlike the obligations during the performance), but protect the economic interests of the weaker party.[38]

Some comparative comments The rules stem from the CAD (Art. 4 (1)(b) CAD) which most legal systems have adopted. According to the CAD this rule should be mandatory (Art. 5 CAD). The PECL-LTCC have also transferred these notions to the franchise and distribution contracts. This also corresponds to most national legal systems in which 'obligations to warn' in relation to all long-term commercial contracts result either from an analogy to the transposed CAD or from good faith.

Signed Written Documents in Accordance to Art. 1:402 PECL-LTCC

Contents of Art. 1:402 PECL-LTCC In relation to all long-term commercial contracts, Art. 1:402 PECL-LTCC stipulates that each party shall be entitled to receive from the other, on request, a signed written document setting out the terms of the contract. The written document can be requested either at the conclusion of or during the contract and even within a reasonable time after the contract has ended.[39] The of this provision are mandatory. This is obvious from its meaning and purpose and the clear commentary to a preliminary version of this article.[40] An express clarification would nevertheless have been very welcome.

---

38 Riesenhuber (2003b), p. 192.

39 The term 'written document' must be broadly interpreted. Cf. Art. 1:303 (1) PECL, which stipulates that notice may be given by any means, whether in writing or otherwise (telex, fax, e-mail), provided that the form used is appropriate to the circumstances.

40 See the commentary to Art. 1:111 (which is almost identical to Art. 1:402) of the 5th draft of the PECL-LTCC.

Analysis of function and influence on party autonomy At first glance, this rule appears to be a formal requirement but in effect it constitutes an obligation to inform. Unlike a genuine requirement of written form, this provision does not make the validity of the contract dependant on the use of written form. Rather, Art. 1:402 PECL-LTCC requires an existing contract. The function of the article is to provide a party with information ('obligation to present evidence') and to facilitate giving evidence.

The requirement of a signed written document does not amount to a mandatory substantive rule since, up to a point, the contractual freedom of the contractual parties is not adversely affected in any way. Party autonomy is therefore not affected. Rather, it is a mandatory information rule which merely confirms a decision by private autonomous individuals. Unlike the pre-contractual duty to inform (likewise a mandatory information rule), which seeks to effect the decision of the parties as to whether and under which conditions a contract is to be entered into (market transparency), the requirement of signed written documents serves a different purpose. Rather, it seeks to enable the contractual parties to make the correct decision as to whether they should let a solicitor or court examine their contractual rights.[41] Therefore, it primarily functions as evidence (i.e. judicial evidence) for the parties (the 'duty to prove evidence').[42] However, this does not alter the fact that both concern mandatory information rules, whereas each performs a somewhat different function.

Some comparative comments The model for this article was Art. 13 CAD. In relation to commercial agency it displays almost the same contents and is also mandatory (Art. 13 (2) CAD).[43] The Study Group generalised this notion for all long-term commercial contracts and thereby reproduces the legal situation in the Member States more or less accurately. Accordingly, as far as commercial agency is concerned, a signed written document is recognized as an information duty owing to the transposition of the CAD in Member States. However, in most Member States (e.g. Germany) the provisions transposing Art. 13 CAD are accordingly applied to long-term commercial contracts.[44]

Conclusion: the PECL-LTCC and their Impact on Party Autonomy

This investigation has shown that the PECL-LTCC draw a distinction between four information duties which must be observed in the case of all types of contract. They are all based on the extremely important duty of co-operation relating to long-term commercial contracts (Art. 1:202 PECL-LTCC) and each serves different aims:

41 Riesenhuber (2003b), p. 201.

42 Riesenhuber (2003b), p. 200.

43 However, there are other examples of information duties derived from secondary law. Cf., e.g., Art. 6 (3) of the Sale of Consumer Goods Directive.

44 Von Hoyningen-Huene (1996), § 85 *Handelsgesetzbuch*, no. 1.

- The pre-contractual obligation to inform aims to create market transparency.
- The obligation to inform during the performance facilitates the performance of the contract.
- The obligation to warn primarily aims to protect the economic interest of the contractual partner.
- The entitlement to receive a signed written document facilitates the obligation to provide evidence.

This investigation has also shown that although all the information duties under consideration are essentially mandatory, they do not necessarily entail a restriction of party autonomy. Rather, it has been established that the pre-contractual obligation to inform and the right to receive a signed written document as a mandatory information rule do not affect party autonomy but merely enable the contractual parties, as private-autonomous individuals, to make a decision.

However, even the obligation to inform during the performance and the obligation to warn, both of which have been classified as mandatory substantive rules, cannot be said to influence party autonomy to a very significant degree. Only some information duties are mandatory which, in any case, result from the nature of long-term commercial contracts as an especially close form of co-operation (Art. 1:202 PECL-LTCC) and which are essential for the success of any system of distribution.

Accordingly, the following can be stated: the information duties of the PECL-LTCC respect party autonomy to a large degree. One must not be tempted to conclude that the largely mandatory character of information duties automatically restricts party autonomy to a considerable degree.

Outlook: The Information Requirements in the PECL-LTCC – A Model for a European Civil Code?

The chances that the information model of the PECL-LTCC will act as a model for a European Code in whatever shape or form are not bad.[45] In this respect, three aspects are worth mentioning:

The first pertains to legal policy. The PECL-LTCC pay the greatest regard to secondary European law and the status quo in most national legal systems. This indicates that they are more likely to be accepted in the Member States.

A further argument, which suggests a relatively wide acceptance of the information model of the PECL-LTCC (at least within the business community), is that party autonomy is not significantly restricted despite the mandatory character of the information duties considered.

The final and very important argument is that of increased legal certainty. The highly developed information system of the PECL-LTCC with their general and

---

45 Of course, this statement only relates to the information duties investigated here and not to the other areas regulated by the PECL-LTCC.

special information duties means that the PECL-LTCC are superior to most national information duties in terms of precision and contributes to better and more exact information being provided to the party concerned. This, in turn, promotes legal certainty and, ultimately, party autonomy. Unfortunately, this positive effect is at least partly cancelled out by the uncertainty concerning the mandatory character of some information duties (the specifications of the general obligation to inform during the performance and the requirement of a signed written document). However, such 'technical' deficits can be avoided in a future European regulatory framework and therefore do not significantly prejudice the basic function of the PECL-LTCC in acting as a model.

To put it in a nutshell: whether a European Civil Code becomes a reality and whatever its shape and form, one may still have recourse to the PECL-LTCC which – some technical defects notwithstanding – generally constitute a cogent information system. They can serve not only as a model for long-term commercial contracts but for other contracts as well. Therefore, one awaits further developments with great interest.

References

Bar, von, C. (2000), 'Die Study Group on a European Civil Code', in Gottwald, P., Jayme, E. and Schwab, D. (eds.), *Festschrift für Dieter Henrich zum 70. Geburtstag* (Bielefeld: Gieseking), pp. 1-11.

Bar, von, C. (2001), 'Deliktsrechtskonzept der Study Group on a European Civil Code', *Zeitschrift für Europäisches Privatrecht*, vol. 9, pp. 515-532.

Blase, F. (2001), *Die Grundregeln des Europäischen Vertragsrechts als Recht grenzüberschreitender Verträge* (Münster: Quadis).

Bortolotti, F. (2001), 'Franchising Contracts in Italian Law', in Schulze, R. (ed.), *Franchising im Europäischen Recht* (Baden-Baden: Nomos), pp. 113-123.

Ferrier, P.D. (2001), 'La Franchise en Droit Français', in Schulze, R. (ed.), *Franchising im Europäischen Recht* (Baden-Baden: Nomos), pp. 103-111.

Feuerriegel, S. (2002), 'Das Unidroit-Modellgesetz über die Offenlegung beim Franchising', *Außenwirtschaftliche Praxis*, vol. 6, pp. 1-6.

Flohr, E. (1998), *Franchise-Vertrag* (Munich: Beck).

Gandolfi, G. (coordinator) (2002), *Code Européen des Contrats* (Milano:Giuffré).

Grigoleit, H.C. (2003), 'Irrtum, Täuschung und Informationspflichten in den European Principles und in den Unidroit-Principles', in Schulze, R., Ebers, M. and Grigoleit, H. C. (eds.), *Informationspflichten und Vertragsschluss im Acquis communautaire* (Tübingen: Mohr Siebeck), pp. 201-230.

Grundmann, S. (2000), 'Privatautonomie im Binnenmarkt – Informationsregeln als Instrument', *Juristenzeitung*, vol. 55, pp. 1133-1143.

Grundmann, S., Kerber, W. and Weatherill, S. (2001), 'Party Autonomy and the Role of Information – an Overview', in Grundmann, S., Kerber, W., and Weatherill, S. (eds.), *Party Autonomy and the Role of Information in the Internal Market* (Berlin: de Gruyter), pp. 2-38.

Grundmann, S. and Stuyck, J. (eds.) (2001), *An Academic Green Paper on European Contract Law* (The Hague: Kluwer Law International).

Hagemeister, R. (2004), *Der Handelsvertreter im englischen Recht und seine Ansprüche bei Beendigung des Vertretervertrages* (Münster: Lit).

Heutger, V. (2003), 'Konturen des Kaufrechtskonzeptes der Study Group on a European Civil Code – Ein Werkstattbericht', *European Review of Private Law*, vol. 4, pp. 155-173.

Hoyningen-Huene, von, G. (1996), in *Münchner Kommentar zum Handelsgesetzbuch (§§ 1-104 HGB),* volume I (Munich: Beck).

Janssen, J. (2001), 'The Legal Nature of Franchise Agreements in the Netherlands', in Schulze, R. (ed.), *Franchising im Europäischen Recht* (Baden-Baden: Nomos), pp. 93-102.

Jeanmart, J. (2001), 'The European Code of Ethics for Franchising: Its Role as a Source of Reference – Legal and Ethical – for Franchising in Europe', in Schulze, R. (ed.), *Franchising im Europäischen Recht* (Baden-Baden: Nomos), pp. 277-282.

Kerton, R.R. and Bodell, W. (1995), 'Quality, Choice and the Economics of Concealment: The Marketing of Lemons', *Journal of Consumer Affairs*, vol. 29, pp. 1-28.

Kroll, W. (2001), *Informationspflichten im Franchising* (Frankfurt am Main: Peter Lang).

Küstner, W. and Thume, K.H. (1998), *Handbuch des gesamten Aussendienstrechts*, volume III, 2. edn. (Munich: Beck).

Lando, O. and Beale, H. (eds.) (2002), *Principles of European Contract Law*, Part I and Part II combined and revised (The Hague: Kluwer Law International).

Martinek, M. and Semler, F. (1996), *Handbuch des Vertriebsrechts* (Munich: Beck).

Najork, E. and Schmidt-Kessel, M. (2003), 'Der Aktionsplan der Kommission für ein kohärenteres Vertragsrecht: Überlegungen zu den von der Kommission vorgeschlagenen Maßnahmen', *Zeitschrift für Gemeinschaftsprivatrecht*, pp. 5-11.

Pellisé de Urguiza, P.C. (2001), 'Le Contrat de Franchise en Espagne: Classification, Phase Précontractuelle et Exécution Contractuelle', in Schulze, R. (ed.), *Franchising im Europäischen Recht* (Baden-Baden: Nomos), pp. 125-148.

Peters, L. (2001), 'The Draft Unidroit Model Law: Genesis and Contents', in Schulze, R. (ed.), *Franchising im Europäischen Recht* (Baden-Baden: Nomos), pp. 255-273.

Radley-Gardner, O., Beale, H., Zimmermann, R. and Schulze, R. (2003), *Fundamental texts on European Private Law* (Oxford: Hart Publishing).

Riesenhuber, K. (2003a), *System und Prinzipien des Europäischen Vertragsrechts* (Berlin: De Gruyter).

Riesenhuber, K. (2003b), *Europäisches Vertragsrecht* (Berlin: De Gruyter).

Schulze, R. (2003), 'The Acquis Communautaire and the Development of European Contract Law', in Schulze, R., Ebers, M. and Grigoleit, H.C. (eds.), *Informationspflichten und Vertragsschluss im Acquis communautaire* (Tübingen: Mohr Siebeck), pp. 15-28.

Staudenmayer, D. (2003), 'Der Aktionsplan der EG-Kommission zum Europäischen Vertragsrecht', *Europäische Zeitschrift für Wirtschaftsrecht*, vol. 14, pp. 165-171.

Unidroit (ed.) (1994), *Principles of International Commercial Contracts* (Rome: Unidroit).

Unidroit (ed.) (2002), *Draft Articles for a Model Franchise Disclosure Law*, Study LXVIII, at http://www.unidroit.org/english/franchising/modellaw/main.htm.

Westphal, B. (1994), *Die Handelsvertreterrichtlinie und deren Umsetzung in den Mitgliedsstaaten der Europäischen Union* (Cologne: no publisher).

Wormald, C. (2001), 'The European Franchise Federation (EFF) and the European Code of Ethics for Franchising – An Introduction', in Schulze, R. (ed.), *Franchising im Europäischen Recht* (Baden-Baden: Nomos), pp. 275-276.

Study Group on a European Civil Code

Principles of European Private Law Long-Term Commercial Contracts: Commercial Agency, Distribution, Franchise*

Edited by Martijn W. Hesselink

TEXT OF ARTICLES

Chapter 1: General Provisions

Section 1: Scope of Chapter 1

Article 1:101: Scope

This Chapter applies to commercial agency, franchise and distribution contracts and with appropriate modifications to other contracts where one party, engaged in business independently uses its skills and efforts to bring another party's products on to the market.

---

* 8th draft of principles concerning commercial agency, franchising and distribution, as approved by the Coordinating Committee of the Study Group on a European Civil Code. The working team consists of: Professor Dr. Martijn W. Hesselink, Dr. Jacobien W. Rutgers, Odavia Buenodiaz, LL.M. (Leuven), DSSA, Manola Scotton, meester Muriel Veldman.

Section 2: Obligations

Article 1:201: Pre-Contractual Information

(1) Each party must provide the other party with adequate information a reasonable time before the contract is concluded. If it does not, paragraph 3 applies.

(2) Adequate information means information which is sufficient to enable the other party to decide on a reasonably informed basis whether or not to enter into a contract of the type and on the terms under consideration.

(3) If a party's failure to comply with paragraph 1 leads the other party to conclude a contract when the first party knew or could reasonably expected to have know that the other party, had it been provided with adequate and timely information, would not have entered the contract, or would have entered the contract only on fundamentally different terms, the remedies for mistake under PECL Chapter 4 apply.

(4) Parties may not derogate from this provision.

Article 1:202: Co-Operation

(1) In commercial agency, franchise and distribution contracts and in other long-term commercial contracts the obligation to co-operate (Art. 1:202 PECL) is fundamental and particularly intense. It requires the parties in particular to collaborate actively and loyally and to co-ordinate their respective efforts in order to achieve the objectives of the contract.

(2) Parties may not derogate from this provision.

Article 1:203: Information during the Performance

(1) During the contract each party must provide the other in due time with all the information which the first party has and the second party needs in order to achieve the objectives of the contract.

(2) Parties may not derogate from this provision.

Article 1:204: Confidentiality

(1) A party who receives confidential information from the other, must keep such information confidential and must not disclose the information to third parties either during or after the end of the contract period.

(2) A party who receives confidential information from the other must not use such information for other purposes than the objectives of the contract.

(3) Any information which a party already had in its possession or which has been disclosed to the general public, and any information which must necessarily be disclosed to customers as a result of the operation of the business is not be regarded as confidential information for this purpose.

Section 3: Ending and Termination

Article 1:301: Contract for a Definite Period

(1) A contract for a definite period ends upon the expiry of the period determined by the contract. Unless the parties agreed otherwise, such a contract cannot be ended unilaterally beforehand, except in the case of ending for an urgent and important reason (Art. 1:304).

(2) A party is free not to renew a contract for a definite period. However, if the other party has given notice in due time that it wishes to renew the contract, the party who wishes not to renew the contract must give the other party notice of its decision not to renew within a reasonable time before the expiry of the contract period.

(3) A contract for a definite period which continues to be performed by both parties after the contract period has expired becomes a contract for an indefinite period.

Article 1:302: Unilateral Ending Contract for Indefinite Period

(1) Either party to a contract for an indefinite period may end the contract by giving notice of reasonable length (Art. 6:109 PECL).

(2) Whether a notice is of reasonable length depends, among other factors, on

(a) the time the contract has lasted,

(b) reasonable investments made,

(c) the time it will take to find a reasonable alternative, and

(d) usages.

(3) A notice period of one month for each year during which the contract has lasted, with a maximum of 36 months, is presumed to be reasonable.

(4) The notice period for the principal, the franchisor or the supplier is to be no shorter than one month for the first year, two months for the second, three months for the third, four months for the fourth, five months for the fifth and six months for

the sixth and subsequent years during which the contract has lasted. Parties may not derogate from this provision.

(5) Agreements on longer notice periods than those laid down in paragraphs 2 and 3 are valid provided that the agreed period to be observed by the principal, franchisor or supplier is no shorter than that to be observed by the commercial agent, the franchisee or the distributor.

(6) The aggrieved party is not entitled to specific performance of the contract during the notice period. However, the court may order specific performance of contractual and post-contractual obligations which do not depend on co-operation.

Article 1:303: Damages for Non-Observance Notice Period

(1) In the case of the non-observance of the notice periods mentioned in Art. 1:301 (2) and Art. 1:302 (1), the aggrieved party is entitled to damages.

(2) The general measure of damages is such sum which corresponds to the benefit which the aggrieved party would have obtained during the non-observed period of notice.

(3) The yearly benefit is presumed to be equal to the average benefit which the aggrieved party has obtained from the contract during the previous 3 years or, if the contract has lasted for a shorter period, during that period.

(4) The general rules on damages for non-performance (Arts. 9:510 et seq. PECL) apply accordingly.

Article 1:304: Termination for Non-Performance

(1) A party may terminate the contract for non-performance only if the other party's non-performance is fundamental within the meaning of Art. 8:103 (b) and Article 8:103 (c) PECL (Art. 9:301 PECL).

(2) *Parties may not derogate from this provision.*

Article 1:305: Indemnity for Goodwill

(1) When the contract comes to an end for any reason (including termination by either party for non-performance), a party is entitled to an indemnity from the other party for goodwill if and to the extent that

> *(a) the first party has significantly increased the other party's volume of business and the other party continues to derive substantial benefits from that business, and*
>
> *(b) the payment of the indemnity is reasonable having regard to all the circumstances.*

(2) The grant of an indemnity does not prevent a party from seeking damages under Art. 1:303.

Article 1:306: Stock, Spare Parts and Materials

If the contract is ended, terminated or avoided by either party, the principal, franchisor or supplier must repurchase the commercial agent's, franchisee's or distributor's remaining stock, spare parts and materials at a reasonable price, unless the commercial agent, franchisee or distributor can reasonably resell them.

Section 4: Other General Provisions

Article 1:401: Right of Retention

In order to secure its rights to remuneration, compensation, damages and indemnity the commercial agent, franchisee or distributor has a right of retention over the movables of the principal, franchisor or supplier which are in its possession as a result of the contract, until the (former) principal, franchisor or supplier has fulfilled its obligations.

Article 1:402: Signed Written Document

Each party is entitled to receive from the other, on request, a signed written document setting out the terms of the contract.

Chapter 2: Commercial Agency

Section 1: General

Article 2:101: Scope

This Chapter applies to contracts under which one party (the commercial agent) agrees to act on a continuing basis as a self-employed intermediary to negotiate or to conclude contracts on behalf of another party (the principal) and the principal agrees to remunerate the commercial agent for the commercial agent's activities.

Section 2: Obligations of the Commercial Agent

Article 2:201: Negotiate and Conclude Contracts

The commercial agent must make reasonable efforts to negotiate contracts on behalf of the principal and to conclude the contracts which the commercial agent was instructed to conclude.

Article 2:202: Instructions

The commercial agent must follow the principal's reasonable instructions, provided they do not substantially affect the commercial agent's independence.

Article 2:203: Information during the Performance

The obligation to inform (Art. 1:203) requires the commercial agent in particular to provide the principal with information concerning:

(a) contracts negotiated or concluded,

(b) market conditions,

(c) the solvency of and other characteristics relating to clients.

Article 2:204: Accounting

(1) The commercial agent must maintain proper accounts relating to the contracts negotiated or concluded on behalf of the principal.

(2) If the commercial agent represents more than one principal, the commercial agent must, in particular, maintain independent accounts for each principal the commercial agent represents.

(3) If the principal has important reasons to doubt that the commercial agent maintains proper accounts, the commercial agent must allow an independent accountant to have reasonable access to the commercial agent's books upon the principal's request. The principal must pay for the services of the independent accountant.

Section 3: Obligations of the Principal

Article 2:301: Entitlement to Commission During the Contract

(1) The commercial agent is entitled to commission on contracts concluded with clients during the period covered by the agency contract, if

(a) (i) the contract with the client has been concluded as a result of the commercial agent's efforts; or

(ii) the contract has been concluded with a third party whom the commercial agent has previously acquired as a client for contracts of the same kind; or

(iii) the commercial agent is entrusted with a certain geographical area or group of clients, and the contract has been concluded with a client belonging to that area or group, and

(b) (i) the principal has or should have performed the principal's obligations under the contract; or

(ii) the client has performed the client's obligations under the contract or justifiably withholds the client's performance (Art. 9:201 PECL).

(2) The parties may not derogate from paragraph 1 sub b) sub ii) to the detriment of the commercial agent.

Article 2:302: Entitlement to Commission After the Contract

(1) The commercial agent is entitled to commission on contracts concluded with clients after the agency contract has ended, if

(a) (i) the contract with the client is mainly the result of the commercial agent's efforts during the period covered by the agency contract, and the contract with the client was concluded within a reasonable period after the agency contract ended; or

(ii) the conditions of Art. 2:301 (1) would have been satisfied except that the contract with the client was not concluded during the period of the agency, and the client's offer reached the principal or the commercial agent before the agency contract ended, and

(b) (i) the principal has or should have performed the principal's obligations under the contract; or

(ii) the client has performed the client's obligations under the contract or justifiably withholds the client's performance (Art. 9:201 PECL).

(2) The parties may not derogate from paragraph 1 sub b) sub ii) to the detriment of the commercial agent.

Article 2:303: Prevailing Entitlement to Commission

The commercial agent is not entitled to the commission referred to in Art. 2:301, if the previous commercial agent is entitled to that commission pursuant to Art. 2:302, unless it is reasonable that the commission is shared between the two commercial agents.

Article 2:304: Moment when Commission is to be Paid

(1) The principal must not pay the commercial agent's commission later than on the last day of the month following the quarter in which the commercial agent became entitled to it.

(2) The parties may not derogate from this provision to the detriment of the commercial agent.

Article 2:305: Entitlement to Commission Extinguished

(1) The commercial agent's entitlement to commission in accordance with Arts. 2:301 and 2:302 can be extinguished only if and to the extent that it is established that the contract with the client will not be performed and that fact is due to a reason for which the principal is not accountable.

(2) Upon the extinguishing of the commercial agent's entitlement to commission, the commercial agent must refund any commission which the commercial agent has already received.

(3) The parties may not derogate from paragraph 1 to the detriment of the commercial agent.

Article 2:306: Remuneration

Any remuneration which (partially) depends upon the number or value of contracts is presumed to be commission within the meaning of this Chapter.

Article 2:307: Information during the Performance

The obligation to inform (Art. 1:203) requires the principal in particular to provide the commercial agent with information concerning:

- *(a) characteristics of the goods or services,*
- *(b) prices and conditions of sale or purchase.*

Article 2:308: Information on Acceptance, Rejection and Non-Performance

(1) The principal must inform the commercial agent, within a reasonable period, of

(a) the principal's acceptance or rejection of a contract which the commercial agent has negotiated on the principal's behalf; and

(b) any non-performance of a contract which the commercial agent has negotiated or concluded on the principal's behalf.

(2) The parties may not derogate from this provision to the detriment of the commercial agent.

Article 2:309: Warning of Decreased Volume of Contracts

(1) The principal must warn the commercial agent within a reasonable time when the principal foresees or ought to foresee that the volume of contracts that the principal will be able to conclude or perform will be significantly lower than the commercial agent could normally have expected.

(2) The parties may not derogate from this provision to the detriment of the commercial agent.

Article 2:310: Information on Commission by means of Statement and Extract from Books

(1) The principal must supply the commercial agent in reasonable time with a statement of the commission to which the commercial agent is entitled. This statement must set out how the amount of the commission has been calculated.

(2) For the purpose of calculating commission, the principal must provide the commercial agent upon request with an extract from the principal's books.

(3) The parties may not derogate from this provision to the detriment of the commercial agent.

Article 2:311: Accounting

(1) The principal must maintain proper accounts relating to the contracts negotiated or concluded by the commercial agent.

(2) If the principal has more than one commercial agent, the principal must, in particular, maintain independent accounts for each commercial agent.

(3) The principal must allow an independent accountant to have reasonable access to the principal's books upon the commercial agent's request, if

(a) the principal does not comply with the principal's obligations under Art. 2:310 (1) and (2), or

(b) the commercial agent has important reasons to doubt that the principal maintains proper accounts.

Article 2:312: Amount of Indemnity

(1) The commercial agent is entitled to an indemnity for goodwill on the basis of Art. 1:306 which must amount to:

(a) the average commission on contracts with new clients and on the increased volume of business with existing clients calculated for the last 12 months, multiplied by:

(b) the number of years the principal is likely to continue to derive benefits from these contracts in the future.

(2) The resulting indemnity must be amended in accordance with:

(a) the average rate of migration in the commercial agent's territory; and

(b) the average interest rates.

(3) In any case, the indemnity must not exceed one year's remuneration, calculated from the commercial agent's average annual remuneration over the preceding five years or, if the contract has been in existence for less than five years, from the average during the period in question.

(4) The parties may not derogate from this provision to the detriment of the commercial agent.

Article 2:313: Del Credere Clause

(1) An agreement whereby the commercial agent guarantees that a client will pay the price of the products forming the subject-matter of the contract(s) which the commercial agent has negotiated or concluded (del credere clause) is only valid if and to the extent that:

(a) the clause is concluded in writing, and

(b) the clause covers particular contracts which were negotiated or concluded by the commercial agent or such contracts with particular clients who are specified in the agreement, and

(c) the clause is reasonable with regard to the interests of the parties.

(2) The commercial agent is entitled to be paid a commission of a reasonable amount on contracts to which the del credere guarantee applies (del credere commission).

Chapter 3: Franchise

Section 1: General

Article 3:101: Scope

This Chapter applies to contracts whereby one party (the franchisor) grants the other party (the franchisee), in exchange for remuneration, the right to conduct a business (franchise business) within the franchisor's network for the purposes of selling certain products on the franchisee's behalf and in the franchisee's name, and whereby the franchisee has the right and the obligation to use the franchisor's tradename or trademark, the know-how and the business method.

Article 3:102: Pre-Contractual Information

(1) The obligation to disclose pre-contractual information (Art. 1:201) requires the franchisor in particular to provide the franchisee with adequate and timely information concerning:

(a) the franchisor's company and experience,

(b) the relevant intellectual property rights,

(c) the characteristics of the relevant know-how,

(d) the commercial sector and the market conditions,

(e) the particular franchise method and its operation,

(f) the structure and extent of the franchise network,

(g) the fees, royalties or any other periodical payments,

(h) the terms of the contract.

(2) If the franchisor´s non-compliance with paragraph 1 does not give rise to a fundamental mistake under Art. 4:103 PECL, the franchisee may recover damages in accordance with Art. 4:117 (2) and (3) PECL, unless the franchisor had reason to believe that the information was adequate or had been given in reasonable time.

(3) The parties may not derogate from this provision.

Section 2: Obligations of the Franchisor

Article 3:201: Intellectual Property Rights

(1) The franchisor must grant the franchisee a right to use the intellectual property rights to the extent necessary to operate the franchise business.

(2) The franchisor must make reasonable efforts to ensure the undisturbed and continuous use of the intellectual property rights.

(3) The parties may not derogate from this provision.

Article 3:202: Know-How

(1) Throughout the duration of the contract, the franchisor must provide the franchisee with the know-how which is necessary to operate the franchise business.

(2) The parties may not derogate from this provision.

Article 3:203: Assistance

(1) The franchisor must provide the franchisee with assistance in the form of training courses, guidance and advice, in so far as necessary for the operation of the franchise business, without additional charge for the franchisee.

(2) The franchisor must provide further assistance, in so far as reasonably requested by the franchisee, at a reasonable cost.

Article 3:204: Supply

(1) When the franchisee is obliged to purchase the products from the franchisor, or from a supplier designated by the franchisor, the franchisor must ensure that the products ordered by the franchisee are supplied within a reasonable time, insofar as practicable and provided that the order is reasonable.

(2) Paragraph 1 also applies to cases where the franchisee, although not legally obliged to purchase from the franchisor or from a supplier designated by the franchisor, is in fact required to do so.

(3) The parties may not derogate from this provision.

Article 3:205: Information during the Performance

The obligation to inform (Art. 1:203) requires the franchisor in particular to provide the franchisee with information concerning:

(a) market conditions,

(b) commercial results of the franchise network,

(c) characteristics of the products,

(d) prices and terms for the sale of products,

(e) any recommended prices and terms for the resale of products,

(f) relevant communication between the franchisor and customers in the territory,

(g) advertising campaigns.

Article 3:206: Warning of Decreased Supply Capacity

(1) When the franchisee is obliged to purchase the products from the franchisor, or from a supplier designated by the franchisor, the franchisor must warn the franchisee within a reasonable time when the franchisor foresees or ought to foresee, that the franchisor's supply capacity or the supply capacity of the designated suppliers will be significantly less than the franchisee had reason to expect.

(2) Paragraph 1 also applies to cases where the franchisee, although not legally obliged to purchase from the franchisor or from a supplier designated by the franchisor, is in fact required to do so.

(3) The parties may not derogate from this provision to the detriment of the franchisee.

Article 3:207: Reputation of Network and Advertising

(1) The franchisor must make reasonable efforts to promote and maintain the reputation of the franchise network.

(2) In particular, the franchisor must design and co-ordinate the appropriate advertising campaigns aiming at the promotion of the franchise network.

(3) The activities of promotion and maintenance of the reputation of the franchise network are to be carried out without additional charge to the franchisee.

Section 3: Obligations of the Franchisee

Article 3:301: Fees, Royalties and Other Periodical Payments

(1) The franchisee must pay to the franchisor fees, royalties or other periodical payments agreed upon in the contract.

(2) If fees, royalties or any other periodical payments are to be determined unilaterally by the franchisor, Art. 6:105 PECL applies.

Article 3:302: Information during the Performance

The obligation to inform (Art. 1:203) requires the franchisee in particular to provide the franchisor with information concerning:

(a) claims brought or threatened by third parties in relation to the franchisor's intellectual property rights.

(b) infringements by third parties of the franchisor's intellectual property rights.

Article 3:303: Business Method and Instructions

(1) The franchisee must make reasonable efforts to operate the franchise business according to the business method of the franchisor.

(2) The franchisee must follow the franchisor's reasonable instructions in relation with the business method and the maintenance of the reputation of the network.

(3) The franchisee must take reasonable care not to harm the franchise network.

(4) The parties may not derogate from this provision.

Article 3:304: Inspection

(1) The franchisee must grant the franchisor reasonable access to the franchisee's premises to enable the franchisor to check that the franchisee is complying with the franchisor's business method and instructions.

(2) The franchise must grant the franchisor reasonable access to the accounting books of the franchisee.

Chapter 4: Distribution

Section 1: General

Article 4:101: Scope and Definitions

(1) This Chapter applies to exclusive distribution, selective distribution and exclusive purchasing contracts.

(2) A distribution contract is a contract whereby one party (the supplier) agrees to supply the other party (the distributor) with products on a continuing basis and the distributor agrees to purchase them and to sell them in the distributor's name and on the distributor's behalf (distribution contract).

(3) An exclusive distribution contract is a distribution contract whereby the supplier agrees to supply products to only one distributor within a certain territory or to a certain group of customers.

(4) A selective distribution contract is a distribution contract whereby the supplier agrees to supply products, either directly or indirectly, only to distributors selected on the basis of specified criteria.

(5) An exclusive purchasing contract is a distribution contract whereby the distributor agrees to purchase products only from the supplier or from a party designated by the supplier.

Section 2: Obligations of the Supplier

Article 4:201: Obligation to Supply

The supplier must supply the products ordered by the distributor, insofar as it is practicable and provided that the order is reasonable.

Article 4:202: Information during the Performance

The obligation to inform (Art. 1:203) requires the supplier to provide the distributor with information concerning:

(a) the characteristics of the products,

(b) the prices and terms for the sale of the products,

(c) any recommended prices and terms for the resale of the products,

(d) any relevant communication between the supplier and customers,

(e) any advertising campaigns relevant to the operation of the business.

Article 4:203: Warning of Decreased Supply Capacity

(1) The supplier must warn the distributor within a reasonable time when the supplier foresees or ought to foresee that the supplier's supply capacity will be significantly less than the distributor had reason to expect.

(2) In exclusive purchasing contracts, parties may not derogate from this provision.

Article 4:204: Advertising Materials

The supplier must provide the distributor at a reasonable price with all the advertising materials the supplier has which are needed for the proper distribution and promotion of the products.

Article 4:205: The Reputation of the Products

The supplier must make reasonable efforts not to damage the reputation of the products.

Section 3: Obligations of the Distributor

Article 4:301: Obligation to Distribute

In exclusive and selective distribution contracts, insofar as it is practicable, the distributor must make reasonable efforts to promote the sales of the products.

Article 4:302: Information during the Performance

In exclusive and selective distribution contracts, the obligation to inform (Art. 1:203) requires the distributor to provide the supplier with information concerning:

(a) claims brought or threatened by third parties in relation to the supplier's intellectual property rights,

(b) infringements by third parties of the supplier's intellectual property rights.

Article 4:303: Warning

In exclusive and selective distribution contracts, the distributor must warn the supplier within a reasonable time when the distributor foresees or ought to foresee that the distributor's requirement will be significantly less than the supplier had reason to expect.

Article 4:304: Instructions

In exclusive and selective distribution contracts, the distributor must follow reasonable instructions from the supplier which are designed to secure the proper distribution of the products or to maintain the reputation or the distinctiveness of the products.

Article 4:305: Inspection

In exclusive and selective distribution contracts, the distributor must provide the supplier with reasonable access to the distributor's premises to enable the supplier to check that the distributor is complying with the standards agreed upon in the contract and with reasonable instructions given.

Article 4:306: The Reputation of the Products

In exclusive and selective distribution contracts, the distributor must make reasonable efforts not to damage the reputation of the products.

Index